The Runaway Church

The Runaway Church

Peter Hebblethwaite

COLLINS

St James's Place, London

1975

William Collins Sons & Co. Ltd
London · Glasgow · Sydney · Auckland
Toronto · Johannesburg

First published 1975
© Peter Hebblethwaite 1975

ISBN 0 00 211648 0

Set in Monotype Plantin
Made and printed in Great Britain by
Richard Clay (The Chaucer Press) Ltd,
Bungay, Suffolk

Contents

Foreword

The purpose of this book is to chronicle and interpret the last decade of the Roman Catholic Church. Friends, foes, critical well-wishers and even casual newspaper-readers are all aware that the familiar landscape has been radically transformed. There are new attitudes abroad in the Church, and a new vocabulary to express them. The Second Vatican Council (1962–5) was the watershed. It initiated changes in every sphere of the Church's life, but subsequent developments were far from harmonious and not always what had been expected or predicted. The Council set in motion a process which, once started, the official Church was powerless to halt. Denounced as disobedience, hailed as the wave of the future, this process has brought us to what may be called the Runaway Church of today.

Of course one can argue endlessly about what should and should not figure in such an account, and still more about its interpretation. With the whole world as one's field and such controversial material to be dealt with, there will no doubt be complaints about omissions and selectivity. When Sir Walter Raleigh embarked on his rather more ambitious *History of the World*, he wrote: 'He who follows contemporary history too close along the heels may haply get kicked in the teeth.' I hope that readers of this story will at least be able to say: 'Yes, that's how it was.'

A litany of indebtedness would take up too much space. But thanks to all those from Cracow to Chicago who have stayed up late to talk it over and shared the hope for the Church which makes faith possible.

Oxford, July 1975

Chapter 1

Its End Was Its Beginning

The Church is necessarily outward-looking, not primarily introspective and conservative, but primarily an
indomitable adventurer into new fields. What else
could she be, since she is, as St Augustine taught us,
the incorporation of Christian love or charity? . . .
Charity has the audacity of the great military geniuses,
who know by instinct that a strategy of defence can
never in the end win a campaign

BISHOP CHRISTOPHER BUTLER
Searchings, pp. 260–1.

The most momentous event in the history of the Roman Catholic
Church in this century, the Second Vatican Council, came to an
end ten years ago. Countless books have been written to explain
what the Council did and why it was important, but there has been
little detailed analysis of the impact it made on the everyday life of
the Church. Yet the shock-waves from the Council spread rapidly
and reverberated round the world, and their results were not
always what was expected or intended. 'We shall only know what
the Council means', said one expert on the day it ended, 'ten years
from now.'

Ten years on, it is still not easy to say exactly what happened.
The only point of general agreement is that nothing could be the
same afterwards. Indeed, the very terms 'pre-conciliar' and 'post-
conciliar' came to express not simply a difference in chronology,
but a difference of attitude, outlook and basic convictions so deep
that it seemed the two could never meet or be reconciled. It is hard
to avoid caricature in discussing these contrasting attitudes, all the
more since, as polarization grew, journalists and sometimes theologians dealt in Aunt Sallies which they identified with 'the forces
that are ruining the Church'. Few bothered to heed Toynbee's

warning in *A Study of History:* 'It is hardly possible to write two consecutive lines of historical narrative without introducing such fictitious personifications as "England", "France", "the Conservative Party", "the Church" . . .' Hasty categorization must be avoided. But however inadequate they are, and however much they become slogans hurled at one's opponents, the terms were not utterly meaningless.

Lumped together under the heading 'pre-conciliar' were the following attitudes: an excessively rationalist approach to theology which thought of revelation in terms of 'inside information' about God; stress on purely individual piety; a view of the liturgy in which the congregation were merely spectators; a suspicion of other Christians and an inbuilt sense of superiority over them; thorough-going opposition not only to Communism but to all the other isms which solicited or dominated the modern world. All that was dismissed as 'pre-conciliar'.

'Post-conciliar' meant the contrary of all these deplorable features. So it came to mean: seeing revelation as the response of man to God's perpetually renewed summons and invitation; a readiness to loosen up scholastic categories by means of more 'existentialist' ideas (and this lead to a more 'Protestant' approach to faith as trust for example); a view of the liturgy that stressed its communal aspect and of other Christians which emphasized dialogue and what was in common; an 'opening to the world' and a readiness to learn from it. At its best the transition from pre-conciliar to post-conciliar was one from arrogance to humility, from unjustifiable certainty to legitimate doubt, from security to hesitation, from swagger to stammer, from triumphalism to sharing in 'the joys and the hopes, the griefs and the anxieties of the men of this age' (*On the Church in the Modern World*, 1). Normally it would be thought superfluous to congratulate a group of human beings on admitting that they belonged to the human race, but for the Roman Catholic Church such an admission was both startling and transforming: it was a way of saying that it was neither so privileged nor so special as had been supposed.

Of course the distinction between pre-conciliar and post-conciliar should not be pushed to the length of absurdity – though in the excitement it frequently was. The Council was transformed into one of those pills which appear to work a miraculous change between 'before' and 'after'. There was an underlying continuity between pre-conciliar and post-conciliar, and if one tries hard enough one can see how the seeds of almost every conciliar doctrine were sown in the years which preceded it. The 'liturgical movement' did not begin with the Council: it plunged its roots deep into the preceding pontificate (*Mediator Dei* appeared in 1947) and even further back into the reign of St Pius X who, when not pursuing Modernists, advocated 'frequent communion' against Jansenist hesitations and scruples. Nor is it difficult to show that the much-vaunted understanding of the Church as organism rather than organization, as living body rather than juridical fortress, reaches back to the encyclical *Mystici Corporis* of Pius XII. And one could show more generally that the Council adopted and extended to the whole Church the best thinking of parts of the Church. To use the rather laboriously mixed metaphor of the Council itself – it was speaking of liturgy – the Council can be considered as 'the summit toward which the activity of the Church is directed; at the same time . . . the fountain from which all her power flows' (*On the Sacred Liturgy*, 10).Towards that summit, which must have seemed not only distant but inaccessible, had toiled so many French and German theologians in the three decades before the Council. Now their hour had struck. Indeed, it would be possible to claim that the Council's 'changes' were superficial, concerned with form rather than substance, and that deep down all is the same. Yet though the contrast between 'before' and 'after' should not be turned into an opposition, as though the Church had turned a somersault, it nevertheless exists and cannot be spirited away by any dialectical finesse.

It is a Catholic habit – it used to be a boast – not to be content with half-measures: in the post-conciliar period this tendency to absolutize led to a conflict rather like a medieval morality play in which the evil was unutterably evil and the good unalloyedly good. There were different ways of interpreting the script, but the commonest was the progressive myth in which His Eminence Cardinal Preconcilio swaggered and orated, closing down the latest catechetical centre, forbidding the sale of the Dutch *New Catechism*, and generally behaving in an obscurantist and reactionary manner. The trouble was that His Eminence Cardinal Preconcilio really existed. He could appear in the guise of Cardinal Siri of Genoa, who declared that 'the Council was the greatest mistake in recent ecclesiastical history' (and by 'recent' he meant in the last five hundred years); or he might appear as Dr McQuaid of Dublin, who on his return assured the people of Ireland that they need have no fears: the Council would make no difference in Ireland; or he might take the looming shape of Cardinal MacIntyre of Los Angeles, who hounded the nuns of the Immaculate Heart of Mary out of his diocese; or he could be represented by the Archbishop of Southwark, who told an astonished group of hard-working teachers of religion that in his diocese there was only one teacher of religion, himself.

There were more candidates for the role of Cardinal Preconcilio than for that of Cardinal Dopoconcilio. Cardinal Dopoconcilio did not use his title, wore a simple black soutane with a wooden cross. He was frequently accused of being a Communist because he said that the Church should be on the side of the poorest and the oppressed. Sometimes he appeared as Dom Helder Camara, of Recife, Brazil – the world's most celebrated bishop and four times candidate for the Nobel Peace Prize; and sometimes as Cardinal Pellegrino of Turin, who was known to criticize the Roman Curia publicly (everyone did so *privately*, of course, which according to Cardinal Heenan was the best method for getting it changed: but if all the private grumbles and criticisms of the Curia had been effective, it would by now be a very different institution); and another candidate, at least until he fell into the arms of the charismatic movement, was Cardinal Suenens whose Flemish bluntness and flair for publicity made him almost the embodiment of Cardinal Dopoconcilio. It also made him enemies. So the stage was set, the roles were assigned, and the drama began to unfold.

There were quarrels, defections, bitter words spoken, irreparable things done and said. There was confusion and shouting. An analysis of what was going on could lead either to the conclusion that the Church was on the brink of self-destruction, and that the folly of a handful of men had brought it to this pass; or that it stood on the edge of a new era. An editorial in *New Blackfriars* compared the constitution *On the Church* to Magna Carta and spoke ironically of 'the great breakthrough into the thirteenth century'. An English bishop said that but for the Council, the Church would have been like the Loch Ness monster: rumoured to exist, of venerable antiquity, actually seen by some, but not of much relevance in the contemporary world. Incompatible and contradictory claims were made. Newspapers talked imprecisely of crisis and fanned the flames. The spectacle of disagreement was sometimes squalid and disedifying, all the more since it came from a body which previously had appeared so 'monolithic'. How was it possible for the well-ordered and disciplined army to be turned into an apparently disorganized rabble? How did the Church become the runaway Church, lurching out of control?

Part of the answer is that the bishops were responsible. Bishops can so easily become the scapegoats, and it is fashionable to complain of lack of leadership. But as John Courtney Murray once said, 'Some people say the American bishops should give us a lead: I'm not so sure – after all, who knows where they would lead us?' No, the point here is simply that the Vatican Council presented the spectacle of bishops arguing vehemently among themselves and doing so before the eyes of the world's press, who gleefully reported all the twists and turnings of the disputes. Priests, religious and laity promptly set about emulating the bishops. Moreover, there were a lot of bishops in Rome at the same time, and there were so many that the bishop was 'demythologized'. He ceased to be a remote and magical figure in a very special hat, and became instead the man who waited at the bus stop like everybody else. This was a welcome trend in that it made bishops approachable; but it also made them considerably less imposing.

The well-publicized disagreements in St Peter's, disedifying though they were on one level, were also welcome in that they were more honest than the smooth façade of apparent unity imposed in the reign of Pope Pius XII, which was purchased only at the price of silencing theologians and gagging dissent. Yves Congar, OP, was exiled from Le Saulchoir to Cambridge and Henri de Lubac,

SJ, was forbidden to teach or even to live in a house where there were students. The result was that both of them did more work than ever before, and both had emerged at the Council as influential and respected figures. The stimulating clash of opinions was better than the anxious imposition of uniformity. What began in Rome spread outwards through the whole Church. The example of Paul standing up to Peter was frequently proposed later in the period as a model, particularly after *Humanae Vitae* in 1968; and the theory was put around that the Holy Spirit manifested himself quite especially in dissent. 'Controversy', declared the manifesto of the Catholic Renewal Movement in Britain, 'is the living proof of the activity of the Holy Spirit within the Church.'

But there is a world of difference between justifying outspokenness and *Honesty in the Church* (Dan Callahan's significant title for a book published in 1965), and making an apologia for dissent. In the long run a squabbling Church could never be 'the sacrament of Christ's salvation', as the Council had grandiosely described it. These Christians would have to be seen to love each other at some level, or else, instead of that witness to the love of Christ they were supposed to provide, they would in fact be providing a counter-witness. The comment so frequently made on ecumenism – that a divided Church could only muffle and obscure the message it had to transmit – applied to the inner life of the Roman Catholic Church as well. It was sometimes said, as consolation, that the most divergent views were reconciled in the Mass, in the Eucharist, that Cardinal Ottaviani and Hans Küng could embrace one another as brothers in this transcendent act; but even if that were true – and in a sense it was – this eucharistic communion could represent no more than a lull, a temporary truce, in a conflict of minds and attitudes which went much deeper than anyone knew at the time.

It was possible, all the same, to present the Church's new and manifest turbulence as a sign of vigour and vitality. Only in a body in which people really *cared* could disagreement be so keen. The grey pall of indifference which settled over so many religious questions in the late twentieth century was not found in the Roman Catholic Church. But this was an ambivalent argument. It is perfectly true that Roman Catholics – or at any rate an articulate minority of them – cared, and cared passionately, about the Church, its structure and its future, and as a compensation for the abuse of other Christians, now officially discouraged as contrary to the spirit of ecumenism, they 'introjected' their conflicts and found their enemies within the Roman Catholic Church. But the fact that both groups cared cannot ultimately be the reconciling principle, since they cared about such different values. Religious conflict is more severe and demanding than ordinary secular conflict. This is not simply because of *odium theologicum* or celibacy, which means that priests can give their total and undivided attention to controversy, undistracted by any humanizing concern for their families. Religion always involves the whole person, mind, heart and imagination; it involves – and indeed is – the assertion of the ultimate. For all these reasons it arouses passions. It is not trifling, like a hobby, or replaceable, like a suit of clothes. Touch religion, and you touch the depths of the whole person. Hence the particular prickliness and touchiness which surround religious questions.

The post-conciliar disputes gave ample evidence of the truth of this principle. And whatever the immediate questions under discussion, the real quarrel was between two conflicting notions of the 'sacred' or the 'holy' which struggled with each other and still do so in a conflict which remains unresolved. One view stresses the 'vertical' element in faith, the relationship to God; and it selects certain persons, institutions, objects, which in a privileged way are held to give access to the divine clearly and unmistakably. Thus the priest will be regarded as a 'holy man' set apart, and only his 'sacred hands' can touch the 'sacred vessels', while the liturgy can be celebrated only in a specially set aside place (a church) and not in profane settings. The image of the sacred and separated priest affects, quite naturally, that of the bishop, who is still more separated and sacred, and this in its turn colours the appreciation of the Pope, who represents the ultimate point along this line of thinking. One can go no further in definitive, authoritative and final teaching than the Pope; and so he is endowed with infallibility, which is not essentially a form of ecclesiastical arrogance but rather a way of saying that the Pope is the ultimately sacred thing on earth (like God, he can neither 'deceive nor be deceived'). The sacred conceived in this way demands total commitment from its officials and consequently celibacy, since to share the common fate of humanity would make them less sacred.

The other view of the sacred refuses to localize it in persons, places and things. Its favourite text is John 4, where Christ says that worship in the future will not take place in temples but will be 'worship in spirit and truth'. But the end of Temple worship at Jerusalem also means the end of the priesthood as a separated, sacred caste: in future there will be 'a chosen race, a royal priesthood, a holy nation, God's own people' (1 Peter 2:9). The fact that Christianity implicitly went back on this principle is often attributed to a 're-Judaizing' process: it proved extremely difficult to live with a view of the sacred as omnipresent and to seek and find God in all things; the temptations of religion (as opposed to faith) impelled men to give the sacred a home, a dwelling, a *locus* in the general blur of the secular. Vatican II gave some basis to the idea that the sacred is simply the secular but seen in the light of God when it urged lay Christians not to allow their hope to remain locked up in the depths of their hearts, but to express it continually 'in the framework of secular life' (*On the Church*, 35). Likewise it asserted that since the Incarnation nothing and no one can be 'purely secular' any more (*On the Church in the Modern World*, 22).

The alternative starting-point gives totally different answers, whatever the question under discussion. Priesthood, for example, ceases to be the attribute of a specialized sacred elite but becomes a *function* which the community needs – and this opens the way not only to married priests and women priests but to 'part-time' priests as well. The sacrament, instead of being a sacred rite to be viewed with profound religious awe, parachuted down from above into the grey ordinariness of our everyday lives, becomes the summing-up of the high points of human existence. The role of the Church in politics is no longer seen as that of exhorting the nations to morality from some superior position and deploring their inevitable failures, but as sharing in the rough and tumble, sustained only by hope. But the overall distinction which can be made is between an attitude in which the Church has nothing to learn from the world, and one in which the Church has much – though not everything – to learn from the world. This distinction is not the same as that between Cardinal Preconcilio and Cardinal Dopoconcilio, though it overlaps with it.

In this sense, then, the Council was not an end but a beginning. In so many instances it papered over the obvious cracks in a laudable effort to secure unanimity. Pope Paul himself always sought compromise texts to which the vast majority of the Council Fathers could assent, if not with enthusiasm then at least with resignation. He wanted, as he said, *'des convaincus, pas de vaincus'*. It was to be a matter of convictions, not of victors and vanquished. This beautiful dream, perhaps the result of an over-idealistic view of the Church, quickly faded, and the cracks opened into yawning chasms. The ambiguity of the conciliar texts meant that it was always possible to interpret them in divergent ways. Thus, for example, defenders of the papal monarchy could point to the fact that the teaching of Vatican I on papal prerogatives was repeated in its entirety and therefore was in no way to be whittled down; but those who wanted to see the papal office as a function serving the unity of the whole Church could point out that this traditional doctrine was set in a fresh context, that of the co-responsibility of all the world's bishops, and that consequently it was in principle modified. A Church which values consistency, they could argue, cannot develop a doctrine by contradicting itself, but only by setting a newly noticed truth alongside an older established one. The same ambivalence is found very obviously in the question of ecumenism, which was simultaneously described as the work of the Holy Spirit (and this in Christian language is the highest seal of approval on any event or person) while the position of the Roman Catholic Church as 'the one true Church' was reasserted. Where was the emphasis to fall? The reader could bring his own tone of voice to his reading and still claim to be 'faithful to the Council' (this was the ambition of everyone, at least during the early part of the period).

With hindsight one can see how naïve was the claim to 'implement' the Council by a series of subsequent instructions, and how naïve it was to imagine that the whole Church would march in step

and with linked arms towards its fulfilment. Rome has showered
document upon document on the rest of the Church, but their very
number muffles their effect and for the most part they are now
received with an indifference which is sometimes stoical and sometimes scornful. Thus there is a great contrast between the *consciously intended* goals of the Council and its *actual effects*. It constantly laid down principles which, if taken seriously, would drag
the barque of Peter out into new and uncharted seas. To say, for
example, that the Church's teaching office was 'not above the word
of God, but serves it' (*On Divine Revelation*, 10) was a far-reaching
commitment. To make the liturgy intelligible by using vernacular
languages seemed a modest aim, but the vernacular revealed
oddities and inconsistencies which the decent obscurity of the
Latin had veiled. To say the religious life should be a 'sign' to all
mankind seemed innocent enough, but it meant that monks and
nuns from now on would have to be judged (and judge themselves)
by the most stringent criteria: if religious life was *defined* as the
following of the three vows of poverty, chastity and obedience, then
provided these were kept, there could be little discussion about it;
but once it was presented as a 'sign' to the world, then its contradictions became apparent – it was not, for example, a sign of the
Gospel for a vast convent surrounded by high walls to exist in the
middle of a Bogotá slum.

Indeed, more generally, the Church had presented herself as a
sign, as 'the sign or sacrament of salvation', and once more that
aroused expectations and severe demands for self-reform. There
could be no finer description of the Church's purpose than the one
given by the Council: 'For it is the function of the Church, led by
the Holy Spirit who renews and purifies her ceaselessly, to make
God the Father and his Incarnate Son *present and in a sense visible*'
(*On the Church in the Modern World*, 21). But the hopes aroused by
this text, and others like it, could so easily be dashed by the petti-
ness of ecclesiastical bureaucrats and the manifest presence of 'sin'
in the Church. Even though the Council had admitted that the
Church was 'in constant need of purification' ('*semper purificanda*' –
and note that Luther's phrase '*semper reformanda*' was avoided), it
didn't do to indicate with too much zest particular areas that were

in need of purification, as Herbert McCabe, OP, found early in 1967 when he mentioned one or two areas of corruption and was dismissed from his post as editor of *New Blackfriars*. But the lament is not that the high hopes of the Council failed: it is rather that they were bound to fail, and yet that they set up a movement in the Church which is irreversible and to some extent uncontrollable.

It is at this point that the rulers of the Church, from Pope Paul downwards, have been seized with alarm, for they fear that the situation is slipping out of control despite repeated warnings and ineffectual threats. Pope Paul has personalized this drama, this feeling of being led where he would not go. The day before his coronation he went down to the church of San Carlo alla Corso in Rome to take part in a 'farewell service' for his compatriots from Brescia. The theme of his sermon was 'What will become of me?' (*'Che cosa sarà di me?'*) His answer was that he did not know, but that, like Peter, he would be led. 'Another will gird you and carry you where you do not wish to go' (John 21:18). Pope Paul has been carried whither he did not wish to go, oscillating between the assertion of a principle and the acceptance of its consequences. He has made splendid ecumenical gestures, and recoiled from their application. The fact that he has been blamed by both the right wing and the left wing convinces him that he is a moderate – and to be a moderate is the ambition of many churchmen, who would like to be, in Cardinal Suenens' phrase, 'in the extreme centre'. For Pope Paul and for all Roman Catholics the question has been the same: how much learning from 'the world' is possible and desirable? The fact that after a brief flirtation with his predecessor's slogan *'aggiornamento'* Pope Paul should have abandoned it in favour of the more decorous and less menacing 'renewal' is significant. 'Renewal' is a churchly exercise in which the Church looks to its origins and revitalizes itself by contact with its spiritual sources; *'aggiornamento'* stresses the needs and legitimate demands of the world.

There can be no doubt that the Council stated the importance of learning from the world – much to the annoyance of the Cardinal Archbishop of Palermo who thought that it was humiliating and undignified for the Church to admit that it had anything to learn from anyone. The Church, says the Council, 'knows how richly she has profited by the history and development of humanity' (*On the Church in the Modern World*, 44) and, even more strikingly, she 'admits that she has greatly profited and still profits from the antagonism of those who oppose or persecute her' (ibid.). The Bishop of Cuernavaca in Mexico had spoken about the need to learn from Marx and Freud, Cardinal Suenens had warned against the repetition of 'another Galileo affair' in which the Church would be in opposition to science; and there was to hand a theoretical framework which enabled the Church, if it so desired, to move out of its introspective preoccupations. Known as 'the signs of the times', this theory was the Roman Catholic equivalent of the World Council of Churches' dictum that 'the world provides the agenda for the Church'. It posited that the Holy Spirit can speak to the Churches (the phrase comes from Revelation 1:10-11) not only through scripture and tradition but also through events, trends or tendencies of the modern world. True, it was not a matter of embracing them uncritically, but the message of the Gospel was to latch on to something that was already there. This was in fact a roughly 'Catholicized' version of Paul Tillich's 'theology of correlations', in which philosophy provides the questions which theology alone can answer. 'It is the task of the entire People of God', says the pastoral constitution, 'to hear, distinguish and interpret the many voices of our age, and to judge them in the light of the divine Word' (*On the Church in the Modern World*, 44). The difficulty lay in cashing these ideas.

In so many instances the leaders of the Church found themselves urging courses of action which, if taken literally, seriously and above all applied to the Church itself, would lead to embarrassing consequences. So for example, it was all very well to make full and responsible participation of all the citizens the norm of good government and to declare it 'in full accord with human nature' (*On the Church in the Modern World*, 75), but where did that leave the Church's own habits of government, which had traditionally prized unquestioning obedience and authority more than 'participation'? Both were interestingly modified, in that obedience was qualified as 'mature', while authority was seen as existing not for its own sake but 'for service'. This is a possible synthesis which emphasizes that liberty and authority do not face each other with a frown, but are complementary and require the middle term of 'community': liberty exists in its context, and authority is exercised for its good. But after some spasmodic attempts there was a partial relapse into older habits. The Council had urged 'responsible parenthood', but that turned out to be a compromise or a play upon words. Splendid documents proclaimed the need for public men to be accessible to the press in order to be accountable to the people. But the Vatican itself continued to exercise the tightest control over its own publications and to refuse entry to journalists, except the most tame. In so many ways the Church ran the risk of being hoist with its own petards, petards which it had lovingly and laboriously prepared at the Vatican Council. The task of transforming an auto-cratic institution into a participatory community proved more diffi-cult than anyone had imagined.

Fear and anxiety make bad counsellors. The Council made possible and proclaimed an openness to the world which had subse-quently been modified out of recognition. It has died the 'death of a thousand qualifications'. In Roman style an adjective is fre-quently used to undermine a noun. Thus to be in favour of 'sound ecumenism' sounds like being in favour of ecumenism, but the implications of 'sound' cut it down to size and make it the equiva-lent of 'officially approved'. Similarly, 'healthy criticism' is needed in the Church, while 'unhealthy criticism' must be avoided like the plague. In this way the rhetoric of Vatican II has been maintained, while its substance has been drained out. At crucial turning-points there has been a reversion to authoritative methods and the separ-ated sacred. 1968 was the decisive year. For then the Pope declared the work of the specially appointed commission on birth-control 'inadequate' and went contrary to it, settling alone a question that had been withdrawn from the competence of the Council. Quite apart from the merits of the case, this action signified that there was to be no real change in the *modus operandi* of the Roman Catholic Church, and that the supreme sacred representative would con-tinue to decide; but at the same time the chosen ground was one

in which separated sacred persons, who are by definition un-
married, have no experience, and their keenness to pronounce on
this subject discredited them more generally. People felt that
although the church leaders might have arcane specialized knowledge which could be relied upon in strictly theological questions,
here was a question within ordinary experience, which did not
regard contraception necessarily as the enemy of married love. The
1971 Synod which dallied with the idea of the ordination of
married men represented another decisive choice; at first it seemed
that a majority was building up in favour, whether as a good thing
in itself (as the Canadians maintained) or to remedy the obvious
pastoral need for more priests (the commoner argument). The word
came down from above that the ordination of married men – which
would have struck a sharp blow at the separated sacred – was not
acceptable, and the question was buried in a special commission.
Once again, it was not simply the decision in itself that caused distress, but the way the machinery specially set up had apparently
been treated with contempt.

   Ten years after the Council the Vatican declared itself firmly in
favour of the separated sacred. The first evidence was the 'Third
Synod'. (It was literally the fourth, though technically the third,
because the 1969 Synod was not in the series and so did not count.)
After the confusions of the previous synods it was limited to a
single topic, that of 'Evangelization'. This splendid theme went to
the heart of the meaning of the Gospel for today. But the Synod
was bogged down in procedural difficulties, and never managed to
find its own voice. There was an attempt to give 'salvation' a secular dimension and to interpret it in terms of social and political
liberation, but this move was powerfully resisted. 'Salvation' remained safely spiritual.

   But the 1974 Synod was in any case overshadowed by the celebrations announced for the Holy Year of 1975. Nothing could give
more categorical expression to the assertion of the separated sacred
than the Holy Year. It is based on a Jewish idea. And just as the
Jews had a separated tribe of priests, so they set aside a year 'of
special public observance, with abstention from work, a return to
the original distribution of land, the cancellation of debts and the

freeing of Hebrew slaves'. It is possible, though difficult, to press these ideas for contemporary relevance. But the ritual itself provided a classic expression of unrepentant, world-defying Roman Catholicism. On Christmas Eve, Pope Paul with three stout hammer blows unsealed the Holy Door of St Peter's through which pilgrims had to pass to gain the Holy Year indulgence. A shower of unexpected dust tumbled down. Next day, Christmas Day, three 'specially designated cardinals' opened similar Holy Doors in three other major basilicas. The whole idea is splendidly medieval, and Dante took part in the very first Holy Year, and the jostling crowds of Rome led him to put it in the *Inferno* (18:28); in 1975 the *sindaco* or mayor of Rome was more worried that the traffic of the city would finally seize up altogether.

He need not have worried, for the response to the Holy Year was lukewarm, and the expected millions did not appear. A brave front was put on, a stiff Roman upper lip was maintained, the discouraging statistics were explained away, the spiritual reality and success of 'reconciliation' in depth was asserted in the official rhetoric, but something had gone wrong. Cardinal Maximilian de Fürstenberg, president of the Central Committee of the Holy Year, explained that the idea was born 'under the prompting of the Holy Spirit on the feast of Pentecost 1973'. It was like an ironical commentary on Pope John's prayer that the Council would be a 'new Pentecost'. Moreover, it was plainly false, since the date of a Holy Year is determined by the bull of Pope Paul II, *Ineffabilis Providentiae*, which itself was based on an earlier text of 1300. Cardinal de Fürstenberg went on, with no awareness of the irony of what he was saying: 'Of course, even granting the primacy of the Spirit, there is needed a certain amount of organization, a co-ordination of services, both to serve the Spirit and to meet the needs of the Church as community.' The Spirit is commended for having got the thing going; but then the organization men take over.

Pope Paul had hesitated before embarking on the risk of the Holy Year. 'We have asked ourselves', he said on 9 May 1973, 'if such a tradition should be maintained in times which are so different from times gone by.' But he swallowed his scruples and went ahead, no doubt with memories of the last Holy Year of 1950 in his mind. But the analogy cannot be sustained. In 1950 Pope Pius XII joyously celebrated the Holy Year and could do so because it summed up the spirit of the Church as it then was: any critical voices there might have been were gagged. But by 1975 the Holy Year no longer expresses the mood of the Church. Indeed, one can go further and say that it contradicts the Church's self-understanding as shown in Vatican II. It is based on a medieval idea, it strongly asserts Catholic identity over against Protestants, it revives, in however muted a form, the use of indulgences which played such an important symbolic role in the beginnings of the Reformation; and so, notwithstanding protestations and qualifying afterthoughts to the contrary, it is not the most ecumenical of events. Moreover, it is not only other Christians who are indifferent or worried. The fact is that the Church is no longer so Rome-centred, and as a result the Holy Year of 1975 appeared as something of an anachronism, deliberately cultivated to encourage a party or faction within the Church. It was a far cry from the high hopes of ten years previously. What went wrong? What happened to the high hopes? How did this gap open up and broaden between official pronouncements and Christian experience?

Chapter 2

They Have Robbed Us of Our Liturgy

If the poet writes 'wood' what are the chances that the
wood of the Cross will be evoked? Should the answer
be 'none', then it would seem that a great impoverish-
ment of some sort would have to be admitted

DAVID JONES
Anathemata, pp. 23–4.

The way people worship tells us more about their view of the
sacred than any other human activity. The prayers we use, the
clothing we wear, the attitudes we adopt, the buildings we put up –
all these are a living source of implicit theology. This was summed
up in the old maxim: *'lex orandi, lex credendi.'* As people worship,
so do they believe.

Judged in this light, Catholic theology came off badly. For
between the Council of Trent in the sixteenth century and the
Second Vatican Council, Catholic liturgy was fossilized to a remarkable degree. This was a conscious act of policy. The papal bull
of 1570, *Quo Primum Tempore*, enjoined that the Roman Missal
should endure for all time, and that no jot or tittle in it should be
altered or amended or dropped. And Pope Pius V added dire
threats about what would happen to those who contravened his
instructions. Of course there were limits to the attempt to impose
complete uniformity in worship. There remained irreducible differences between Mass celebrated in a Central European church of
baroque splendour and Mass celebrated in an English country
house where the priest arrived in disguise and departed in haste.
There was a difference of style and spiritual outlook: a light,
spacious building, with rich paintings and *trompe-l'oeil* effects,
saints and putti, an orchestra and a Haydn setting put the Christian
in one frame of mind; quite another was evoked by oak panelling,
quiet devotion and a sense of illegality. These cultural and social

differences remained, and there were many more. The contrast between 'the blessed mutter of the Mass' and the theatrical unfolding of the divine drama in baroque has affected judgements to this day. But for all the difference of styles, there was a deep unity of content and structure. The words were the same, whether muttered or proclaimed or polyphonically sung.

Nearly four hundred years after Pius V's bull, the Second Vatican Council changed all that. To some the liturgical changes seemed overdue and obvious, once the *meaning* of the liturgy had been grasped; to others they were unequivocally threatening and calamitous, the loss of a great heritage. All agreed that they were significant. Few emulated the cussedness of the ex-Indian army officer who campaigned in favour of the Vernacular Society before the Council, only to join the Latin Mass Society as soon as the aims of the Vernacular Society were realized.

Opposition to liturgical change was found chiefly among elites, whether social or intellectual. The late Duke of Norfolk was occasionally described as 'the leading English Catholic layman', though he acquired the title in virtue of his birth rather than through notable achievement. Though a Roman Catholic, he was Earl Marshal and therefore responsible for many royal and Anglican ceremonies. He was a stickler for precision and punctuality. He would stand there, stop-watch in hand, endlessly regulating those stately comings and goings, wheelings and bowings which make up a royal occasion like a marriage or a coronation. He did not like the liturgical changes introduced by Vatican II. Here is how the obituary in *The Times* put it, with customary understatement: 'It need hardly be added that he did not welcome the liturgical changes which followed the Second Vatican Council, and he let it be known that when he was received in private audience by the Pope after the canonization of the Forty Martyrs, he left the Pope in no doubt that the changes were widely unwelcome in England, and urged him to make no more changes.' One could certainly challenge the Duke's right to speak in the name of English Catholics – a word he always pronounced, like others of his class and generation, with an intrusive 'r' ('Cartholic'). It was likely that he was projecting on to his fellow countrymen his own feelings of distaste.

But what was it, deep down, that he so disliked? And what was it that rallied in common disappointment Evelyn Waugh and François Mauriac and so many other writers? In the first years of the decade there was much talk of 'the changes in the Church'. When the phrase was used without further qualification it usually meant liturgical change. 'No more changes', said the Duke to the Pope. Liturgical change, then, summed up and symbolized all the other 'changes' and caused deep forebodings about the future. Liturgical change was the one that could be most easily grasped and comprehended. This was the one that touched most people most immediately. This was the one that came home.

The real significance of liturgical change, and its threatening nature, lies here: if change was possible in the sphere of a liturgy which for centuries had remained invariable, then change would be possible in any area of religious life; and that thought led to another which did not long remain unexpressed: where will it all end? Once more Catholics proved to be victims of arguments which they had previously put forth with too much enthusiasm. That the liturgy had not changed for centuries was not just a statement of fact – it was an apologetic argument. Bossuet's *Histoire des Variations des Eglises Protestantes* provided the classic text in how Protestants, having unwisely abandoned liturgical unity, had lapsed into doctrinal chaos and splintered into innumerable sects. In contrast the waves of error and diversity would lash in vain against the rock of Peter.

To this sense of enduring permanence in time, was added the argument about universality in space: the Latin liturgy was held to be the great bulwark against ecclesiastical nationalism, a consolation for the tourist arriving unexpectedly for Mass in a strange place, and the cause of the Church's unity. 'The Mass', everyone said, as though it were a self-evident truth, 'is the same the whole world over.' Just before the Vatican Council an English bishop wrote a pastoral letter in which he declared that whatever else happened at the forthcoming Council – and he did not expect that much good would come of it – the Last Gospel would never be touched. The 'Last Gospel' was the Prologue to St John's Gospel which, as one had to inform those under twenty, was always read at the end of Mass.

These arguments – uniformity in time, universality in space – had held the field for so long and now were discarded so rapidly that many were left breathless at the suddenness of the change. A whole new series of considerations began to be brought into play to legitimate the 'changes' and justify the reformers' zeal. The 'new' arguments were in fact far from recent, and were stock-in-trade in much of the writing that came from German-speaking countries. Pius Parsch in Vienna and Odo Casel in Germany had made the liturgy central in Christian living, and they were not alone. It was sometimes suggested that the 'liturgical movement' of the late thirties was a Christian response to Communism and, nearer home, to Nazism. In answer to these false collectivisms, Christians rediscovered the social nature of their redemption. We are saved as a people.

A similar movement had developed in France and spread outwards from the Abbey of Solesmes. But to prevent the liturgical movement from remaining too monastic and remote from the life of twentieth-century urban man, the French bishops set up a 'Centre de Liturgie Pastorale'. Its exact title is of importance. Throughout the fifties it was argued that the liturgy had to become *pastoral*, and that it should have a *teaching* function. Manifestly it would fail in its pastoral function and be hindered as teaching if its language was obscure and its gestures remote. Anyone familiar with these discussions would not have been in the least surprised when the 'changes' began to burst upon the Catholic world. But, as is frequently the case, there was concerned surprise as old ignorance met new knowledge for the first time.

Many who were desolated by the new liturgy thought it had come about as a result of a plot. Sinister deeds were attributed to Cardinal Lercaro, Archbishop of Bologna, who was president of the Liturgical Consilium specially set up to oversee the changes. In 1966 an Italian man of letters, Tito Casini, wrote a violent pamphlet, *La Tunica Stracciata*, in which he described the Cardinal as 'the most formidable menace, after Martin Luther, to the Church's integrity and unity'. He was further compared, most unfavourably, to a termite or white ant. Lercaro's right-hand man, Fr Bugnini, Secretary of the Consilium, also came under attack until he was made bishop and removed to comparative safety.

The notion of a conspiracy can be excluded. It was the product of disappointed fantasy. There was no mystery about how the Consilium worked, according to the brief of the Council and with the support of Pope Paul. It made 'changes' in the light of a few simple principles. It was neither trying to restore some lost, primitive liturgy – which everyone agreed was undiscoverable, even if it had existed – nor to start from scratch with a *tabula rasa*. Liturgical change came about because, once certain principles were laid down, an irresistible logic meant that further, and sometimes unexpected, consequences would follow. There was a dialectic of change.

The pivot on which everything turned was 'active participation'. It was not an original expression. As long ago as 1903, St Pius X had used it in a *motu proprio* encouraging church music. But to borrow Newman's phrase, there was a long road from notional to real assent. By 1963, 'active participation' had become the key term. The liturgy was no longer seen as the private act of the priest, to which the laity were admitted as onlookers, but as the public act by which the whole People of God shared in the prayer and sacrifice of Christ. It was seen as the act by which Christ took possession of his People, confirmed their unity and set them off on their tasks in the world. Once more these ideas were not new. The novelty lay in saying that this participation was not any mere 'following in the mind', but should be expressed in word and music and gesture. An old Jesuit had made a distinction between 'the training in faith, hope and charity' and the *expression* of faith, hope and charity. What he and a whole tradition had dissolved, the Liturgical Constitution of Vatican II put together again. The expression of faith could no longer be individual and interior. It summoned the whole person, body and soul, mind and heart, and evoked a response.

But once the principle of participation had been clearly stated, and given the decline of Latin as a common language, then the requirement of the vernacular plainly followed. Latin provided an additional element of estrangement or distancing between the worshipper and his Lord. It was removed, though not altogether at first. In the constitution *On the Sacred Liturgy* there is a curious distinction between parts of the Mass belonging to the priest (which remained in Latin) and 'parts which pertain to the people' (which slid into the vernacular) (54). This was another doomed distinction which did not long survive. Moreover, the use of the vernacular brought out oddities and inconsistencies which the Latin had long veiled, and so the use of the vernacular implied also a complete re-ordering of the liturgy 'in such a way that the intrinsic nature and purpose of its several parts, as also the connection between them, can be more clearly manifested' (50). Liturgical reform became a vast package which had to be taken as a whole.

Distinguish clearly between the liturgy of the word and the eucharistic rite: but then the *homily* follows, clearly envisaged not as the priest moralizing or talking about whatever comes into his head but as a relevant commentary on the scripture of the day. Place this stress on scripture: but then a demand for more variety and richness in choice of readings will follow. Establish the *function* of the several parts: but then the penitential rite will have to be more sharply distinguished from the introductory greeting, and a whole panoply of acclamations, responses, psalms, antiphons and hymns are needed to flesh out the varied responses. Re-ordering also implied simplification. As the constitution put it: 'The rites should be distinguished by a noble simplicity; they should be short, clear, and unencumbered by useless repetitions; they should be within the people's powers of comprehension, and normally should not require much explanation' (34).

In the five years after the Council the Roman Catholic Church was like a vast workshop in which these principles were put into practice in a patchwork, piecemeal manner. It began even before the Council ended, with the instruction *Inter Oecumenici* (dated 26 September 1964), and was completed by two further instructions (1967, 1970) and another on 'Sacred Music' (1967). At the start, there were even two bodies which competed with each other in a most unedifying manner. No sooner had the Liturgical Consilium introduced the 'bidding prayers' (what Anglicans know as 'prayers of intercession') than the Sacred Congregation of Rites showed that it had no less reforming zeal by reducing the words spoken at communion to '*Corpus Christi*', with the ratifying response '*Amen*'. These demarcation disputes only came to an end with the fusion of the two bodies in the newly named Congregation for Divine Worship. The simplification of the liturgy turned out to be a complicated and laborious matter.

Manifestly there was some discrepancy between the liturgists' vision and what actually happened in parishes around the world. But some truths quickly became evident everywhere. An absolutely central place was given to the Mass, the Eucharist, and other sacraments like marriage, priestly ordination and confirmation were set in the context of the Mass and took place after the reading of the Gospel. This led to the decline or total extinction of other church services. In most places Benediction became a distant memory. It also became apparent that what was involved was much more than a series of minor adjustments to age-old ceremonies: it involved a whole way of looking at the Church and its role in the world. The Council of Trent had confined itself to pruning liturgical excesses. Vatican Council II was the first council to try to think out the liturgy from basic principles.

One of the most important landmarks in the process of reform came at the first Synod of Bishops in October 1967. The bishops were invited to be present at the *Missa Normativa*, the immediate ancestor of the present liturgy. It lasted three-quarters of an hour, and was graced with a homily by Fr Bugnini. Reactions were mixed. There were some expressions of discontent. The aged Cardinal Browne, former Master General of the Dominicans, confessed that he could find nothing in it 'against faith or morals' which, coming from him, was high praise. Everything conspired against success: the unlikely fiction was that the bishops were ordinary Italians at Mass on a Sunday morning. But despite this implausibility – and liturgy needs a setting of authenticity if it is really to work – the majority were impressed and 71 voted in favour, 62 in favour but with modifications, and 41 disapproved. Archbishop Dwyer of Birmingham, England, explained afterwards what had been going on: 'The aim of the new liturgy is to restore the balance between individual and community spirituality. At Mass every Sunday the whole community is to take an active part in what is going on. Everyone there will be instructed, will be trained. He will be instructed in his duty to God and his neighbour. In a solemn, ritual religious act he will be trained to realize that all men are his brothers, that no man is an island.' If the Church is a vast learning community, then the liturgy is its school. Archbishop Dwyer added: 'The liturgical reform is in a real sense the key to the *aggiornamento*. Make no mistake about it: the revolution begins here.'

Others too were beginning to echo the words of the aristocrat to Louis XVI: 'Sire, this is not a revolt, it is a revolution.' Rightwing tracts pictured the Liturgical Consilium as a horde of barbarians who vandalously massacred the heritage of the past for the sake of a dubious notion of modernity, or else as doctrinaire zealots, locked up in a double-glazed ivory tower, and remote from ordinary parish liturgies where babies cried, small children noisily dropped toys, and even adults were known to cough and sneeze. In fact the identity of the members of the Consilium could easily be looked up: it had 48 members and over 200 experts who toiled away in 42 subcommittees. They were on the whole neither remote from life nor brutal, insensitive Philistines who destroyed the past out of sheer vindictiveness. They were aiming at something wholly new in the Roman Catholic Church: a liturgy which would be valid for the *present* though in obvious continuity with the past; and a liturgy for the *people*, not an elitist consolation for aesthetes. And since the way Christians worship reflects the way they think about the Church, the conflict was partly one between an 'elitist' and a 'populist' understanding of the Christian community.

There were other immediate theological and practical implications. The priest no longer stood with his back to the people, and no longer addressed his words to a wall at the end of the church. He turned to face them, at an altar which was brought forward. The adaptation was often awkward in buildings designed with a different liturgical style in mind, but modern churches – like the new cathedrals at Liverpool and Clifton – gathered the people round three sides of the altar. It was the equivalent of smashing the proscenium arch and adopting theatre-in-the-round (and both theatre critics and liturgists began to speak about involvement and participation). The exact significance of this change has been the subject of much confused debate. The priest was no longer placed as a *mediator* somewhere between the congregation and God; he became – and vocabulary soon caught up with the change – more of a 'president of the assembly' than a mediator. Critics claimed that in this way the 'sense of mystery' was lost; to be able to see the priest's face, his grimaces, twitchings or even smiles, was a distraction. He became less of an 'instrument' and more a person in his own right. New demands were made upon him in clarity of diction and dignity of gesture. He could no longer get away with slovenliness. But it was not so much that the 'sense of mystery' had been lost; it was rather that it had been re-located. Christ came in the midst of his people directly (according to Matthew 18:20). The liturgy became the immediate expression of the Church as the gathered community. A further consequence was that the priestly gestures, now that they became visible, would have to be simplified. No longer could the priest dash reverent signs of the cross over the bread and wine. Ritual was condemned to become more meaningful.

The use of the vernacular carried the 'populist' process a stage further. It brought with it a whole crop of difficulties, many of them still unresolved. The new official texts continued to be composed, and thought out, in Latin. But in view of the mobility of people in contemporary society, it seemed obvious that a particular language group should have a common translation. English is the most widely spoken language in the world, and an International Committee for English in the Liturgy was set to work. The initials ICEL soon became familiar and dreaded. At a meeting in Rome in 1968 they tried to lay down the principles on which they worked. The first difficulty was that the Council had granted to the episcopal conferences the right to authorize translations (*On the Sacred Liturgy*, 36), and so ICEL could not *impose* any particular translation, and did not wish to. And even apart from that, episcopal conferences varied in the sense of urgency they brought to the task of using the new versions: some wanted to make haste and use provi-

sional translations, while others preferred cautious delay. Despite
its sense of modesty, ICEL did hope that its texts would be universally adopted. Hence Article II stated: 'No international text can
hope to satisfy fully the desires and expectations of every conference in a language group. In order that ICEL may serve as an
effective instrument for an international linguistic group, member
conferences must be ready to subordinate preferences in style and
language for the sake of achieving a generally acceptable uniform
text and to accept the verdict of a two-thirds majority of the member conferences' (Report to the Episcopal Conferences, December
1968). Already the ponderous unwieldy prose of that statement
served warning that trouble lay ahead.

The translations provided by ICEL have been described as flat,
prosaic, neutral and, on occasions, ludicrously comic. As a response
to 'The Lord be with you', 'And also with you' is neither elegant
nor expressive nor illuminating. It reduces the exchange to a polite
greeting. 'We had not counted', wrote Michael Novak, 'on the
use of suburban supermarket English; on the watering down of
Christian mysteries to the level of "human potential" movements
and "sensitivity"' (*Commonweal*, 29 November 1974). One of the
most severe critics of the translations is Ian Robinson, who has no
right-wing axe to grind. His main concern is with the survival of
the English language. After the Lord's Prayer, the priest is directed
to say:

> Deliver us, Lord, from every evil,
> and grant us peace in our day.
> In your mercy keep us free from sin
> and protect us from all anxiety.

'Peace in our day' has an unfortunate evocation of Neville Chamber-
lain's ill-fated 'peace in our time', and on the last phrase Robinson
comments: 'I can't imagine a more irreligious wish than to be
protected from all anxiety, about, for instance, one's salvation: it is
prayer to be delivered from religious life into hebetude' (Ian
Robinson, *The Survival of English*, p. 54). It is easy to make great
sport with banalities and false associations. But it may be that
Robinson's strictures are more of a comment on the present state of

the English language than on the work of ICEL. Committee translation is difficult enough, but when the language itself seems incapable of evoking religious feelings, then too much blame should not be heaped on the hapless translators. We have a language that is exposed to political manipulation and advertising sleight-of-hand. It is a blunt instrument for talking about God, his splendours and intervention in human history.

Yet that is the task of the liturgy. What is true of language is true of music. Active participation implied that there should be singing, as an involvement of the whole person. 'He who sings, prays twice over', said St Augustine. Vatican II did not set out to abolish 'the glories of Catholic music', but its effect was to make the choir, as a specialized group performing intricate music, a rarity. One by one great choirs were disbanded or ruined by economic difficulties. 'Bare ruined choirs, where late the sweet birds sang.' However, three qualifications must be added straight away. First, choirs of quality had never been numerous. Secondly, 'the glories of Catholic music' suggested an ever-flowing, ever-broadening stream of musical talent deployed throughout the centuries, whereas the truth was that in most places, and for much of the time, nothing of note was happening (cf. Colin Mawby, 'Music as a Pastoral Aid', in *The Tablet*, 11 May 1974, p. 470). And thirdly, the function of a choir in the new liturgy was quite different. It was not a matter of systematically destroying the specialized, experienced and competent group of musicians, but of subordinating them to the liturgy as a whole.

What happened in practice varied from country to country. Holland was fortunate in that composers like Flor Peters had already been working from the fifties on a liturgical music that was bright and singable. In the sixties the Jesuit Huijbers was able to build on and develop this tradition. In the German-speaking countries there had long been the tradition of the *Singmesse* in which everyone joined in singing paraphrased texts of the liturgy. A jazz composer of distinction, Peter Janssens, produced music that was indisputably modern yet reverent. Everywhere the musical traditions which had previously been given scope outside the liturgy were pressed into service, ranging from a remarkable Mexican

Mass sung in the cathedral at Cuernavaca to the African *Missa Luba*. The Centre de Liturgie Pastorale in France had encouraged composers like Lucien Deiss and Joseph Gelineau. Gelineau's simple modal settings of the Psalms were based on an amalgam of Debussy and negro spirituals; his translated version of the Psalms into a kind of sprung rhythm worked well enough in French, but could be performed in a disastrously tumpety-tump way by the time it reached the English-speaking world.

The demands the new liturgy made for simplicity and singability meant that vast quantities of highly forgettable music were produced not only year by year, but even Sunday by Sunday. This was not necessarily to be deplored. There is a kind of musical journalism which meets an immediate need without aiming at imperishability. The spectacular success of rock musicals like *Godspell* and *Jesus Christ Superstar* brought worried comment from bishops but confirmed the trend towards pop and the omnipresent guitar. A French priest wrote a book about Johnny Halliday, a pop singer, and enthusiastically declared that the twanging of the guitar was to this generation what the sound of the great organ had been to our ancestors. The judgement was a little premature. But the guitar divided parishes that were vaguely 'folk' on the one hand, from those on the other who remained faithful to the more staid organ, though even they extended their repertoire to include Protestant hymns.

Serious composers became discouraged: they were invited to write music for texts which might be abandoned in the next change, they had to write music of an elementary nature, they could never be sure of performance, and they were often, as men brought up in a musical tradition, nostalgic for the *Agnus Dei* and other familiar forms of the past. Yet the new liturgy needed composers desperately. Indeed, their opportunity was great. By distinguishing more clearly than ever the *function* of the different parts of the Mass, the new liturgy challenged the composer's skill, resourcefulness and imagination: the entry song sets the mood, and is not the same in Lent and Pentecost. The response to the readings should be more of a contemplative, musing assimilation of what had gone before. There is room too for variety in form:

with now a simple refrain for the congregation, alternating with a more complex choral part. From March 1975 the 'standard' ICEL texts came into force, and one reason for composers' reticence was gone.

Two other reforms caused widespread controversy. Communion under both kinds, which had been one of the demands of the Reformation, was envisaged by the Liturgical Constitution and was extended still more widely by the instruction *Eucharisticum Mysterium* (25 May 1967). Nevertheless, it confined itself to listing a number of special cases – a marriage, a retreat, the relatives of a priest at his ordination Mass, and, delightfully, abbesses and religious on the day of their blessing or profession, as well as on the day of their jubilee. This seemed to imply that a grudging concession was being made, and it was at variance with the instruction's own statement of principle: 'When Holy Communion is received under both kinds, the *sign* is more expressive, for under the form of both kinds the sign of the Eucharistic Banquet appears more perfectly' (32). Precisely. But the doctrine of the 'more expressive sign' meant that communion under both kinds could not be restricted to special occasions. Though it could prove difficult to administer communion under both kinds to large congregations, the practice became more and more widespread.

Communion in the hand became another unexpected subject of controversy. Opponents complained that it was irreverent, and warned darkly of the dangers of the black mass. Advocates replied that only babes and birds were spoon-fed and that the mature, adult Christian ought to receive Christ in a mature, adult way. By 1971 the hierarchies of most Common Market countries, along with Japan, French Somaliland and Yugoslavia, had secured permission for communion in the hand, on the sensible condition that it was not imposed on anyone against their will. But it proved impossible to halt the practice elsewhere, despite episcopal disapproval. When Cardinal Heenan declared in a pastoral letter that the 'experiment' should cease in his diocese, one priest said that in his parish they were no longer experimenting: the experiment had succeeded, and so they would continue.

But any account of liturgical change which confined itself to

what was officially approved would be misleading. The Council
gave an impetus to a movement which developed a life of its own,
inevitably. For once the idea of *adaptation* to different types of
congregation was accepted, then it would be difficult to set arbitrary limits to the degree of adaptation and each group could claim
the right to a liturgy adapted to its own needs. Moreover, the very
possibility of the centralized reform of the liturgy began to be
doubted; and indeed it was optimistic to imagine that texts written
in Latin would immediately prove satisfactory when translated into
the innumerable world languages. The creative possibilities were
not being tapped. Participation was needed not merely in the
liturgy, but in the formation of the liturgy; and those communities
which used liturgical committees to prepare next Sunday's worship
were invariably more successful than those in places where it was
simply imposed and accepted, as though parachuted down from on
high. There was much that a liturgy committee could do, even
within the limits laid down. But adaptation and creativity led to
'experiments' that were not approved.

The notion of 'experiment' had a curious history. Clearly, there
will be no liturgy of any value unless it can be tested out somewhere,
and it must be tested in a real community. The Congregation for
Divine Worship accepted two types of 'experiment' only: the first
were initiated by the Congregation itself, which invited comments
from local hierarchies on proposed new rites; and the second were
'experiments' for which permission had been secured from the
Congregation, but only after writing in detail describing the
'experiment'. The first type of 'experiment' has produced the
revised rites now in use (from infant baptism to funerals). The
second type has produced very little, since the procedure proposed
is cumbersome in the extreme, and few groups had the leisure,
even if they had the inclination, to write up lengthy accounts of
what they were proposing to do. In any case there was a fairly
radical opposition between the bureaucratic methods and the
immediate needs which could be met by a combination of genial
inspiration and slap-happy improvisation. But a good deal of
experimentation was 'undue', measured by the standards of the
Sacred Congregation. Sometimes local bishops themselves author-

ized 'experiments'. More often they intervened to halt Mass being celebrated by a priest in a boiler suit. A cartoon in *The Critic* in 1968 showed the Last Supper: 'Wait till the diocesan chancery hears about this' was the ironical caption. Roman documents multiplied warnings against 'excesses'. *Notitiae*, house organ of the Consilium, warned in 1967: 'Things must not be done out of turn. When the time for creating arrives, it will not then be necessary to observe the restrictions of literal translation. But at the moment we are still at the stage where we have a chance to appreciate better all the richness of our liturgical heritage and to continue to live off it' (*Notitiae*, 1967, nos. 31-3, p. 296).

The crucial question was: how much creativity is to be allowed to the local community? Some seized it without waiting. Readings were taken from any place except scripture, ranging from Dag Hammarskjold to Solzhenitsyn or the newspaper or K. Marx. There were said to be over 350 canons in use in Holland. One of them, by Huub Oosterhuis, was described, with complete accuracy, as a canon for agnostics. 'Lord,' it humbly asked, 'if you exist, come among us.' Volumes of eucharistic prayers were published, but they did not catch the moving spirit, since by now the self-respecting priest was a man who had devised his own eucharistic prayer and was capable of improvising in public.

Again, the effects could be remarkable especially in small groups where a book with a set text could so easily form a barrier to experience; but there could equally well be much fumbling among stereotypes and biblical reminiscences. These developments, which on the whole were only possible with small groups, were difficult to use in the parish church: and thus, in a way which was exactly contrary to the aims of the Council, the gap between a liturgical elite and the masses was increased.

The demand for freedom and creativity was one thing: the do-it-yourself liturgical kit another. There have been invented liturgies with rice and tea instead of bread and wine, intended to symbolize solidarity with the oppressed people of Vietnam. Andrew Greeley has listed some of the more bizarre manifestations of creativity in which all sense of tradition is not only lost but gaily trampled upon. In one university community in America priest and congregation smoked marijuana after the homily in order to 'facilitate' the Spirit. A new funeral rite begins with 'The Battle Hymn of the Republic', which is followed by readings from the dead man's favourite authors. The Gospel is replaced by 'a story or anecdote' about the deceased. The five senses of the corpse are anointed with oil and then 'everybody anoints everybody else'. Flowers are handed round and 'whoever wants to can put his flower on the dead man, making a little ceremony out of it'. The bread and wine are given to the corpse, the glass is then wrapped in a napkin and smashed. 'Swing Low, Sweet Chariot' brings the proceedings to a merciful close ('US Catholics, 1972', in *The Month*, May 1972, p. 135 et seq.).

It is not sheer perversity which leads to such things. There is a theory designed to justify them. Harvey Cox, ever a faithful recorder of trends, had first claimed that man was moving beyond 'the religious stage' (in *The Secular City*), but by 1974 he had rediscovered the importance of ritual and myth. The effects were somewhat startling, and in *The Seduction of the Spirit* he describes a liturgical experiment, called oddly 'Byzantine Easter', which took place in a Boston discotheque at four o'clock in the morning. Cox (Baptist) devised it, and was helped out by an Episcopalian priest, two United Church of Christ ministers (one a woman), a Melkite priest and a Roman Catholic priest. The congregation of some two thousand placed upon the altar 'pumpernickel, cinnamon buns, doughnuts, twinkies, long French loaves, matzos, scones, heavy black bread and raisin tarts'. They next began to paint 'peace signs, fishes, crosses and assorted graffiti on one another's faces and bodies'. Cox explains that there was an attempt at popular liturgy of participation (as opposed to a 'spectator' liturgy) and hence there was dancing with light-and-music collages and 'physical encounter movements'. The aim was to revive the powerful old symbols of Christianity and bring them more directly into the service of human liberation. The music ranged from the 'Hallelujah Chorus' through the theme march from the film *Z*, and ended with the Beatles singing 'Here Comes the Sun', at which point someone opened the back door and 'by some miracle of celestial timing, the sun was just beginning to peek over the Boston extension of the Massachusetts turnpike'. Two Boston policemen, dismissed by Cox as 'custodians of convention', brought the proceedings to a halt because it seemed to them 'more like a debauch than a religious service'.

The practical effect of such way-out liturgies was to give the participants a fugitive thrill and to discredit 'legitimate' experimentation and adaptation. And they were based on a fundamentally false appreciation of the nature of ritual, which is never a purely spontaneous expression of man's 'interiority' (as Cox claims) but rather an inherited social experience which is repeated and strengthened in rites. Mary Douglas has shown in her book *Natural Symbols* that the tendency towards more spontaneous forms of worship, far from being a sign of religious enlightenment, is a reflection of a society in which social relationships are breaking down and are increasingly loosely structured. This argument based on the nature of religious ritual does not mean rejecting the whole of the positive achievements of the liturgical movement, but it does suggest that liturgy needs to move round 'fixed points' which the historical community that is the Church recognizes as its objective signs, 'the intersection of the timeless with time' as Eliot put it. We live in a world that is full of noisy *signals*, and the mass media assault from all sides. But the liturgy is made up of *signs* which have transforming significance for the confused, perplexed humanity that we are. Vatican II had a largely practical approach to the liturgy: it was based on a theory that was coherent enough, but rather narrow; and the experience of a decade has shown that it would have made fewer mistakes if it had paid more attention to psychology and sociology. But that would have made an unwieldy process even more cumbersome. In touching worship, the Council touched what is deepest in man's religious life. That is why apparently trivial questions could arouse so much passion and assume such vast significance. The Archbishop of Birmingham was right. The revolution began here.

Chapter 3

We Are All Co-responsible Now

Authority, if it is to be effective, must gain consent,
and consent can only be gained where those involved
have been able to take part ... if not in the final
decision, at least in the steps leading up to it

CARDINAL SUENENS
interview in *Informations Catholiques Internationales*, 15 May 1969.

If Cardinal Suenens did not coin the word, he certainly popularized it: co-responsibility. It was the title and theme of the book he
published in 1968 (*Coresponsibility in the Church*). The word acted
as a clarion-call. Yet it never seemed quite at home in English. It
sat stiffly there, squat and foreign, like some ogre sent to mock the
high aspirations towards which it pointed. And though towards the
end of the decade 'co-responsibility' had come to have a hollow
ring, some such term was needed to hint at the active involvement
of everyone in the life of the Church.

It was another consequence of the Council's fateful decision to
make the 'People of God' the central concept in understanding the
Church. For the gifts of the Holy Spirit are showered on all, and
there is a radical equality in grace which no subsequent claims of
office could destroy. What these doctrines asserted theoretically,
the revised liturgy brought home. Ideally, if not always in practice,
the new liturgy expressed the mystery of the Church as the People
of God, summoned by the proclamation of the Gospel, gathered
round the altar of the Lord, nourished by his body and blood and
sent out on its mission to the world, its unity reaffirmed. And if
'active participation' was the watchword of the revised liturgy, it
was only to be expected that there would be a search for some way
of expressing the participation of the laity in church order and
government.

A layman is a *laos*-man, a member of the People of God. No

longer passive and inarticulate, he was to be brought into the coun-
sels of the Church. The move was resisted by some priests,
accustomed to 'knowing better' and being the only religious authority for their area. But they were dismissed as antediluvian ob-
scurantists, and a network of consultative bodies was set up at all
levels, ranging from the parish council at the base to the synod of
bishops at the summit. Never before in the Church's history had so
much paper been moved around by so many people; never had
there been so much conferring, talking, consulting and reporting
back. It was easy for bishops to scoff at the unwieldiness of it all,
and to make the ever-popular appeal for an end to talk and a
beginning of action. In the 1970s Cardinal Heenan rarely missed an
opportunity to pour cold water on the futility of so much talk.
Addressing a conference of church leaders held in Birmingham in
1972, he began dispiritingly: 'Although in no way cynical, I have
to confess that I am never over-confident of hearing God's voice at
conferences – neither here today, nor for example at the meeting of
our Bishops' Conference in Westminster. God can and does use
councils and conferences as channels of his grace, but it has so far
been my experience that God's voice is more likely to be heard in
our daily prayer or while we are about our daily work' (quoted in
David Edwards, *The British Churches Turn to the Future*, p. 26). The
ecumenical audience was taken aback by the vigour of the attack.
But why should Cardinal Heenan feel threatened by the need to
consult? It is so much more comfortable to follow the habit of a
lifetime, to make up one's mind in the quiet of prayer and persuade
oneself that one is following the voice of God. All the endless talk
and discussion was disturbing because it put an end to the idea of
an all-wise, omnicompetent and omniscient bishop with special
access to God, and set him in the context of the whole Church seen
as a learning and participating community. Once there had been a
clear and rigid distinction between 'the teaching Church' and 'the
Church that was taught'. Now everyone was to be involved in the
learning process.

Such a transforming miracle could not come about overnight, or
even in ten years. Nor could 'participation' suddenly spring into
existence by a kind of metaphysical proclamation that it was a

Good Thing. It had to be made to happen. Structures were needed, and since none existed, they had to be invented. The Church had very little experience of serious and systematic consultation. Once more it set forth on uncharted seas with not much of a map and an unsteady compass. It was paradoxical and ironical that the very decade which saw the growth of anti-institutional feeling in the Church should also witness a proliferation of newly devised institutions, all designed to give some content to the idea of 'co-responsibility'. Jean Ladrière, Professor of Philosophy at Louvain University, argued the unfashionable case for institutions. Without them there was no way of inserting individuals into the community of the Church, and above all no way of giving them access to its decision-making centres. It is sometimes necessary to establish institutions where they do not exist, *in order* to preserve freedom.

So new bodies were invented where none had been. The parish pastoral council was the basic group. It was deliberately called 'pastoral' to stress that it was not concerned merely with repairing the parish pump so much as with the spiritual and missionary activity of the local community. It put lay expertise at the service of the parish. The idea caught on more rapidly in the 'Anglo-Saxon' world than among the Latins and the Slavs. Handbooks and guides multiplied. The American Commission on Pastoral Councils published *Guidelines for Parish Councils: A Manual for Training.* Robert Brodrick estimated that by 1973 there were in the United States more than half a million people serving on elected bodies; and he added that this 'grass-roots' movement had to be recognized as a 'grace-rooted' movement. The somewhat paradoxical result was that those Catholics who might in the past have been found in the ranks of 'Catholic Action' now found themselves serving on various councils and committees. The attempt to 'open the Church to the world' had tended to make it more introverted.

On the next level came the diocesan pastoral council. Not all dioceses managed to have one, far from it. Where a diocesan pastoral council did exist, it could spend much energy on time-consuming procedural questions, the exact competence of the body was not always clearly defined, and some of those elected could not take time off from work to attend. This gave them a middle-class

emphasis. There was much frustration. But the vision of what a
pastoral council could be was well sketched out by Archbishop
Beck of Liverpool when he inaugurated his own: 'The Church's
life does not flow down from the Pope through bishops and clergy
to a passive laity; it springs from the grass-roots of the People of
God; and the function of authority is co-ordination, authentication
and, in exceptional cases, control . . . It is part of my responsibility
to sanctify as well as teach and govern this archdiocese. To do this
I shall need the help of all. There will be many subjects on which I
shall want advice. This may include matters of administration,
finance and organization. But fundamentally our concern must be
with apostolic activity and sanctity – with the holiness of the People
of God' (quoted in 'The Liverpool Diocesan Pastoral Council' by
John Fitzsimons, in *The Clergy Review*, September 1968, pp. 661–
72). In theory, then, pastoral councils were neither a sop thrown to
the laity nor a panacea; they were to gather and co-ordinate all the
apostolic forces of a diocese. But the two parts of Archbishop
Beck's statement illustrate the difficulty of the enterprise. There is
a striking contrast between the loftiness of the aim and the rather
restricted nature of the agenda. What exactly lay within the competence of the diocesan pastoral council? Liturgical decisions –
communion in the hand or Saturday-evening Mass – belonged
somewhere else, and the experience was repeated in other fields.
The diocesan pastoral council could be tempted to conclude that it
was wasting its time and so ought to disband. The alternative of
struggling wearily on as a formality was too ghastly to contemplate.

    Part of the problem was that there were so many other 'structures
of dialogue' competing for the bishop's attention. Priests were
supposed to be brought together in a 'senate', and there was the
conference of major superiors to contend with (it assembled the
heads of religious orders). No bishop who was keen to learn need
ever fail for lack of advice. It came to him from all directions. His
ecumenical commission would take care of that area, special commissions would be at work on relations with Jews or Moslems,
while the bishop might find his five-minute sermon on television
roughly torn to pieces by the mass-media commission. If he ven-

tured into theology relying on memories of his seminary days, the Theological Commission would be on the watch; if he tried out a political judgement the Justice and Peace Commission would be up in arms, and as for the question of social welfare, well, there was another committee to deal with that. The bishop's role was maintained, because the theory was that none of these bodies had any decision-taking authority as such. They were supposed to contribute to wise decision-making, to have the last but one word, while leaving the last word to the presiding bishop.

One result of the proliferation of consultative bodies was that 'experts' were given great influence in the Church. The word is put in quotes because it was used very loosely. 'Expert' could refer to anyone who claimed to have devoted some time to thinking about a question or even, at the limit, to have read a book about it. Many 'experts' were competent only in relation to the ignorance which surrounded them. In a blistering attack on 'experts' – whom he calls 'the professionals' – James Hitchcock alleged that they had attained unchecked influence in the Church and a quasi-autonomous status. He referred to bodies in the USA such as the Catholic Theological Society, the Canon Law Society and the Federation of Diocesan Liturgical Commissions. All of these constituted pressure-with-interest groups in the Church which, on this analysis, rendered the 'ordinary' laity impotent yet over-organized, coordinated but cowed; while the bishop himself was increasingly isolated and insulated, being surrounded by ever more layers of bureaucracy (cf. *The Critic*, October–December 1974, p. 10).

Now it is true that where there is a real shift of power, it will be at someone's expense. Power abhors a vacuum, and if the bishop cedes it, then it will not simply ebb away but pass into other hands. But few in the post-conciliar period liked to think of the Church in terms of power: it made such an ugly contrast with the notion of ministry as service and the Church as a participating community. But even if one adopts a sociological view of the Church – as Cardinal Felici, the man responsible for the revision of canon law, did at the 1974 Synod – the Hitchcock thesis cannot be generalized. Powerful professional interest groups did act as lobbyists for causes within the Church, but they did not win all their battles. Catechists, for example, certainly formed a vigorous, talented and self-perpetuating group in Britain. Most of them had studied together at Corpus Christi College in London or Lumen Vitae in Brussels. But their cohesion and like-mindedness could do nothing to prevent the staff of Corpus Christi from being dismissed *en bloc* at the end of 1971; and despite protests, Lumen Vitae was unable to remove the ban placed on Giulio Girardi in autumn 1974. Power swayed and tottered a little, but it was not fundamentally displaced. Furthermore, in England at least, some members of commissions were chosen not for their expertise but in the hope that they would be able to represent the non-expert view of 'the man in the pew'. Even if not all consultative bodies were thus rendered docile, the fantasy of timid bishops being pushed around by overbearing expert groups cannot be universally sustained.

The problems of participation came to a head most dramatically in Holland. Holland was one of the few countries to stage – if that is the right word – a national pastoral council. This, it was hoped, would crown the work of the diocesan pastoral councils at the national level. In Britain no national pastoral council was ever convened, on the grounds that not all dioceses had set up diocesan pastoral councils; that distant day is still awaited. But the Dutch, with their democratic temper, small number of bishops and excellent communications system, had forged ahead and evolved the most intricate, ambitious and certainly notorious national pastoral council. Its example is worth studying in some detail because in the short space of three years it moved from high optimism to collapse. From the outset its aim was to involve as many people as possible in the Church's decision-making process. The Dutch theologians who worked on the project frankly admitted that, finding no ecclesiastical models that were of any use, they had learned from the experience of large firms like Philips and General Motors which faced the same problem: how could people be made to feel involved in an excessively large institution? So they built up towards the pastoral council from the parish level. There were over 15,000 groups, involving 15–20 people each. Next came post boxes to which the shy could write. And finally organizations were brought in. 'All the Church is responsible for all the Church', said

Piet Smulders, one of the theologians who worked on the constitution. It was a grand idea.

The Dutch Pastoral Council met in six sessions between 1968 and 1970. It was watched with great interest abroad, not only because of the controversial nature of the themes discussed, but because it was widely regarded either as a model for others or a dangerous sign of future trends. Holland became the laboratory of the Church. One can trace in successive statements by Cardinal Alfrink, the Dutch primate, how the conception of the pastoral council was gradually whittled down, without however managing to satisfy Rome. In January 1968 he explained its purpose in terms not very different from those used by Archbishop Beck: 'The bishops intend to give the entire People of God, on all levels, a chance to express its opinions and give advice. The idea is that out of this common discussion the strategy which the Church needs for today will emerge.' But of course 'policies' do not simply 'emerge': someone had to devise the agenda, prepare reports, lead debates. By April 1969 Cardinal Alfrink had shown himself sensitive to the objection that the bishops seemed to have abdicated their responsibilities. 'The Pastoral Council', he explained, 'is neither a mere talking shop leading nowhere, nor is it a parliament which can take legislative decisions, for if it were a mere talking shop, it would not take the laity seriously, and if it were a parliament, it would not take the bishops seriously.' By January 1970 his tone had become gloomy and full of – justified as it turned out – forebodings: 'In our country we are still trying to learn the difficult art of dialogue. The bishops will do everything in their power to keep that dialogue open and to win understanding for what the Church in Holland is trying to do.'

In particular he hoped for understanding in Rome. From the start the Pastoral Council had been an experimental and therefore provisional body. At its final plenary session on 8 April 1970 Cardinal Alfrink explained that its work would be continued in a permanent pastoral council. By 31 August 1971 the statutes of the new organism were published. They explained its purpose in these words: 'The scope of the Permanent Pastoral Council is to foster the cohesion of all Dutch Catholics in the development of a common pastoral strategy.' The statutes then added the dangerous explanation: 'This Council is a strategic body, and therefore more than a consultative body.' The statutes were sent to Rome for approval.

The silence was long, deep and ominous. The first hint of an answer was indirect. The official Roman canon law review, *Communicationes*, gave an outline in June 1972 of the proposed new legislation governing episcopal conferences and national councils. It brought the Dutch no cheer. Everything they had tried to realize was rejected point by point. The Church's government and pastoral policy were not a matter for discussion: they were to be kept firmly in the hands of the bishops. Everyone else – the whole *galère* of vicars-general, religious superiors, priests and laity – was granted merely a consultative voice. That summer Cardinal Alfrink went to Rome and on his return he gave a television interview to explain what had happened (14 August 1972).

The Roman canonists objected particularly to the fact that the members of the Council were to be directly elected by the people rather than nominated by the bishops. But it was above all the diminished role of bishops which aroused Roman alarm. The Dutch proposals had not sufficiently safeguarded the authority of the bishops, and they were made subservient to this 'democratic' assembly. The Dutch bishops, who now had a Rome-appointed 'conscious conservative' in their midst (appointed on 30 December 1970, and the description is his own), obediently gave way and salvaged what they could from the wreckage by announcing, on 2 December 1972, the setting up of a new body to be prudently called the 'National Council for Pastoral Deliberation'. It was a pale ghost of the Pastoral Council and never aroused comparable enthusiasm.

In his TV interview Cardinal Alfrink contrasted two views of authority in the Church: the *dominating* view of authority, which he held to be a thing of the past, and the *dialogal* approach, which he continued to hope would be the path of the future. This recalled Erich Fromm's distinction between *inhibiting authority*, which knows best and represses, and *rational authority*, which is self-authenticating and releasing. The Dutch intention, Cardinal

Alfrink insisted, 'was not to create a parliament in the democratic sense of the word, but to set up a dialogue in which everyone at his own level had his share of responsibility'. The problem for the Dutch bishops was that they had a twofold responsibility: towards Rome and towards their own people. They were forced into a corner in which loyalty to the one meant disloyalty to the other.

Thus all the talk about 'democracy' in the Church proved to be premature and off the point. In fact no one advocated that the Church ought to be a 'democracy', though it was post-conciliar orthodoxy to say that the Church ought to be 'more democratic' in its decision-making structures. The distinction is important. If, on the other hand, a speaker declared that 'the Church is not a democracy', he was usually trying by this platitude to assert its unique origin, purpose and constitution, and to express his preference for the Church as an autocracy, with a clear chain of command down from the Pope to the last layman. Two views of authority and two views of the Church clashed in this debate, and they remained alongside each other in uneasy juxtaposition. Cardinal Suenens had sketched out a dream of harmony: 'Within the Church there is at one and the same time a principle of unity (monarchy), a pluralism of hierarchical responsibilities (oligarchy) and a fundamental equality of all in the communion of the People of God (democracy)' (*Coresponsibility in the Church*, p. 190). But that was stated with altogether too much neatness, and it did not explain how the One, the Few and the Many were to be related to each other. And where three factors have to mesh in together, there were bound to be border disputes and quarrels about demarcation lines.

But there was a more radical weakness still in the array of consultative bodies. They were frequently reminded that they were *merely* consultative. That was dispiriting. The pastoral council or the senate of priests could laboriously arrive at a decision, only to find it rejected without any, or any adequate, reasons being given. This painful experience could be had not only on the humbler levels of consultation where, in any case, the matters considered open to discussion were trivial, but right up to the highest level of consultation in the Church. The International Theological Commission was set up to give the central teaching authority access to better advice than was available from the Congregation for the Doctrine of Faith, but its indigestible and worthy reports were not used in any question that mattered. Karl Rahner resigned from it in 1974. The experience of the pontifical commission on birth-control is so well-known that it need only be mentioned here: a clear recommendation of an expert commission was set aside by the Pope. To avoid a repetition of such regrettable events, when a commission on the role of women in the Church was set up in 1974 its ground rules were laid down in advance, and it was forbidden to discuss the possible ordination of women to the priesthood.

In this way the Church, in its central government, ensured for itself the worst of all worlds. For to reject advice that had been deliberately sought seemed far worse than not to have asked for it in the first place. Here 'conservatives' in the Church were more far-sighted: they realized that even to appear to be 'consulting' on a disputed question would raise hopes – or fears – of change. Do not consult if you want a quiet life. The mood of disenchantment in the Church was increased by the contrast between the immense labour of consultation and its hoped-for benefits, and its somewhat meagre results.

Bishops themselves were not exempt from such feelings. The Synod of Bishops, the highest level of consultation in the Church, met four times, in 1967, in 1969 (an extraordinary session), in 1971 and in 1974. Each meeting had its own characteristics. In 1967 optimism ran high and some useful work was done despite the overloaded programme: it was expecting too much to dispatch the revision of canon law, seminary reform, doctrinal dangers, liturgy and mixed marriages within six weeks. But no one was too distressed because this first attempt was regarded, in Cardinal Conway's phrase, as a 'trial run'. The 1969 Synod was convened in the atmosphere of crisis engendered by *Humanae Vitae*, and an attempt was made to explore the implications of 'collegiality'. The Synod was reassuring in that it falsified dire predictions about the Church's imminent collapse. The 1971 Synod was in every sense the best prepared. It had two manageable themes, 'Justice in the World' and 'The Priestly Ministry'. Moreover, in 1971 draft texts had been distributed well in advance, so that any bishops who wished to could consult their own churches before setting off for Rome. The Canadians were one hierarchy which eagerly seized this opportunity, and as a result their speeches had a freshness and weight not found elsewhere. There was a brief window opened on a type of synod which would really involve the whole Church, and be built from the ground upwards. The Church is the only international organization which could even envisage such a grandiose project.

However, the 1971 Synod, though a high point, was also a disappointment. Its conclusions were carefully manipulated, the significant minority in favour of the ordination of married men was disregarded, and the deliberations of the Synod seemed to have such little impact on the life of the Church that enthusiasm waned when it came to the preparation of the 1974 Synod. Its theme, 'Evangelization', was as outward-turned as could be, but the whole affair was a confused shambles which aroused little interest in the world outside and was forgotten almost as soon as it was over. Moreover, in his final speech, Pope Paul took the Synod to task for certain injudicious statements. He told the Synod that it was 'dangerous to speak of diversified theologies according to continents and cultures'. What was odd was to summon a body for purposes of consultation, and then to rebuke it on the morning it ended, before there had been time to consider the nature of its advice. Yet the bishops put a brave front on it, most of them doggedly maintaining that the 1974 Synod had been a great success. If it really had been such a success, there would have been no need to protest so much. It is undeniable that the 1974 Synod is the one which had the least impact on the general life of the Church. What began in 1967 as a hopeful exercise in consulting the whole Church through the bishops has declined into a routine exercise in letting people from the remoter provinces have their say, and then carrying on exactly as before. The waters close swiftly in.

However, there was one useful function which the Synod of Bishops continued to perform: it provided a vivid reminder of how different the 'local churches' had become. This was the most important consequence of the attempt to put into effect co-responsibility. The relative autonomy given to episcopal conferences with their accompanying councils and commissions meant a growth in the national consciousness of the local churches – at least where country and episcopal conference coincided (the majority of cases). There have always been deep differences between national churches, but a vigorous attempt had been made, particularly after Vatican I, to impose a standard pattern on them all. The result was that in this period the differences, although they existed, were smoothed out as far as possible and regarded as regrettable defects. The Roman colleges and universities provided a patterned education and docile men to fill the far-flung bishoprics. They learned Italian, which would be useful when they had to visit the Curia. The attempt to impose uniformity in the liturgy was carried into every field. It was this which had given the Church the appearance of a staid monolith, with the same type endlessly repeating itself like Gutenberg characters marching across the page.

Yet the diversity had always been there, lurking just below the surface, a result of the complicated interplay between history and the relationship of the Church to political power. The Church fulfilled and fulfils different functions in different countries. In Poland it kept alive a sense of the nation, its language and its culture throughout the century and a quarter when the country was partitioned; but in nearby Moravia, now north-western Czechoslovakia, Catholicism had been imposed by the Austrians in the eighteenth century and it appeared as the instrument of oppression rather than the safeguard of identity. And in America the Church had protected and integrated the immigrants who poured across the Atlantic.

All these differences and many more have always existed. What was new in the Council's position was that diversity came to be regarded as a positive value rather than a regrettable fact. It was no longer necessary to apologize for diversity. The central insight was that Catholicity did not imply uniformity. The constitution *On the Church* was quite explicit: 'Moreover, within the Church particular Churches hold rightful place. These Churches retain their own traditions . . . The chair of Peter . . . presides over the whole assembly of charity and protects legitimate differences' (13). The local churches were given their charter and legitimation. The

Council's formulation suggested that Rome would protect them –
but from whom? The main threat came from Rome itself, which
grew increasingly alarmed as diversity ceased to be a theory and
became an accomplished fact. There was furious back-pedalling.

But it was too late. The new values were expressed in a whole
new vocabulary. Theologians like Karl Rahner argued that the idea
of 'the local church' was one of the central insights of Vatican II.
The Church, with all its tasks, is really present at the local level,
and we do not have to wait until we have assembled all the separate
parts into one vast whole before we can begin to speak of 'the
Church'. It exists in and for Harlem and Notting Hill and Dar es
Salaam. It is on the local level that 'the Church' ceases to be a
vast shadowy abstraction looming somewhere overhead and comes
home. The differences that inevitably resulted were placed under
the barbarous neologism of 'pluriformity' which never quite made
the grade in English. 'Pluralism', however, did and received the
accolade of a special study from the International Theological
Commission. 'Pluriformity' referred to diversity of practices,
'pluralism' to diversity of theological approaches. The African and
Asian version which came to be used in the seventies was 'indigen-
ization'. This was a rescue operation on a word (*indigène*) which
turned an insult into a badge of honour. It paralleled the political
development of the newly emerging nations. All these clumsy new
words referred to something that was really happening.

But was it a runaway development? Were the local churches
careering wildly out of control, and threatening the principle of
unity? The vigorous response of Rome to the Dutch experiment
was a sign that it feared the consequences of too much emphasis on
the autonomy of the local churches. The argument swung inde-
cisively to and fro, with the Dutch arguing that they were within
the bounds of legitimate diversity, that unity had signs other than
uniformity, and that they had merely followed up the impetus
given by the Council. Less spectacular differences had crept in
unnoticed elsewhere. The gap between what had once been called
'the centre and the periphery' widened. The implications of saying
'We are all co-responsible' were felt keenly and dramatically.

Chapter 4

Behind the Dog-collar

The priesthood has adopted and adapted to itself some
of the most prominent NT roles and, consequently,
enfolded a tremendous idealistic wealth – the spiritual
ideals of the disciples of Jesus, the spirits of dedicated
service, embodied in Paul, the tried and true virtues
of the presbyter-bishop, the dignity of the sacramental
ministry associated with the bread of life and the cup
of the new covenant. In short, the priesthood aspires
to what was regarded as a model of Christian
behaviour by various stages of NT thought

RAYMOND E. BROWN
Priest and Bishop: Biblical Reflections, p. 44.

Any attempt at Church renewal which did not take into account the
clergy would be doomed to failure. The Church has other full-time
professionals at its service, principally the vast though decreasing
army of nuns and a small but increasing number of laypeople, but
the day-to-day task of leadership in the Christian community is in
the hands of priests. This remains true, even though the 'image' of
the priest is battered and bruised as a result of the events of the last
decade. Cardinal Heenan disapproves of talk of the 'image' of the
priest. When a priest is doing his job properly, when he is visiting
the sick, hearing confessions, and preparing his sermons, then he
has no time and less inclination to brood over the 'image' which he
projects. This may be reassuring for some priests. But there has
been enough self-questioning on the part of priests themselves for
it to be impossible to dismiss so rapidly the question: what exactly
is a priest?

In practice priests, both before and after the Council, did so
many different things that the search for common features might
seem frustrating: they could be teachers, professors, writers, bee-

keepers, musicians, occasionally poets, diocesan or Vatican bureaucrats – the list is far from complete. There was also a breed of what
were called 'hyphenated priests' – such as 'priest-workers' or 'priest-
scientists'. But the vast majority of priests were unhyphenated.
They worked unobtrusively in parishes and were devoted to the
'pastoral ministry', though even that still did not describe exactly
what they did. It was, therefore, not easy to make the move from
what a priest did to what, in essence, he really was. Moreover, just
as there were cultural differences in the liturgy, so cultural expectations coloured the priest's style, outlook and status in society.

In America and in Britain a certain type of priest predominated:
he was, at best, the father of his immigrant flock, keeping it in
order, reminding it of home, consoling, strengthening, building up
the community. He was never, in the English-speaking world, a
civil servant paid by the State, as he was in the Austro-Hungarian
empire and in France until 1902, and still is today in West Germany. Nor was he usually in the West the political leader he quite
frequently was in Latin America. But beneath all this diversity of
activity and style, the Council of Trent had discerned a common
'essence', an ontological state, which defined the priesthood and
left no room for argument: he was someone who had the power to
'effect' (a clumsy word, but Trent's word, 'confect', is even uglier)
the sacraments of the Eucharist and Penance. This 'power' was not
shared by the laity, from whom he differed essentially. He acceded
to this state by the sacrament of ordination, which endowed him
with a 'character' or 'seal upon the soul' which could never be
removed, even by sin (a theme Graham Greene was to exploit with
his whisky priest in *The Power and the Glory*). His spirituality
consisted in making himself worthy to celebrate the Eucharist. He
knew clearly what his task was and where his duties lay. All was
well.

Since the Council all has not been well. There has been a profound *malaise* among priests, which alternating bursts of optimism
and defensiveness cannot long conceal. Part of the explanation of
the *malaise* is not so much theological as sociological. As Archbishop Grégoire told the 1971 Synod in the name of the Canadian
bishops, the priest has experienced 'a gradual stripping away of

fields of activity and competence'. The priest as helper of those in trouble has given way to the professional social worker. The priest as the one of superior education who leads his flock and forms their opinions is under stress in a time of higher education and the competing mass media. The priest's competence as a marriage counsellor began to be challenged on the grounds that as a celibate he does not know what he is talking about. As a religious expert, he has to face competition and criticism from laymen for whom his seminary training seems to have been largely a training in irrelevance. And if all these functions have been stripped from him or at least are questioned, he is left with one undisputed task – that of administering the parish and its plant, and the realization of that could plunge him into even deeper gloom since it is hard to see anything especially priestly in counting the collection, seeing that the rates are paid, and installing the new heater.

Archbishop Grégoire added another reason for priestly discomfiture: 'the resistance that priests meet with among the faithful towards any authority or teaching which is based on anything other than competence.' In other words, the priest discovered that he could not compensate for his own ignorance or inadequacy by an appeal to authority. He would have to 'commend authority', to use a Pauline phrase (2 Corinthians 4:1–2). Moreover, he had another special difficulty. In the general Christian identity crisis, he was more exposed than anyone else, since he was publicly accountable for the Church's teaching. If a layman disagreed with *Humanae Vitae*, he could keep silent and suffer no perceptible harm. But if a priest disagreed (and the Andrew Greeley study of *American Priests* reported that 43% of them rejected its teaching), this would not pass unnoticed. As the public witness of the Church, he was more manifestly committed to its officially declared public teaching. And if what he said in public differed from his private advice, then further difficulties would arise. Even the National Conference of Priests of England and Wales, which no one could accuse of being a revolutionary body, was aware of the dangers of such a discrepancy. Fr Joseph O'Carroll noted at its 1974 meeting: 'The problem is that the decisions we make privately in the confessional are not the decisions we would make publicly to our bishops.'

'Murmurs of assent', said the anonymous correspondent in *The Times*, 'cut him off in mid-sentence before he could go on to explain what the bishop would do' (*The Times*, 9 September 1974).

Obviously the Council did not set out to make the priest's life more difficult. On the other hand it cannot candidly be said that it devoted much thought to the question of the priesthood. Its collective mind was engaged elsewhere. It emphasized the collegiality of the bishops and the importance of the laity as the 'People of God'. This left priests squeezed in between the upper and nether millstones of the exalted bishop and the emerging layman. Even so, the Council implied a theology of ministry which was to have profound effects. For the Council of Trent had not said the last word, and, as Raymond E. Brown suggests in the quotation at the head of this chapter, the riches of the Christian tradition were such that different aspects of the priesthood could be brought to light.

The first new emphasis of Vatican II was the doctrine that, while bishops have the fullness of the priesthood, priests share in the ministry of the bishops. There had been an age-old scholarly dispute about whether the priest should be seen as a scaled-down bishop or the bishop as a boosted priest. Some theologians had taken the priesthood as their starting-point, and then added on episcopacy as a further extension of sacramental power (the bishop alone could confer the sacraments of confirmation and ordination). The Council adopted the alternative starting-point, which sees the fullness of priestly consecration in the bishop, who receives his mission from Christ (via a series of mediations), while priests are granted a subordinate share in that ministry, as brothers and co-workers in the bishop's pastoral ministry. This particular piece of doctrine was vividly illustrated in the restored rite of concelebration, in which the 'brotherhood of priests' gathered round the bishop and expressed the unity of the diocese.

It was not the intention of the Council to emphasize in this way the contrast between the laity on the one hand and bishops and priests on the other; but it was the effect. For this doctrine declared as peremptorily as possible that office in the Church was derived from mission and, ultimately, from the mission of Christ. It was not derived from the People of God. However, it should be added in fairness that theologians like Edward Schillebeeckx denounced the dualism which thought that mandate and ministry in the Church must come *either* wholly from above *or* wholly from below. The Holy Spirit is at work in the whole Church, and though his gifts have always to be tested and discerned, the mandate can come *from* Christ *through* the community and then be ratified and consecrated by ordination. However theoretical this point may appear, it has great importance for the future.

But while priests were being tied even more firmly to the bishop's apron-strings, the Council also turned them loose in the world. Secular priests, who were increasingly called 'diocesan' priests, were emphatically not monks, and therefore their whole style of life and prayer should not be monastic. The diocesan priest was not to be a detached mystic: 'Let him not be undone by his apostolic cares, dangers, and toils, but rather led by them to higher sanctity' (*On the Church*, 41). This curiously phrased exhortation encouraged the priest to see his life of prayer in terms of service to the community.

But what was of more decisive importance was the shift of emphasis in the understanding of the nature of the priesthood itself. Trent had defined the priest as a man endowed with special powers, but it did not include the preaching of the Gospel in its definition, since that appeared to be a dangerously Protestant idea. Trent in fact rationalized the situation in which a great many priests actually found themselves at the time of the Reformation: they said their Mass, alone or with only a few people present, while their missionary impulse, at least in Europe, was dimmed. But Vatican II found this unsatisfactory. Trent defined the priest in abstraction. It expressed his nature in relation to the sacraments, but not to the word of God which he had to preach nor to the community which he had to serve.

The Council tried to strike a balance between the 'cultic' priest and the minister of the Word. It had no reason to fear Protestant contagion. Word and sacrament were seen as two complementary aspects of the one priestly mission. The priest dispensed the sacraments, but he had also to prepare in depth their reception. Conversely the preaching of the Word led to a desire for the sacraments.

There was a significant change of vocabulary: whereas the Council spoke of 'the ministerial priesthood', by the time of the 1971 Synod noun and adjective had changed places – its theme was 'the priestly ministry'. The emphasis moved away from the *ex opere operato* or quasi-automatic operation of the sacraments towards the need to arouse faith in the recipient. The magical view of the sacraments suffered a blow. This made more stringent demands on the laity, but it also transformed the way the priest looked at himself: he was equally minister of the Word and minister of the Eucharist, and to each aspect there corresponded specific tasks.

As minister of the Word of God, he would have to come to know the Bible in a new way as the illuminating record of the history of salvation. This was very different from the Counter-Reformation approach which had treated scripture as a convenient arsenal from which to quarry proof-texts. Now he had to try to make the Word of God intelligible in another age and another culture, and so rediscover his missionary vocation: he was not simply a keeper in an ecclesiastical museum, but a herald of mankind's future. The missionary task would take him out on to frontiers, where he would have to confront the gropings of his contemporaries with the values of the Gospel. He had also to 'apply' the Gospel to different situations, to let its light fall on human situations, to arouse his own community to an awareness of wider issues, and speak with a prophetic voice. More testingly still, the growing charismatic movement expected him to be a man of prayer who was capable of initiating others into prayer. Students looked for a guru, not an ecclesiastical bureaucrat or a parish administrator. He could no longer get away with the safe, regular and devout administration of the sacraments.

Moreover, even his familiar sacramental and eucharistic role was given a fresh interpretation. As minister of the Eucharist he had the endless task of building and repairing the community which comes into existence as a result of the proclamation of the Gospel. It became a cliché to recognize that community was threatened by the sheer size of modern cities, their impersonality and indifference, their relentless, divisive competitiveness. The Christian community he strove to build up was to provide the human context in which alone the message of the Gospel could begin to be credible. Not that the community he was striving to maintain and encourage was seen as a comfortable, introverted refuge from a wicked world. The community had the task of discerning local needs, and that involved inventiveness and imagination, qualities which had not been prized in the seminary. He was urged to devote himself to the 'new poor', those on the fringes of society – the handicapped, the maladjusted, the old. Of course he could not work this miracle all by himself. But his task was to prod and stimulate the community, and so become, as the formula was, an *enabling* person.

All these tasks could be deduced from considering the priest's role as minister of the Word and the Eucharist. The Eucharist is not so much a sacrament in the Church as *the* sacrament of the Church. It brings the Church into being. It is in the Eucharist, too, that the full dimensions of the priestly ministry, embracing both sacred and secular, can be seen. David P. O'Neill summed them up in this way:

> Here the priest celebrates a peace demonstration, in memory of the demonstration of peace and reconciliation in the death and resurrection of the Lord Jesus.
> Here the priest is a leader in joy and thanksgiving.
> Here the priest teaches men to join hands and share what they have.
> Here the priest celebrates a love festival.
> Here the priest leads men in a freedom song.
> Here the priest tells men that the time for hate is gone, that now is the time for love (David P. O'Neill, *The Priest in Crisis*, p. 215).

This was a much more demanding view of the priest's role. Many priests were simply incapable of understanding it, and fell back into doing what they knew best. Others worked out the full logic of the new emphases. Ministry is for service. This was the key principle. It represented a return to New Testament thinking and was of vital importance in ecumenical discussion. It was no longer possible to view the priest simply as a privileged person in the Church endowed with special sacramental powers. Now, on the contrary, he was seen essentially in his relationship to the community he existed to serve.

This posed a problem for the 'hyphenated priests' (the priest-scholars or priest-scientists) whose relationship to precise communities was intermittent or tenuous.

The 1971 Synod showed clearly that there were grounds for disquiet about the state of the priesthood. The fundamental problem was one of theological method. Bishop Santos Ascarza of Chile outlined the two contrasting approaches: 'The first starts from scripture and the priesthood of Christ in order to determine the purpose, scope and meaning of the priestly ministry once and for all (*semel pro semper*), and then proceeds to draw appropriate conclusions for our time. It is clear but abstract. The other method starts from the signs of the times, the crisis in the priesthood and the conditions in which the apostolate is developing, and then discerns what Christ is asking of us today.' The two methods produce quite different results. The deductive approach had been followed in all the official texts of the decade, most notably in the encyclical *Sacerdotalis Coelibatus* of 1967 which reaffirmed the importance of priestly celibacy. It began from a clear concept of the priesthood as a state of life in the Church. It might be modified in minor details, but not substantially changed. It distinguished the priest unambiguously from the layman.

The alternative view gave the primacy to the whole People of God as a priestly people. Within this people there is a diversity of ministries. Here one can see that the transition from 'ministerial priesthood' to 'priestly ministry' was not just a semantic quibble, for to speak of the 'priestly ministry' was to suppose that there were many ministries in the Church, ministries of healing, teaching, exhortation, consolation, and even administration; and among them was the *priestly* ministry. Those who took this starting-point emphasized that the priestly ministry was a service or a function in the Church, and not so much a state. They were therefore prepared to look at the multiple needs of the Church, and open to experiment and inventiveness. They wanted to stress the primacy of experience: the ministries which the Church needed today could only grow under the influence of the Holy Spirit – they could not be invented by a commission, however eminent, or by theologians, however learned. The New Testament was much vaguer on mini-

stry than the Council of Trent. As Fr Joseph Lécuyer, speaking in
the name of the heads of religious orders, said: 'The threefold
ministry of bishop, priest and deacon does not appear clearly in the
New Testament and is only described with precision from the
start of the second century: one can therefore ask whether there are
not grounds for recognizing the possibility of a different organization of the ministry in the different churches, taking into account
different situations.' Once the familiar categories had been loosened
in this way, it was no longer unthinkable to consider the possibility
of part-time priests and the ordination of women or married men.
 The Synod's discussion concentrated on the possibility of
ordaining married men. The principal argument in favour was a
practical one, based on the needs of the Church, especially in
missionary countries. One of the most eloquent pleas came from
Bishop Anthony Galvin, the man who had disarmed the Pope's
would-be assassin in Manila. He spoke in the name of the bishops
of Singapore-Malaysia: 'We are of the opinion that the institutional
Church shows too little flexibility concerning the ordination of
married men when circumstances would seem to ask for it. Flexibility is not a sign of shaking faith in Christ. It should not be thought
that we are belittling celibacy. Not at all. In fact we think that it is a
splendid mainstay of eternal and divine values when it is lived for
the sake of the Kingdom . . . Christ came to serve, not to be
served. To understand him in a purely static, intellectual and
juridical manner would be not to understand him. The love of
Christ, who had compassion on the multitudes, makes us confront
with courage the problems that besiege the countries we live in . . .
What happens to these nations when the missionaries are withdrawn? Who can tell when and how soon the missionaries will be
withdrawn? Signs are against us: the multitudes wait for compassion. We say this without feelings of rancour or failure.
 'We cannot be accused of despair. However, we are of the opinion that the ordination to the priesthood of mature married men will
provide for the future in a history that cannot be denied its inex-
orable laws. Married men chosen according to local cultural
procedure should be found, men who "have secured for themselves
a sure footing, and great boldness in proclaiming that faith which

is found in Christ Jesus" (1 Timothy 3:13).' But these arguments did not pass unchallenged. The chief counter-argument was that the ordination of married men would constitute 'the thin end of the wedge'. Cardinal Höffner of Cologne alleged that 'any exception from the norm of celibacy would have an explosive effect, so that celibacy would disappear in a short time'. Cardinal Höffner, the supreme exponent of the deductive method, was the dominating personality at the 1971 Synod. His views prevailed. Although his aim was to defend priestly celibacy, he cannot be said to have shown much confidence in its capacity to survive if the ordination of married men could undermine it so swiftly. The Synod was in the end invited to vote on two propositions which made clear how limited was the area for manoeuvre. The first received 107 votes and read: 'Always preserving the right of the Supreme Pontiff, the ordination of married men is not admitted even in particular cases.' The second proposition received 87 votes: 'It belongs to the Supreme Pontiff alone, in particular cases, for reasons of pastoral need and taking into account the good of the universal Church, to grant priestly ordination to married men of mature age and good life (*maturae aetatis et probatae vitae*).' The vote was designed not so much to decide between the alternatives as to reveal the mind of the Synod. In the final document the results appeared in a footnote for the record. There were no practical consequences. The other tentative suggestions on part-time priests and the ordination of women were barely discussed and have been even more firmly blocked.

Although a few token priests were present, the 1971 Synod was essentially a discussion about priests by bishops. Meanwhile priests themselves had been assiduously analysing their situation, both officially and unofficially. It was one thing to gather round the bishop in the authorized senate of priests, and quite another to form unofficial pressure groups. While the senate of priests might be discussing pension schemes or a retiring age for parish priests or – as in one Polish diocese – an appropriate present for the bishop on his jubilee, the unofficial groupings were much more radical. In France the movement called 'Echange et Dialogue' came into being on 3 November 1968. Its fifty-five priests had been inspired by 'the events of May' which had shaken the Gaullist regime earlier that year. They mounted the sacerdotal barricades and proclaimed that 'the Church is in urgent need of revolution'. They advocated three 'rights' for priests: the right to work like everyone else, the right to political commitment, and the right to marry. The denial of these 'rights', they believed, was stifling their humanity. Many of them proceeded to exercise their newly claimed rights in defiance of the Church, and the movement continued as a semi-tolerated group. At its 1973 congress it gathered over a thousand people in Lyons, where they studied ways of 'undermining the ecclesiastical system' and set about 'unmasking the Church's ideology'.

A comparable political emphasis was found in many groups of Latin-American priests. In Argentina there were the Priests for the Third World (Sacerdotes para el Tercer Mundo), founded in 1967, who declared in their manifesto that 'true socialism is Christianity lived in its integrity'. Mexico saw the emergence of a group called Priests for the People (Sacerdotes para el Pueblo), who defended themselves against the charge that they were dividing the Church on the grounds that 'the division already exists: we merely take cognisance of its existence'. With one eye on the frequent hierarchical claim to speak on behalf of 'those who have no voice', they frankly stated: 'We do not propose to speak in the name of the people – we propose to enter into solidarity with the people in their struggle for liberation.'

Back in Europe, the French had considerable influence on the Assemblée des Prêtres Solidaires, which held a series of meetings between 1969 and 1971. At Chur in 1969 they timed their meeting to coincide with the Symposium of European Bishops, and while the bishops met in the inaccessible fortress of the local seminary, situated on the top of a hill, the priests assembled in a temperance restaurant, the Rätisches Volkhaus, down in the valley below. They climbed the hill to applaud a speech of Cardinal Suenens on the flexibility of the Christian priesthood throughout history, but otherwise there was no communication between the two assemblies.

The protesting priests had little better fortune in Rome later in 1969 when they addressed a respectful letter to Pope Paul. Equally respectfully, Pope Paul replied that he could not accept their request for an audience for four reasons: many of them were at odds with their bishops, and he could not receive them without consulting their bishops; the documents they had kindly forwarded to him contained many dubious opinions; their representative nature had been challenged; and finally, to give them an audience would inevitably be interpreted as a sign of approval. It was a courteous but firmly dismissive reply. There would be few clearer instances of the runaway Church than these muddled and dissident priests. They were not in the end proposing new ministries in the light of an alternative theological approach: they were dissolving the priestly ministry altogether. Being unable to define their particular and specific function as priests in the Church, they woke up laymen. Sometimes this was a conscious choice, embraced in the name of service seen on another level. Camilo Torres, regarded by many as a prophetic figure, had put it precisely, if paradoxically, when he was granted laicization after a five-minute interview with Cardinal Concha of Bogotá. 'I took off my soutane to be more truly a priest . . . We cannot have a supernatural life without charity, and our charity must be efficacious. In the last judgement our eternal destiny will be determined in so far as we have given food, drink, lodging, clothing, refuge and welcome to our brothers' (24 June 1965). Within six months he was shot by a military patrol.

The 'Anglo-Saxon' version of these movements was less heroic, less global and sweeping in its condemnations, more restrained in its rhetoric. It was inclined to be 'activist' and reformist rather than revolutionary. In America the National Federation of Priests' Councils (NFPC), representing 115 out of the 152 dioceses of continental America, tried hard to maintain contact with the bishops. In the spring of 1970 the president of NFPC said in a statement aimed at the US Bishops' Conference: 'As we present our ideas to you we want to assure you that we do not wish to be interventionists but collaborators . . . We share with you a common sense of frustration and failure that, despite all our efforts, we have done very little. We too, the rest of the People of God, have sinned against credibility, courageous communication and col-

legiality' (23 April 1970). This statesmanlike tone and the characteristically post-conciliar catalogue of sins were to be welcomed,
but at its annual convention held in Baltimore the following year
the NFPC skated on thin ice in adopting the following resolution:
'We ask that the choice between celibacy and marriage for priests
now active in the ministry be allowed and that the change begin
immediately.' The NFPC had begun to win some sort of grudging
acceptance from the bishops, but after that resolution John C.
Haughey predicted that it would probably 'be treated like the skunk
at the party' (*America*, 3 April 1971). Weakened by the loss of some
of its more prominent members and discouraged by the surrounding inertia, the NFPC has continued to exist and to pass
much the same resolutions. Meeting at St Petersburg Beach,
Florida, in March 1975, it laid particular stress on the restoration
to the active priestly ministry of priests who had been laicized.

Departures from the ministry became a familiar and distressing
part of the priestly story throughout the decade. Even the official
statistics of the *Annuario Pontificio* chronicle the decline in
numbers. Its 1974 edition gives the number of diocesan priests as
270,737, which was 2396 or 8·8% less than the previous year. The
decrease was most significant in North America (down 14·8%),
South America (down 12·4%) and Europe (down 11·1%), while
gains were noted in Africa, Asia and Central America. The all-
round decrease was partly due to the excess of deaths over ordinations, but it owed a good deal to the loss of those priests who had
'returned to the lay state'. The official Church was uncertain in its
attitude to the laicized priests. 'Defection' was a common way of
describing what they had done, and one Maundy Thursday Pope
Paul compared them to Judas. Yet at the same time dispensations
began to be given with greater ease if not always greater speed.
While 'defection' might be an accurate term for someone who had
betrayed and now despised what he once held dear, it did not seem
appropriate for those of good will who wanted to continue an
unobtrusive Christian life. Moreover, the *sensus fidelium*, which
here might be translated as 'the common sense of the faithful', did
not reject the ex-priests or regard them as so many Judases.

The whole vocabulary surrounding this question was confused

and unclear. What did it mean, for example, to speak of 'leaving the priesthood', when the traditional view was that the sacrament of ordination conferred a 'character', a permanent seal or *sphragis* on the soul? It could be bound up or placed in cold storage but not destroyed. Again, if one spoke of 'leaving the ministry', there was still an element of unclarity, since there are so many levels of ministry in the Church. The theoretical difficulties complicated the practical question of what to do with these men who had often spent years in the service of the Church and had not forfeited their knowledge or competence overnight. The Vatican discouraged any employment of them in Catholic teaching institutions. Most of them were capable of teaching religion, if nothing else; but religion was precisely what they were forbidden to teach. One of the persistent causes of conflict between the Vatican and Holland was the high proportion of ex-priests teaching in the Amsterdam Theological Institute. The Dutch bishops temporized and talked of dialogue. In some cases teaching posts were secure because they were governed by a civil contract. But the question remained: was to be an ex-priest an irremediable disgrace, for which the only remedy was to lie low and pretend to be dead? Or was it a permissible option which did not destroy a man's usefulness to the Church? And was there anything to be learned from them? One of the few officials in Rome who believed that the Church had something to learn from this experience was Fr Pedro Arrupe, General of the Jesuits. In a letter to his Latin-American brothers he said that there were two sorts of departure: in some cases there was a personal psychological problem which could only be solved in this way; but others were a symptom of a *malaise*, an indication that something was wrong with the way the Jesuit life or the priesthood was being lived.

But the official view was that there was nothing at all to be learned from such cases. They were unfortunate, unhappy, and best forgotten. 'One rotten apple affects the whole barrel', remarked an English bishop, urging the Roman Congregation to make all speed. The latest Roman instructions, conveyed in a rescript or letter to bishops and religious superiors in 1971, complained fussily that some applicants were not filling in their forms properly. They were providing inadequate or insufficient grounds. It was not enough, for example, to cite the mere desire to get married; nor was it any use attempting a civil marriage, still less fixing the date of a religious ceremony. What, then, was recommended? If a long history of conflict with authority could be mentioned, together with a deep disturbance of faith, then the Sacred Congregation would be most satisfied. It is clear that if the 'right' answers are given, they will show on analysis that the Church is simply releasing its trouble-makers and those who were in any case losing their faith. It will also be possible to claim that the problem of priestly identity has nothing to do with celibacy. It is like playing a game with marked cards: the answer is known in advance.

It would of course be monstrously unfair, and a different kind of manipulation, to suggest that all or even a majority of priests found the pastoral ministry irksome, teetered on the verge of departure or were daily afflicted by a deep sense of crisis. That would be nonsense. And in any case we would not know. The priest bears his scars in private. Enough of them were leaders in joy and reconciliation, enough of them led men in a freedom song, enough of them proclaimed forgiveness and the death of hate for the Gospel to reach another generation. There was imagination and innovation in the priestly ministry. The new liturgy enabled a priest to synthesize all the activities of the parish community and to make his preaching come home with social or political relevance. There were new ministries which recognized that the territorial parish in a commuter suburb was not the best place to find people, and that specialized groups could profit from specialized priests. This principle, which had always been recognized for universities and hospitals, was extended in some cases to airports and department stores, to immigrant workers and down-and-outs.

There were many reasons for optimism about the priesthood. They were well expressed by Cardinal Enrique y Tarancón in his report to the 1971 Synod. He insisted that the crisis of the priesthood, which he did not deny, was not to be attributed to ill-will or tottering faith, but was part of the very real difficulty of being faithful to the Gospel and finding a new language for faith in the changing world of today; and it is the best men who feel mos-strongly the pressure of this challenge. This is why the priest feels drawn to secular work or to politics. He is reluctant to confine his mission to the automatic dispensing of the sacraments and he cannot think of his spiritual life apart from his ministry. He actively seeks co-responsibility with his bishop, and instead of an opposition between clergy and laity, which produced clericalism and its mirror-image, anti-clericalism, we are moving towards an understanding of the complementary relationship between priest and people. Without vision, the priestly people perish, and Cardinal Tarancón's optimism was bracing and honest. But each of the positive factors he mentions carries with it a shadow. What is certain is that the old moulds of priestly spirituality were cracked by the Council, and that the task of devising a new pattern for the ministry is as yet unfinished. That is why the state of the priesthood today remains deeply ambiguous, and judgements on it can swing between the two extremes. As Eugene C. Kennedy, the American priest-psychologist, wrote towards the end of the period: 'We have never had it so good and never had it so bad. Pastoral work is the scene of some of the Church's most creative activity and some of its most quiet despair' ('Ministry', in *National Catholic Reporter*, 25 April 1975).

Chapter 5

Guarding the Guardians

What is needed is not reiteration of the old language
of authority, but the development of a new one . . . It
is this conflict between two notions of how authority
works – the old, certain one, and the new, growing and
still only semi-articulate one – that has created the
crisis from which we are suffering

ROSEMARY HAUGHTON
Dialogue, pp. 27–8.

It was not an easy time to be a bishop. They received advice,
solicited and unsolicited, from all sides, and a fair quota of abuse.
They were caught in the middle of the process of polarization, and
while 'those behind cried "Forward", those before cried "Back"'.
Or as the Bishop of Versailles put it in an expansive moment: 'A
bishop today is like a driver with two passengers – one has his hand
on the brake while the other has his foot on the accelerator.' But the
bishop could not dither in uncertainty or take refuge in benign
neutrality, hovering between factions. He had, in due time, to
govern. The change in the exercise of authority referred to by
Rosemary Haughton above did not mean its abolition. It was a
paradox, not always understood at the time, that the requirement
of greater participation in decision-making involved *more* qualities
of leadership rather than less, and that the authoritarian bishop
had not been exchanged for a doormat.

The Council had tried to sketch out a portrait of a bishop, 'a new
image for the pastor in our time' said Archbishop Veuillot of
Paris in introducing the text. His central task is the building up of
community, the *ministerium communitatis*. To achieve this, he has –
and the order is important – to teach, to sanctify and to govern. He
is a teacher before he is a diocesan manager. In *The Documents of
Vatican II* Bishop Paul J. Hallinan was able to echo Karl Rahner's

confident prediction: 'The Christian of the future will not feel himself reduced in stature or oppressed by his bishop . . . He will know that even in the community of the faithful there must be those who are responsible for binding decisions and action, and the spirit of Christ which animates all will be with such men. As for the bishop, there will be nothing else for him, as in the ancient Church of the martyrs, but continually to invite such voluntary obedience and understanding for his decisions, in love and humility' (p. 395). That is moving enough, but sometimes the discourse of theologians seems to move in the stratosphere, and there is bound to be a measure of jolting and bumping as we come down to earth. Bishops could not be transformed by documents declaring that they ought to be so transformed.

Yet a new style of bishop began to emerge, less authoritarian and more spiritual, less managerial and more pastoral, less fussy and more direct. Some bishops – not all – began to be embarrassed by large houses and expensive cars, and got rid of them. Cardinal Lercaro in Bologna turned his episcopal palace into a home for orphans. The visitation of a parish, instead of being merely an occasion to check up on the parish priest, became a real opportunity to meet people and to visit the sick of the parish. The possibility of resignation meant that a bishop did not have to cling to office, and Cardinal Léger set an example by leaving Montreal and going to work in a leper colony. There were other signs of changed attitudes. Few bishops expected their rings to be kissed, though not all emulated Archbishop Roberts, former archbishop of Bombay, who used to say to gushing ladies: 'You may kiss my ring, madam, but I must warn you that it is in my hip pocket.' Many bishops wore the ring given to them to mark the end of the Council: it took the form of a mitre. Bejewelled fingers were no longer in vogue. Simplicity in dress, life-style and manner was the rule.

Detailed evidence of the changed attitudes is bound to be patchy and difficult to document. Yet one can quote, as an example among many, the address given by Archbishop Winning who became archbishop of Glasgow in autumn 1974. Speaking to his priests, he pleaded for trust and openness: 'What I want to encourage above all is a spirit of friendliness and freedom . . . When I speak of friendliness and freedom, that means I never wish that any of you should walk in fear of me as your superior. Fear inhibits: it destroys friendship and mutual trust. Fear also enslaves . . . When a spirit of fear exists, the work of the Church is stultified: the clergy are reluctant to use their own discretion, for fear of unfavourable reactions.' Archbishop Winning also stressed that there was a place for criticism in the Church, that although it obviously ought not to be 'destructively critical', nevertheless it ought not 'to be confined to the smoke-filled rooms of our familiar friends' (10 September 1974). These admirable intentions remain to be tested in the fire of experience, but they represent a fair summary of the spirit which the new style of bishop wished to create.

But beyond these lofty aspirations, the main practical effect of the Council was to make the bishop a much busier man. Quite apart from the multitude of committees and commissions which hedged him in, and the extra time needed to visit the parishes, he was also expected to play a role on the national level through the episcopal conference. Vatican II encouraged the setting up of episcopal conferences (*On the Bishops' Pastoral Office in the Church*, 36). This may seem an unexciting proposal. There is nothing particularly stimulating in the notion of bishops meeting each other if they want to. Let them have freedom of assembly like anyone else. But although there had always been meetings of bishops from time to time, fear of creeping Gallicanism had made the Vatican reluctant to allow them to have too much autonomy and influence. In France, for example, it was said in the early years of the century that although there were bishops, there was no episcopacy. As an organized body, they did not exist. That cannot be said since Vatican II. Once bishops meet, there is pressure upon them to make statements. Their statements have sometimes been of great importance. The Latin-American Bishops' Conference (CELAM) at its 1968 meeting at Medellin committed the Church to a programme of social reform which was to have far-reaching consequences.

The bishop was no longer seen in isolation, but at the centre of a complex web of shared responsibilities. His main function had not changed: he symbolized in his person the unity of the diocese; but this did not mean that he was expected to be omnicompetent or the source of all initiatives. He was the conductor of the orchestra, not the leading soloist as well. He was to be, in a phrase of Cardinal Suenens, 'a centre of discernment'. His special grace or charism was thought to be an ability to 'discriminate' the good spirit from the bad, and so to edify the Church. Discrimination is especially needed in time of crisis, and, said Cardinal Marty of Paris, 'we need bishops for a time of crisis, new Athanasiuses'.

The new Athanasiuses, however, were now able to lay down their burden at the age of seventy-five. A retirement age for bishops was something new, and the theoretical justification provided for hanging on to office had been that the bishop was a father to his diocese and 'fathers do not resign'. But Cardinal Suenens had dealt with this pseudo-difficulty in a speech to the Council: 'While a father always remains a father, responsibility for the undertakings within the family gradually passes to the son' (*Coresponsibility in the Church*, p. 104). Besides the argument based on episcopal paternity, the indissoluble nature of the bond between a bishop and his diocese was often used to legitimate gerontocracy: it was compared to the marriage bond. But this argument had been undermined by the habit of transferring men from see to see which, if the analogy were to be rigorously pursued, would suggest a large number of episcopal divorces. Anyway, boldly, in August 1966, Pope Paul published his *motu proprio* which said that bishops ought to tender their resignations at the age of seventy-five.

Now seventy-five is not a particularly youthful age and in most professions (judges excepted) retirement happens a decade earlier. The requirement of resignation at seventy-five, however, meant that it would be difficult for very old men to cling limpet-like to high office, utterly convinced of their indispensability. It was said of Cardinal Browne that when he was made a cardinal, well into his seventies, he flung away his sticks and enjoyed better health at the prospect of helping to keep the Church on the right lines. Not all the old were opposed to the new, and they had their patron and champion in Pope John XXIII who became pope at the age of seventy-six and proceeded to startle the world with his vigour; but any bishop who made that point had the duty to emulate Pope

John, a rather more difficult matter. However, there were two weaknesses in the proposal. The rule did not apply to the cardinals of the Roman Curia, and it was, in any case, only a recommendation, not a strict requirement. Unaccountable deafness was known to afflict some bishops when they timidly offered their resignation to the Pope, such that they did not hear his reply. The diminutive and indestructible Archbishop Sir Michael Gonzi of Malta is thus still at his post and heading for the nineties.

The possibility of bishops resigning inevitably led to speculation about the Pope resigning. Once the taboo had been broken, why should the papacy be the only exception? And since cardinals over the age of eighty were to be debarred from the next conclave, the pontiff was even more isolated. Moreover, the argument based on the impossibility of renouncing spiritual fatherhood had been found wanting in the case of bishops and abandoned. From time to time, rumours of Pope Paul's resignation caused a stir in the press, all the more since in September 1966 he had gone out of his way to visit the tomb of Pope Celestine V, a pontiff who was famous not for his reign but for abandoning it. But all these rumours were quickly scotched by the Vatican Press Office, which interpreted the Pope's references to 'the end of our mission' as an anticipation of his death. It is certainly true that Pope Paul has proved healthier than his own forebodings suggested. During a visit to Cagliari in Sardinia in the spring of 1970 he already spoke of himself as 'one for whom the clock of life and old age point to a forthcoming end'.

But whatever was true of the Bishop of Rome, the possibility of a bishop resigning ushered in the idea that his office could be thought of as a temporary service to the Church with a limited term – six to twelve years was the usual span suggested. In secular society men and women no longer hold office on grounds of seniority or heredity but rather because they are useful and competent; it was argued that bishops in a fast-moving world might well have exhausted their stock of energy and imagination after a decade or so, and could with advantage stand down much earlier than seventy-five. The case was argued by the Catholic Faculty of the University of Tübingen (*Bishops and People*, edited and translated by Leonard and Arlene Swidler). With older bishops retiring, the way was open to appoint younger men, who would therefore be around for a very long time unless something were done to limit them. The Bishop of Rotterdam, Dr Martin Jansen, resigned in 1970 at the age of sixty-five, and he explained that his decision was neither sudden nor born of weariness: 'I believe that the length of time one may hold the office of bishop should not be too long. Eventually every man is threatened by rigidity and routine and the blindness which comes with an official position.'

But whatever reasons bishops might have for wanting to resign – and ironically some of the best men resigned while their less enlightened fellow bishops hung grimly on – the business of appointing bishops remained firmly in the hands of Rome. Talk of consultation made little practical difference, and the role of papal nuncios or apostolic delegates remained decisive. The appointment of bishops remained the principal means of control over the local churches. As Hans Küng ironically put it: 'In so far as Rome had a free hand, new bishops were selected preferably according to the two tried and tested principles of sound moral standards and the uncritical loyalty to Rome which is called "obedience". Fortunately, mistakes were made in some instances, and some men were appointed who subsequently distinguished themselves by their independence of mind, courage and unexpected initiative' (*Infallible?*, p. 17). Küng's irony is not unjustified, for the system was designed to produce safe and solid men rather than inspiring leaders. Cardinal Heenan provides indirect confirmation of what Küng says. Speaking of his own appointment to the diocese of Leeds – communicated to him in Latin – he remarked: 'I knew that prudence was the most highly prized virtue in episcopal candidates and I did not count it among my attributes' (*Not the Whole Truth*, p. 324). He gave way reluctantly and was landed on the people of Leeds. Catholics had little idea of how bishops came to be appointed, but that did not stop them singing '*Ecce Sacerdos Magnus*' with a will. Bishops simply dropped down from heaven by order of the Holy Father.

Systems varied somewhat from country to country but the American model, established by a decree of the Consistorial Congregation in 1916 was not untypical. At the beginning of Lent, though only in odd-numbered years, all the bishops submitted to their archbishop the names of two priests they judged fit for the office of bishop. Before making up their minds, they were urged to seek advice, 'even from priests', though without in any way being bound to follow the advice they were given. The archbishop then added his own names to the by now bulky list, put them in alphabetical order, and called a discreet meeting at which the names were discussed in what was described as 'a moderate tone'. A copy of the proceedings was then forwarded to Rome by the apostolic delegate, and the American records were destroyed. The process was shrouded in secrecy at every step. It was a form of episcopal co-option, but it left great influence in the hands of the Vatican diplomat. He did not hesitate to use it.

As recently as 1973 the papal nuncio in Bonn was caught out intriguing to secure the dismissal of a German bishop. The nuncio, Archbishop Corrado Bafile, in a letter to the Cardinal Secretary of State, Villot, proposed the removal from office of the Bishop of Limburg, Dr Wilhelm Kempf, and his replacement by an apostolic administrator. Ill-health was offered as the pretext. 'It seems', wrote the nuncio with misplaced confidence, 'that such a solution would not cause much reaction in public opinion; there may be some clamour in the press but it will not last long.' The letter was revealed by a minor official in the Secretariat of State. The gaffe was blown and a year later (January 1974) there was yet another Roman document issued on the importance of secrecy. But in Rome everything is a mystery and nothing is, in the end, a secret. The Bafile incident illustrated that even in the post-conciliar Church a papal diplomat was not above intriguing to remove a bishop: this did not inspire much confidence in his handling of names for new appointments. And a diplomat only pursues a course of action which he thinks his superiors will be in agreement with.

Not all papal diplomats behaved quite so crassly, and there have been attempts to make consultation a reality. The Canadian bishops changed their system in 1969. To the list of the 'qualities' required in a bishop as seen by canon law they added some more of their own. A potential bishop, they suggested, should have 'an ability for teamwork . . . a modern mentality, a good knowledge of pastoral needs, ability to express himself and communicate with others, courage and dynamism, respect for the laity, a real sense of the Church today'. When a see falls vacant a special *ad hoc* committee of the bishops' conference consults as widely as possible, and every member of the priests' council and the pastoral council can give reasons in writing why he or she thinks that their candidate is suitable for this particular diocese. After further deliberation, the apostolic delegate forwards a list of three names to Rome. But the weakness of all secret consultations done on a one-to-one basis is that no one ever really knows whether advice has been taken or why it has been disregarded. And the buck can always be passed to Rome, where Cardinal Baggio presides over the Congregation of Bishops and holds the dossiers on possible candidates.

One dramatic example of clash between local requirements and a Rome appointment occurred in Holland in 1970. The resignation of Dr Martin Jansen gave the diocese of Rotterdam a chance to experiment with a new system. Direct election was ruled out from the start because it was feared that it would be divisive; and in any case the 'candidates' were not sufficiently well-known for voting to make much sense. Yet there was a strong desire to involve all the people of the diocese in the choice of a new bishop. The solution was to devise a questionnaire designed to discover the sort of bishop the diocese needed. On a Sunday in February 1970 the question-naire was handed out at Mass, and the homily was based on speci-ally chosen readings (1 Timothy 4:1–13 – Paul's advice to bishops; and Matthew 28:11–20 – the commissioning of the Twelve). Eighty thousand answers were received. They were correlated and published. What emerged was that the people of Rotterdam wanted above all a 'pastor', a 'shepherd': he should be more concerned with the future than the past, have his own ideas, but be capable of listening, taking advice and working with others. The move from this 'profile' to actual names was accomplished by the diocesan pastoral council which accepted suggestions from the priests of the diocese and the lay members of deanery councils.

Eventually the list was boiled down first to eight and then to five names. Leading the field was Dr Cornelius Braun, vicar-general of he diocese, with 30% of the nominations, and second came Dr

Simonis with 15%. The remaining votes were scattered among 'progressive' candidates, which was why Dr Simonis, despite his 15%, went to the bottom of the list of eight and was excluded altogether from the list of five. He did not fit the 'profile'. Chicanery was alleged. On 30 December 1970 Dr Simonis' appointment was announced. There was uproar and a storm of protests. It seemed that the elaborate procedure had been deliberately set aside, and that another blow was being delivered at the Dutch system of consultation. But none of this deterred the Sacred Congregation of Bishops, which behaved in exactly the same way the next time a Dutch diocese, that of Roermond, fell vacant. The maxim of Pope Leo the Great had not been respected: 'On no account is anyone to be a bishop who has not been chosen by the clergy, desired by the people, and consecrated by the bishops of the province with the authority of the metropolitan.'

In the appointment of bishops all the threads and all the roads lead to Rome. The original reason for this centralization, and the reason sometimes produced to defend it today, is the urgent need for the Church to be independent of the State in the appointment of bishops; but this argument applies today only in Communist countries, where the government often seeks to have bishops sympathetic to it, or in countries which have a concordat and where the State claims the right to veto. But arguments used to justify independence from the State can hardly be used appropriately to legitimate ignoring the express wishes of the people of a diocese. So an appeal is made to the 'silent majority' of staunch but inarticulate Catholics who have been brushed aside by the activists and busybodies who bother to sit on committees. So the myth develops of a paternalistic Vatican saving people from themselves. And in such rescue operations the Vatican diplomat plays an important role.

Yet the Vatican diplomatic service was presented in a totally different light in Pope Paul's apostolic letter of 24 June 1969 (*Sollicitudo Omnium*). The primary function is 'to render ever closer and more operative the ties that bind the Holy See and the local churches'; in addition they may have duties towards the state in which they work, and in any case can devote themselves to vague but grandiose causes like peace and collaboration between peoples.

What this high-minded account omits is that the nuncio, pronuncio or apostolic delegate inevitably has something of the Vatican spy; no matter how genial he may be, he still has to send in reports on matters of interest, to keep track of dissident theologians, to scour the press for cuttings deemed offensive to the Holy See. If maintaining links between Rome and the local churches were the only purpose, then it could be achieved more easily by letting each local church have its representative to the Vatican. But the world-wide network of Vatican diplomats means that the Holy See has its own men on the spot to provide it with tailored information.

Thus we reach the most unknown and impenetrable level of ecclesiastical life: the Roman Curia. Most Catholics will have actually seen a bishop; few can claim to have seen a member of the Roman Curia, or even to be able to name any of them. That the Curia was in need of reform was neither the most novel nor courageous of judgements. One of Pope Paul's first acts was to say so himself in a remarkable speech in which he wielded an axe over the heads of astonished curial cardinals (the text can be found in Xavier Rynne, *The Second Session*, p. 338 et seq.). Criticism, he remarked, could be 'a prod to watchfulness and an invitation to reform'. The Curia was invited to reform itself, and the general principles were laid down: the Curia was to be at the service of the world's bishops, and not dominate over them; it was to be internationalized, so that the preponderance of Italians would be avoided; it was to be reorganized to make it more efficient. The mills ground very slowly, and it was not until 15 August 1967 that the *motu proprio* reforming the Curia appeared (*Regimini Ecclesiae*). It introduced diocesan bishops into the Curia, usually seven per congregation, but this was a largely symbolic move since all it really meant was that the occasional bishop travelled to Rome for the annual plenary meetings of his congregation. He could so easily be outsmarted by the permanent staff who controlled the agenda and saw to the carrying out of decisions: outsiders could always be quelled with the argument that although their suggestion might be good for their local church, it would never do for the universal Church of which the Romans had an intimate, though second-hand, knowledge.

However, the reforms of 1967 did something to internationalize the Curia by permitting the use of modern languages. In the nine years from 1961 to 1970 the number of people working in the Curia grew from 1322 to 2260, but the proportion of Italians declined from 56·7% to 37·8%. Another set of proposals was designed to stop officials clinging to their posts, and a shake-up every five years became possible. No automatic promotion could be presumed. And on the death of the pope, all cardinal presidents and secretaries will have to resign. This would give the new pope a freer hand than in the past.

None of these reforms were startling. They were mostly a matter of tinkering with the works. The greatest change came over the Roman Curia simply because the so-called 'new Curia' developed methods of its own which owed little to the traditions of the Roman bureaucracy. Cardinal König, for example, throughout the decade president of the Secretariat for Non-believers, remained in Vienna as archbishop and refused to be centralized. The Secretariat for Christian Unity evolved a system of internal consultation, originally devised by Cardinal Bea, which made serious use of the talented men the Secretariat had always been able to attract – though it did not always manage to keep them. The Commission for Justice and Peace gave more place to lay men and women than any other Roman body, and it became an alternative and sometimes rival source of information, challenging the Secretariat of State on its own ground of information and the judgement of political situations. Some members of the 'new Curia' became globe-trotters which enabled them to see and get to know the Church, but exposed them to the facile charge of neglecting their duties and, by 1975, of overspending.

But the principal result of the 1967 reforms was to enhance the power of the Secretariat of State. This came about in two ways. First there was a need to arrive at some kind of co-ordination where there were overlapping competencies, and the Cardinal Secretary of State was appointed co-ordinator in chief, but he left a good deal of the work to Mgr Giovanni Benelli, who possessed the modestly deceptive title of 'substitute', *sostituto*. Secondly, this immense machine was at the service of the Pope and the *motu proprio* specifically said that 'it is a basic rule that no serious and extraordinary business may be conducted before the appropriate heads have notified the Supreme Pontiff' and that 'all decisions require the Pope's approval' (136). It was a recipe for disaster, since manifestly the Pope – any pope – would be unable to hold together so many threads and his subordinates would constantly play upon the ambiguity of the situation. Precisely what needed the Pope's approval? When in doubt, submit your text, proposal or even letter. They would then disappear into the maw of the office of the Sostituto, whence they re-emerged, some months later, hacked about or modified or accepted, and all this was done in the name of 'the Supreme Authority'. And in many cases it was clear that 'the Supreme Authority' had not seen the document in question. The effect of the restructuring of the Curia was to make the Sostituto the hour-glass linking Pope and Church. Communication, upwards and downwards, has to pass this way.

Archbishop Giovanni Benelli has held this post since 1967. He was only forty-six when he arrived, and has energy to spare. The smallness and continuity of the Roman world is illustrated by the fact that when Mgr Montini himself held the post of Sostituto in the pontificate of Pius XII, he had employed the young Benelli as his secretary and had not forgotten him.

Benelli has all the more influence in that Cardinal Villot, technically his superior at the Secretariat of State, does not have the same passionate zeal for work as Benelli and is more interested in collaboration between episcopal conferences than the hurly-burly conflicts of ecclesiastical politics. Benelli is not an ogre, and indeed he knows how to charm. He is a servant of Pope Paul, and entirely consumed by his task, which he accomplishes with complete loyalty. Any criticisms of his role tend to strengthen it, and any undue influence will be hotly denied. Ill-will will be attributed to the foolhardy critic. An article which set out to show that Benelli was 'at odds with the best recent thinking of the Church' ('The Man who is closest to the Pope', in *The Observer*, 11 and 18 March 1973) was said by a Belgian writer to be 'based on the gossip of doorkeepers and undignified remarks of bodyguards' (*La Libre Belgique*, 17 March 1973). As the author of the offending article, I can swear that I never spoke to a doorkeeper or a bodyguard when in Rome.

The evidence for the fact that Mgr Benelli is 'at odds with the best recent thinking of the Church' is not based on hearsay or anecdote, on which one frequently has to rely in a highly secretive institution, but on a rare speech which he unwisely made. It was published in full in *Civiltà Cattolica*, the Jesuit-edited semi-official cousin of *Osservatore Romano*. The article is called 'The Validity of Pontifical Diplomacy' ('Validità della Diplomazia Pontificia', *Civiltà Cattolica*, 6 May 1972, pp. 268–78). It displays in a paradigm way the mentality which is characteristic of the worst side of the Roman Curia and why it has difficulty in grasping what is really happening elsewhere. As its title suggests, the lecture is a defence of the Vatican diplomatic service, which has been under attack. But Benelli cannot simply point this out and keep his cool, still less give any examples: the fact that the new nunciature in Chile had just been daubed with left-wing slogans would have been very much to his purpose. Instead, he orates and declares that Vatican diplomacy 'has been assailed by a flood of polemics and criticism so characteristic of our age'. That sets the tone of defensive vagueness from the start. Invisible and anonymous opponents are brushed aside with elegant formulations. Nothing is ever identified, no position is clearly stated, no examples of general principles are ever given – a reticence which he justifies on grounds of 'diplomatic discretion'. 'Delicate matters', a favourite Roman phrase, require nuances and hints rather than plain statement. So Benelli is often obscure. But he is precise in one way. His style is that of a jurist who quickly translates the spiritual language of the Gospels ('Feed my sheep') into juridical terms ('the right and duty of Peter'). Scripture is used uncritically, historical sense is lacking, and thus we get the following description of the 'historical basis' of papal diplomatic activity: 'Titus and Timothy, official representatives of St Paul *vis-à-vis* the local churches of Asia Minor and Greece, can in fact be considered as the first apostolic delegates in the strictest and most modern sense of the term.' The prodigious leap from the first century to the present is accomplished in the twinkling of an eye.

But it is in the attitude shown towards the local churches that the pre-conciliar theology of Benelli appears most strikingly. They barely exist. Or rather, they are allowed a somewhat meagre existence, but simply as the recipients of orders and directives from the centre. They are also places where trouble starts, and this is where the papal nuncio can make himself useful: 'Difficult and delicate situations not infrequently arise in the local churches when the representative of the Pope emerges as the most suitable person, and sometimes the only person, capable of instilling the community with that faith and hope which are necessary to continue to resist.' We are vouchsafed no examples and it is very difficult to imagine a scenario in which the papal envoy played the role here attributed to him. The travail of Eastern Europe has been undergone without benefit of nuncio. The over-estimation of the role of Vatican diplomats continues. Alas, he concedes, there are occasionally conflicts and clashes within the local church, and it is the task of the local bishops to sort them out. But – and this is a very revealing passage – 'their intervention can be so problematic and difficult, either because of particular circumstances or because they are themselves involved. The action that pontifical representatives can take in such delicate situations is providential.' The implication here is that local bishops can be so influenced by family, circle of friends or political connections that they lose their independence. This can indeed happen and a useful example would have been the links which bound together Cardinal Santos of Manila to President Marcos. But there is no reason to suppose that the pontifical representatives are magically exempt from pressures. They too have their own views. The only difference is that they can be removed more easily and swiftly.

The exaltation of the role of nuncio and the playing down of the local bishops is a feature of the curial style. While Benelli is thoroughly pessimistic about the local churches, and sees them, warts and all, with unflinching realism, he is thoroughly optimistic about the Vatican representatives. It is this which gives one the feeling of moving in cloud-cuckoo-land. Thus he is able to declare categorically: 'When the nuncio presents himself to the Christian community of a nation, the faithful welcome him festively (*festosa-*

mente).' The truth is that sometimes they do, sometimes they do not, and that usually they are unaware of his arrival in their midst. Benelli is full of 'realism' so long as he is talking about other bodies, but it mysteriously deserts him when he speaks of the Vatican. He had no particular reason for mentioning the World Council of Churches in his lecture, and so his reference to it takes the form of a gratuitous swipe. After explaining that the existence of diplomatic representatives makes possible a 'presence' of the Church in the world of international affairs, he goes on: 'Not all communities are in a position to have such relations, for example the WCC, which lacks an international juridical personality.' There is more 'realism' as he laboriously explains that it is no use dreaming of utopia or claiming that the purity of the Gospel demands that we shun contact with the sinful world. It is the duty of the Church, he declares, 'not to deal with some imaginary and hypothetical world, but with civil society as it really is, in the concrete, as it in fact exists'. The redundancies here indicate the nervousness. As Isaiah Berlin remarked, when a man announces that he is a realist, you may be quite sure that he is on the point of doing something rather shady.

The suggestion is not that Benelli is wicked or over-ambitious: it is simply that he is out of touch and moving in a world that is not inhabited by ordinary Christians. He possesses the title of 'archbishop', though he has never exercised any sustained pastoral office. At the time of the Counter-Reformation the edifying theory was that when a Roman official was not busy at his desk, he was ministering to the galley-slaves. Many curialists try to find modern equivalents but Benelli is much too busy for that. He revealed in his 1972 lecture a set of attitudes which do much to explain the inevitability of conflict between the centre and the periphery – a phrase which came to be used to contrast Rome with the rest of the world. But it did not imply a very high regard for the outlying corners of the empire, and suggested a rather weary Roman senator pulling his toga about him and saying: 'More trouble among the Belgae, dissension among the Picts.' The periphery riposted by taking less and less interest in what emanated from the centre. And bishops – the real bishops who visit the sick and know the priests of their diocese – were torn between the two.

Chapter 6

The Agony of Pope Paul

ARRIGO LEVI: *Russia is perhaps the only country in the world in which the principle of authority remains intact.*

POPE PAUL: *Is that a great strength or a great weakness?*
interview in *La Stampa*, 1968.

It is very difficult to know a pope. Although he is constantly in the public eye, it is not these moments with the crowds which count for him. And although he speaks as often and at as great a length as any politician, the form of a pontifical discourse is not immediately revealing of his innermost thoughts, especially in the ungainly gobbledegook translations that are usually provided. So a pope is at once the most public and the most private of men, constantly on show and yet bafflingly elusive. So many hopes and aspirations come to rest in him, so awesome is his office, that it almost consumes the person of the office-holder. At the same time a pope is not simply the inanimate bearer of pontifical gear, like the dolls in Fellini's film. His personality remains and affects the life of the Church. Pope Paul VI had the daunting task of following Pope John XXIII, concluding the Council his predecessor had started, and holding the Church together in the next decade. The strain shows.

Two anecdotes reveal something of the man. In January 1973 a papal diplomat visited Pope Paul and found him anxious and pessimistic about the Church's future. He tried to console the Pope with the thought that there was a good deal of generosity and desire for authentic religious life among young people, but without success. The Pope said: 'Now I understand St Peter, who came to Rome twice, the second time to be crucified.' He had himself come to Rome twice: the first time to enter the Secretariat of State, where he toiled for nearly thirty years, and the second time to be elected pope after his seven-year period as archbishop of Milan. To be pope is to be crucified. Less melodramatic but no less revealing is the story of the admirable way he presided at a meeting of the bishops of the archdiocese of Paris in September 1971. The meeting came about as a result of a suggestion by Cardinal Marty, who wanted to express 'collegiality' in a concrete way and prevent Paris and Rome drifting apart. After five years the Parisian bishops were to review their work. They did so in Rome, in the presence of the Pope. It was a working session round a table, not an audience. They were impressed by the Pope's grasp of their difficulties. He took a keen interest in the way they had divided the diocese into 'sectors' of activity rather than territorially. But after an hour he went over to his desk, produced a manuscript and said: 'I suppose I had better read out the speech that has been prepared.' The role had taken over again.

Yet Pope Paul had tried desperately hard not to be confined in his role. That was why he travelled. The jet age made possible a globe-trotting pope or, as he insisted from the start, 'a pilgrim pope'. Pope John had travelled, but only within Italy: and if one of the characteristic photographs of Pope John shows him in soup-plate hat at the rain-besplattered window of a railway carriage (thus linking him with Pio Nono who built the railway), one characteristic picture of Pope Paul shows him in an aeroplane half-way round the world. Modernity does not consist in speed of travel, but Pope Paul's journeys helped to shatter the image of a pope imprisoned in the Vatican. The Curial attitude was, 'Let them come to us.' This Pope, shy and awkward with crowds, with his nervous two-handed sawing-of-the-air gesture, would go to the people.

His first journey took him to the Holy Land. By going to the land of Israel (which the Romans had called 'Palestine' in order to blot out the memory of the Jewish people) Pope Paul dramatized the 'return to the sources' which was the basis of the conciliar renewal. It was a gesture which reached back beyond the divisions of the Reformation, and back beyond the division between East and West since in Jerusalem he met and welcomed in a brotherly embrace Patriarch Athenagoras. But in aspiration Pope Paul was reaching still further back, before the Emperor Constantine, to a time when a group of men proclaimed the good news about this man Jesus of Nazareth to slaves and the oppressed in the eastern Mediterranean. And all these hints and suggestions were implicit in his action: he could spell them out in speeches and discourses, and of course he did, but the dramatic impact of the 'event' was more important. Throughout his pontificate Pope Paul was to seek other 'lived parables' which taught simply by happening. And his first journey was the most significant. He went, as he explained, 'to that blessed land where St Peter set forth and to which none of his successors has returned'.

Though not reaching the same sublime heights, the next two visits, to Bombay and the United Nations, maintained the tempo. The Church on the move had a pope on the move. The visit to India was a tribute to a non-aligned nation and to a deeply religious people, and at the same time something of a quest at a time when 'the third world' was just beginning to haunt the West. Pope Paul claims to have learned from his travels: 'We were able to see and virtually to touch the very grave difficulties besetting the peoples of long-standing civilizations who are at grips with the problems of development' (*Populorum Progressio*, 1967). However unlikely the notion that a journey from airport to city centre can really throw much light on the state of a nation, travel – aided by good briefing – made Pope Paul aware of the problems of urban sprawl and shanty-town poverty, and this concern was reflected in the apostolic letter to Cardinal Roy, *Octogesima Adveniens* (14 May 1971). Further journeys to Africa and Latin America confirmed the emphasis on the third world which is characteristic of this pontificate.

The third journey of the Pope, however, was to the United Nations, and once more it was of great symbolic importance. The journey dramatized the dedication of the papacy to the work of peace. The Pope claimed for the Church the role of 'conscience of the nations', proposed indirectly the entry of China into the United Nations and made recommendations on disarmament. There was talk of a 'new triumphalism', as though the papacy, having finally accepted the loss of its temporal power, was now trying to recoup on the international level what it had reluctantly lost on the national and European level. 'Italian' considerations ceased to be so dominating, though from time to time they were revived. The historian Arnold Toynbee is one observer who has been prepared to take the papal work for peace at its face value: 'In his work for peace, the Pope has the whole world for his parish and the whole human race for his flock' (*The Vatican and World Peace*, edited by Francis Sweeney, p. 96). But as Pope Paul remarked himself in his first encyclical, *Ecclesiam Suam*, 'the apostolic art is risky', and the political implications of his support for the United Nations were not lost on right-wing Catholics who regarded it as an impotent and interfering body.

But despite such difficulties – which were inseparable from any sort of action and would not have been avoided by total inaction – there was an impressive logic in the first three journeys of Pope Paul. In *Ecclesiam Suam*, the most personal of his encyclicals and one that presents itself as 'a conversational letter', he speaks of the 'concentric circles' which encompass him (97–117). That presupposes Rome at the centre, surrounded and supported by loyal Catholics, with other Christians forming the next circle and the great non-Christian religions a still wider circle, until finally, at the outermost rim, the unbelieving world is reached. This pattern is frequently reflected in papal rhetoric. It was used at the start of the Holy Year when each of these categories was, in turn, invited to 'come to Rome'.

But in the first half of the pontificate, that comforting Counter-Reformation pattern was smashed. The pilgrim Pope had gone to the sources of faith, to the third world, and to the forum of all the nations. And he had gone, not as though in possession of some magic formula to resolve everyone's problems, but as a seeker after truth who wanted to make some contribution, however modest, to their solution. This change marked the recognition of the truth of Péguy's remark: it was characteristic of the Middle Ages to know clearly who the enemy was and where the frontier lay, but now, said Péguy, 'the frontier is everywhere, the circumference is everywhere'. In other words, the Church does not stand aloof from the concerns of mankind and does not have to surround itself with concentric circles which, inevitably, suggest defensive outworks and fortifications.

This context helps to explain why the visit to Portugal in May 1967 was widely regarded as a set-back and a disappointment. The Pope went to the shrine of Our Lady of Fatima. It was not a happy idea, for Fatima was characterized by precisely the kind of mariological devotion which roused the wrath of Protestants as well as the mistrust of Catholics, taught by the Council to take a more sober view of Mary. The Council placed Mary not on some remote pedestal, but with the Church: she was seen as the exemplar of human co-operation with the divine initiative. It seemed, therefore, to be unwise to set the seal of pontifical approval on a devotion which was, to say the least, secondary, and which was accompanied by startling portents such as the sun standing still in the sky. With its hints of mysterious 'revelations' concerned with Soviet Russia, it was just the sort of pious and mystic pseudo-event to commend itself to Pius XII – which it did.

The visit was not only an ecumenical embarrassment. Fatima happened to be in Portugal, a highly authoritarian 'Fascist' country which had been engaged in fairly uninterrupted colonial wars in its African territories of Angola and Mozambique. A report submitted to Pope Paul beforehand predicted the likely effect, and as a result every effort was made to tone down the political implications of the visit so as not to distress liberal opinion and the developing nations of Africa. Pope Paul tried hard to impose a different meaning on his journey. He spoke once again on the urgent need for peace. He gave an address on 'Our Lady and Ecumenism', and consulted the Secretariat for Christian Unity about it in advance. He tried to eliminate all the 'superstitious' elements in the Fatima story. His visit to Salazar, an inevitable courtesy once he had committed himself to going to Portugal, was brief and no photographers were present. A commentator on Vatican Radio, who was not unprompted, tried to sum up the papal achievement: 'Paul VI purified devotion to Our Lady at Fatima. He swept away the atmosphere of secrecy, of political and social exploitation, of false mystery, of whisperings and gossip. In his discourses the Pope made no mention of the mysterious Fatima that intellectuals [*sic*] had used to put forward their own ideas under the cover of Our Lady.' That was perfectly true as far as the Pope's intentions were concerned. But the principle stated earlier applies: it is the visit itself which bears the meaning, and subsequent interpretations and second thoughts cannot alter that meaning. The general public retained one fact: the Pope had visited a Marian shrine in a Fascist country.

This illustrates a general dilemma faced by Pope Paul. He acted or he spoke, but then the Vatican Press Office laboriously explained that the event or the speech did not really mean what it appeared to mean. A dangerous gap opened up between the rhetoric and the realities. In later visits he tried to establish a link between his presence and the collegial activity of the local bishops. Thus he was in Kampala, Uganda, in 1969, at the conclusion of the first plenary assembly of the African bishops (SECAM). He went further than they expected when he said: 'An adaptation of the Christian life in the fields of pastoral, ritual, didactic and spiritual activities is not only possible, it is even favoured by the Church. The liturgical renewal is a living example of this. And in this sense you may, and you must, have an African Christianity. Indeed, you possess human values and characteristic forms of culture which can rise up to such perfection as to find in Christianity and for Christianity a true superior fullness, and prove to be capable of a richness of expression all its own, and genuinely African.' The African bishops took this as a serious programmatic statement, and were therefore disconcerted to hear Pope Paul say, at the end of the 1974 Synod, that 'it would be dangerous to speak of different theologies for different continents and different cultures'. It may be possible with immense semantic labour to reconcile the two statements, but the danger is that the reconciliation comes to exist only on paper.

The Pope's last journey was to the Far East in November 1970. It took him to Pago Pago in American Samoa, to the Philippines, and to Australia, where the celebration of Mass on Randwick Racecourse, Sydney (bookmakers' stands had been removed by fork-lift trucks), neatly coincided with the anniversary of the arrival of Captain Cook two hundred years previously. Once more there was an attempt to express 'travelling collegiality' as the Pope took part in the final meeting of the Oceanic bishops' assembly. He

heard pleas for a change of Australia's immigration policies from
the Bishop of Tonga, and suggestions on the need to ordain married men from other missionary bishops. There was ecumenical
coolness in Australia, and the Anglican Archbishop of Sydney
boycotted a prayer service. In the Philippines the difficulties were
political rather than ecumenical. Along the route to the cathedral in
Manila demonstrators waved placards proclaiming, 'Santos retire'
(Santos was Cardinal and very close to President Marcos) and
'Explain the unexplained wealth of the Church'. But the demonstrators later distinguished between the Pope, whom they welcomed, and Cardinal Santos, an acknowledged millionaire, whom
they abused. Pope Paul joined the Asian bishops and urged them to
see to it that the Church 'lost its foreign appearance'. 'No one', he
said, 'can speak to an Asian better than another Asian.'

The deliberations with the Asian bishops were, however, overshadowed by an assassination attempt on the Pope's life. The
assassin, a Bolivian called Benjamin Mendoza y Amor, known
locally as 'the mad painter', disguised himself in clerical dress and
got close enough to the Pope to draw a knife on him. Early versions
of the story claimed that Mendoza had been felled by a karate chop
from President Marcos, but the truth was much less dramatic:
Don Macchi, the Pope's secretary, pushed Mendoza away and into
the arms of English-born Bishop Anthony Galvin of Singapore, a
six-foot ex-rugby player who swiftly overpowered him. It was a
bungled attempt at assassination, and Pope Paul forgave the man
and tried to forget the incident.

But having visited the five continents, the Pope ceased to travel.
It was certainly not fear or apprehension which led him to change
his approach: he does not lack courage. Contingency plans for a
visit to Poland were prepared, originally in 1966 for the millennium
celebrations of Polish Christianity, and from time to time the dust
was blown off them. But even though official relations with Poland
gradually improved, especially after Gierek replaced Gomulka in
December 1970, the Communists could never bring themselves to
risk the demonstrations of popular enthusiasm for the Pope which
would certainly have occurred. That dream remained unfulfilled. A
visit to a Communist country would have admirably completed the

symbolic round of papal journeys and illustrated his accessibility to all categories of men. But the journeys ceased in 1970, just as the stream of encyclical letters ceased in 1968, and in the second half of the pontificate the Pope has become stay-at-home and has seen the world outside reflected through second-hand reports. He has lost the initiative which he had in his first six years. By 1975, with the celebration of the Holy Year, he was inviting everyone to come to Rome, and thus re-established the view of the Church which placed Rome at the centre and the rest of the world around it in concentric circles.

To have been a travelling, 'missionary' or 'pilgrim' pope was the first great novelty of his pontificate. To be a pope who consulted beyond the narrow confines of the Roman Curia was the second. Indirectly this has contributed to his travail, for although he made consultation possible by setting up the Episcopal Synod, bringing diocesan bishops into the Roman Curia and establishing commissions to deal with certain urgent and complex questions, he nullified the effect of these moves by reserving two questions to himself and refusing absolutely to share, still less to delegate, his responsibility. Birth-control and clerical celibacy (together with the distinct but related matter of the ordination of married men) remained firmly in his hands and received the answer 'No'. Why? Was it an inability to trust anyone else, a courageous refusal to evade responsibility, or a kind of pontifical messianism which impelled him to shoulder these burdens alone and so become, in Cardinal Suenens' vivid phrase, a kind of 'solitary Atlas'? No doubt all three elements played their part, but the last seems to have been of crucial importance to judge by what he said in a rare interview: 'How easy it is to study, but how difficult it is to decide.' Whether Pope John ever really compared him to Hamlet may be doubted: but Pope Paul has certainly experienced the pain of decision, and chosen to decide alone. By his reluctance to delegate or share the decision on these two questions, Pope Paul drew down on himself the hostility of all those who disagreed; by committing the full weight of his personal authority, he put it at risk and exposed himself to attack. The sign of unity became a sign of contradiction. In both cases he could have striven for a 'collegial' decision, but he chose not to take that course, perhaps because he was not sure what answer the collegial process would give or feared that it would give an answer which he could not personally endorse.

Both the encyclical on priestly celibacy of 1967 and that on birth-control of 1968 were intended to bring controversy to a close. The result was that they gave it new and more acrimonious life. And in both decisions the collegial process was short-circuited. Yet Pope Paul had constantly repeated that collegiality involved 'the harmonious collaboration of the episcopal college', but, as Cardinal Suenens pointed out, collegiality was a concept which the Pope urged on the bishops of the world, but without applying it to himself as head of the college.

Another personal papal initiative led to further trouble. 1968 was declared a Year of Faith and on 29 June, Feast of Saints Peter and Paul, the Pope offered to the world his profession of faith, which came to be known briefly as the Credo of Pope Paul VI. Four times longer than the traditional creeds, it was intended to confirm Christians in their faith and settle their doubts. Vatican Radio commented upon the event in predictably glowing terms: 'We have just been present at an historic half-hour', said the commentator, 'for by this discourse the Holy Father has put an end to the confusion which has raged for five or six years in the Church, and has cut short all useless theological discussion.' That proved to be an over-optimistic verdict, and once more the attempt to put an end to discussion gave it new impetus. The judgement of professional theologians, when they bothered at all, was severe and unsparing. One professor at the Jesuit Gregorian University in Rome commented: 'We can now close down all theological institutes and simply send for the record from Rome.' It seemed that the Pope, having removed key decisions from the college of bishops, was now trying to do the work of theologians as well, and his very sincerity was both touching and frustrating. The 1967 Synod had recommended the drawing up of 'a pastoral and practical declaration on the doctrinal questions which worry the People of God today'. But was the Pope's Credo a non-collegial attempt to meet this collegial proposal? In any event, no other attempt was made.

It was not that anyone, formally, disagreed with the contents of the Pope's Credo. Indeed, in many respects its formulations were admirable, open-minded and in tune with the latest theological developments. It asserted, for example, the infallibility of the college of bishops alongside that of the Pope. It was full of praise for 'the rich diversity of liturgical rites and the legitimate diversity of spiritual and theological traditions which, far from hindering the Church's unity, manifest it all the more'. It held out hope for the salvation of the sincere unbeliever who sought to follow the dictates of his conscience. But at the same time whole passages from the Council of Trent on original sin – transmitted not by imitation but by 'propagation' – and on transubstantiation, not to mention angels and purgatory, were reproduced with no attempt to echo the re-thinking which had been taking place on all these questions. It was a curious way to set about answering the questions of contemporary man. All those brave words at the Wednesday audiences about finding a contemporary language for faith and starting from the real situation of modern man seemed to have been forgotten and replaced by simple assertion. At a stroke, the errors of the *New Catechism*, the Dutch attempt to restate the faith which had long been under fire, were to be banished. As it happened, Pope Paul's Credo was quickly lost sight of in the storm which followed the publication of *Humanae Vitae* only a few weeks later, but the Credo was a warning sign that the Pope, henceforward, was going to throw his personal weight behind those who were alarmed by the consequences of the Council and determined to limit its effects.

Yet paradoxically Pope Paul's exalted conception of his office is matched by deep personal humility. When he carries the heavy cross during the Holy Week ceremonies, he identifies completely with his task. Dissent in the Church causes him worry, he told the cardinals in December 1969, and the defection of priests was his 'crown of thorns'. Pope Paul does not bear the burden of office lightly. He is relentless in his understanding of his office, and re-cognizes that it is, to some, an ecumenical obstacle. At the same time, he has nothing of the dictator and is never overbearing or interfering in the details of administration. He leaves a great deal to his secretaries and to the Substitute: it is they who acquire power and incur unpopularity. His choice of the name Paul implied a programme. Like the Apostle Paul, he wanted to be a pilgrim and a missionary to the Gentiles, to the people who do not know Christ. The journeys of the first half of his pontificate should be seen in the light of this missionary ambition. It is to the modern Gentiles that he tries to speak, even though he sometimes feels that no one is listening. In a phrase of touching honesty he once spoke of the need 'to offer our service to the world, a service that is all the more necessary in that it is not wanted' (24 June 1965). He accepts rebuffs as part of the cross he has to bear.

Pope Paul is an avid newspaper reader. Every morning he skims *La Stampa*, *Corriere della Sera* and *Le Monde*. An efficient cuttings service brings samples of the rest of the world press. He knows what the world is thinking and saying about him, and has occasionally commented on his reading. Just before Christmas in 1968, towards the end of a year in which trouble had assailed him from all sides, he said: 'We try to keep an open mind and to understand the distress and the impatience which have sometimes taken the form of rebellion and challenge.' Pope Pius XII could never have used such language. Pope Paul knew perfectly well that he had been accused of pessimism and neurotic anxiety, and was keen that his motivation should be correctly understood: 'It is not anxiety that leads us to insist on certain themes, but a concern for the Church's orthodoxy and the good ordering of her life.' Nine months later he returned to the same theme. He mentioned that 'a courageous churchman' – immediately identified as Cardinal Suenens – had suggested to him that the Church's central administration had shown great timidity when faced by post-conciliar developments and was 'fearful and uncertain instead of being open-minded and decisive in action'. 'This observation', he added sombrely, 'impelled us to reflect upon ourselves.' He did not report the fruits of his reflections. To be worried about being worried plunges the worrier into still deeper trouble. Despite the attempt to inject a note of optimism into his speeches, the cries of woe and alarm are what stick in the mind.

Pope Paul speaks a great deal in public. As a result, he sometimes reveals more of himself than he would wish to. In one speech, for example, he set out to analyse the likely reactions of his hearers to the word 'service', and his analysis is more revealing about himself than about them. Modern man, he declared, rejects the idea of service and 'does not want to be the servant of an authority or a law'. This seems a travesty of 'modern man', who is perfectly capable of submitting to rational authority, authority which commends itself; and moreover, the idea of 'service of humanity' is very much alive. But Pope Paul missed this encouraging possibility and went on to add that 'modern man's instinct for freedom drives him to caprice, lack of restraint and finally anarchy'. This is a rather rapid downward spiral even for that deplorable individual, modern man. There was no recognition that if 'modern man' suspects authority, this is partly because of the horrors which have been committed in this century in the name of obedience to authority. It is not simply cussedness. Pope Paul so frequently is negative where he could be more positive without any loss of integrity.

Another constant of the pontifical style is the surprising venom of his attacks on 'sociology'. On the whole, they do not worry professional sociologists, who fail to recognize their own work in what is being so vigorously denounced. The onslaught is usually directed against a 'purely empirical' view of the Church or the habit of 'deducing moral norms from sociological surveys'. Here is one example, from December 1969: 'Sociology is fashionable. Its methods appear to be wholly scientific and positive, and it has behind it the authority of statistics. Thus the result of the poll becomes the decisive criterion, not only of what is in the collective mind but of what is the norm.' It is true that in Holland in the period of optimism 'market research' was considered essential before embarking on any apostolic project, and it is also true that disturbing statistics on clerical celibacy and other controverted questions were beginning to appear; but they were regarded as part of the data of the disputed problem, not its solution. The misunderstanding with sociology is unfortunate. As Peter Berger has maintained, sociology is not subversive in the long run. In the short term it is indeed disturbing of settled institutions, since it is unafraid to ask questions and has little respect for authority as such. But in the long term sociology is concerned with the cohesion of society, with the values which animate it, with the role of tradition and continuity, and with the laws of change. By his self-denying ordinance Pope Paul has deprived himself of one helpful way of understanding the changing Church and presiding over its orderly transformation. He has unnecessarily turned a potential ally into an enemy. The same could be said of the other, vaguer and more elusive enemies which are periodically denounced: relativism and historicism, to name but two. Anxiety does not help in the discernment and encouragement of what is good. And prophecies of gloom are frequently self-fulfilling.

It is here that Pope Paul most suffers by comparison with Pope John XXIII, whose optimism and trust seemed almost to create their own object. A good teacher brings out the best in his pupils by building up their confidence rather than presenting them with the catalogue of their mistakes. Pope John was a good teacher. He radiated goodness and brought it into existence. Despite the cheering crowds on his journeys, Pope Paul has never been a truly popular figure and has not succeeded in communicating that warmth which people feel when they meet him privately. He is most at ease in small gatherings. At his first meeting with diplomats it was not merely politeness which led him to say: 'This is almost a family gathering at which after years of absence one sees the faces of friends who awaken cherished memories.' Diplomacy was for so long his milieu. The papacy is his vocation and cross. He has many times spoken of the need to combine the spirit of St Paul with that of St Peter. The theme of the two rock apostles is more than a rhetorical flourish. He hoped to combine the Petrine principle of order, stability, continuity and firmness with the Pauline principle of dynamism, energy and Christ-centred creativity. But after the year of crisis in 1968, the Petrine principle has been increasingly stressed. Concern for order has predominated. Pope Paul's dilemma is that he temperamentally cannot emulate Pope John and temperamentally does not want to emulate Pope Pius XII. He has neither the authority which commends itself nor the authority which imposes itself.

Pope Paul is convinced that he is a moderate. The evidence is that he is criticized by both extremes. The right-wing blame him for liturgical change, a readiness to talk to Communists and 'freedom fighters', his emphasis on the third world. The left-wing say that he had not the courage to carry through the insights of Vatican II and that he has fumbled his opportunities. He is dragged apart as he tries to hold the centre. His long experience has taught him two lessons in particular. First, he does not want to be exposed to the charge made against Pius XII on the Nazi persecution of the Jews: that of not speaking out. Hence the panoramic view of the world and the willingness to utter general truths about any corner of it; though this is modified by his diplomatic habits of not wanting to offend anyone. But secondly, Pope Paul has an agonizing awareness of precedent, and a keen sense of the irreversibility of certain changes in the Church. One cannot, say, permit the ordination of married men as an experiment, and then judge the results a decade later. The 'thin end of the wedge' argument is frequently invoked, and his reluctance to bind his successor comes in to support it. Against this, he has made minor changes which could have more profound effects than are realized. The simple act of debarring cardinals over the age of eighty from the conclave which elects the Pope was an unspectacular decision in itself. But it means that for the first time since the Third Lateran Council in 1179 a limitation has been placed on the exclusive right of the College of Cardinals to elect the Pope. Other limitations can follow, and non-cardinal presidents of episcopal conferences could be introduced into the conclave. A lever has been provided for the future. A small departure from precedent is in principle as important as a large departure. And with the Synod of Bishops an instrument has been provided for the future, which another pope could use in a very different way.

In human terms the office of pope has become impossible to fulfil. The papal office contains within it so many responsibilities that no man can give adequate attention to them all, and the Pope becomes like a juggler spinning a number of plates. Some of them will fall to the ground. He is Bishop of Rome, Primate of Italy, Patriarch of the West, Pope of the Universal Church; it is as though the same person were simultaneously Mayor of New York, President of the United States, and Secretary-General of the United Nations. The tasks proliferate and simply defy human powers. Precisely, it might be said, and that is why the papacy depends ultimately not on the capacity of the individual who holds the office but on the divine assistance which is promised to him. This no Catholic Christian can dispute. But that does not mean that the papacy has to take precisely its present form, with its centralized bureaucracy and diplomatic representatives. The existing situation has come about as a result of a long process of history: to present it as divinely established is abusive and inhibits any idea of serious change. The paradox is that papal authority is all the stronger for being less self-assertive, that it gains when it sees itself in terms of service rather than power, and is prepared to learn as well as teach. If the unity of the wider Church needs symbolizing here below, the Pope is the traditional and available symbol of that unity. Anglicans and Orthodox have recognized this. It is less well known that Lutherans have reached the same point. 'Our Lutheran teaching about the ministry and the Church', says an official report, 'constrains us to believe that recognition of papal primacy is possible to the degree that a renewed papacy would in fact foster faithfulness to the Gospel and truly exercise a Petrine function within the Church' (Lutheran/Roman Catholic Dialogue on Papal Primacy, 48, 4 March 1974; published in *One in Christ*, 1974, no. 3). The way to the future is not closed.

Chapter 7

Whatever Happened
to the Theologians?

A Catholic theologian spends many years in discovering a new insight and then just as many years in
proving that it is not really new

MARK SCHOOF
'Dutch Catholic Theology',
in *Cross Currents*, Winter 1973, no. 4, p. 426.

Meanwhile, whatever was happening in the Vatican, the Church
had not stood still, and the change could be seen most strikingly
among the theologians, those with the professional task of articu-
lating the Christian faith. From being remote or even dusty
scholars whose work was rarely noticed outside the narrow circle of
their colleagues, they were pushed to the centre of the stage,
involved in brightly lit controversy and sometimes collided with
the *magisterium*, the teaching authority of the Church. Hans Küng's
clash with Rome will be described at the end of this chapter. A
more illuminating starting-point will be the changed understanding of the theologian's role which flowed quite naturally from the
changed self-understanding of the Church. A gap was bound to
open up between officials at the centre and theologians at the periphery, because the theologians were quicker to respond to new
needs, usually worked in a strongly ecumenical context, and were
more courageous (some said foolhardy) in their attempted restate-
ment of Christian faith.

The changed role of the theologian can best be seen by taking a
rapid cross-section and asking what a theologian thought he was
doing in 1955, 1965 and 1975. How did he see his task? In 1955 he
was a man who quite simply 'handed on what he had received'. He
did not expect the theological landscape to change in a startling

manner or to be suddenly convulsed. He expected it to look much the same at the end of his long and laborious career as at the start. He taught from handbooks or manuals which distinguished with enviable clarity what was 'of Catholic faith' and what was merely 'theological opinion'. 'Adversaries' appeared early on in his theses. Their ideas were sketchily presented and rapidly dismissed. Scripture and the Fathers were used, without much critical sense, to 'prove' the theses that were advanced. The theologian might differ from the manual on minor points, and indeed he had to if he were to appear a serious scholar and not just a conformist nonentity; but the area of permitted disagreement – today's pluralism – was extremely restricted.

By 1965 the situation had changed utterly. Those theologians, mostly French and German, who had been burrowing away at the sources of theology since the 1930s, moved out of obscurity. Those who had been under a darkening cloud ever since Pope Pius XII had proscribed 'the new theology' in his encyclical *Humani Generis* of 1950 were now much in demand. The work of Yves Congar on ecclesiology and ecumenism, that of Henri de Lubac on the supernatural, that of Chenu on the 'world' and work, became respectable and urgently needed. The Council, said Pope John, would have to learn from history, and the three theologians mentioned were all formed in rigorous historical methods, even if Anglo-Saxon scholars complained about the inaccuracy of their footnotes. 'You need fifteen years', Congar used to tell his students at Le Saulchoir, 'to get to know St Thomas properly.' And he expected them to get to know St Thomas properly, not in vain. The theology which prevailed at the Council was predominantly European. In an engaging book entitled *The Rhine Flows into the Tiber*, Fr Ralph Wiltgen endeavoured to show that the Council was the result of a plot by Rhineland theologians who combined together to pull wool over the eyes of the world's bishops. There was no conspiracy, but there was certainly a hegemony of continental theologians. John Courtney Murray was an exception to this rule. It is fair to say that in 1965 the Anglo-Saxons on the whole accepted the European predominance, and that by 1975 they no longer do. Nor do the Africans and the Latin Americans.

But in 1965 theology was still dominated by men like Congar, Chenu, de Lubac and Karl Rahner. The former victims of the Holy Office, who had been forbidden to teach and occasionally to publish, were now held in high honour. After a concelebration at the end of the Council, Pope Paul embraced Henri de Lubac and thanked him for his work. These theologians did not agree on everything. But between them they represented a trend which can be expressed in a series of shorthand formulae: from the essentialist to the existentialist; from the juridical to the personalist; from the a-historical to the historical; from the exclusive to the inclusive; from deductive theology to inductive anthropology; from defensiveness to dialogue. None of these slogans provided a precise criterion; but all indicated a direction, and dozens of minor theological works proclaimed the new trends.

But there was an even more decisive change at the Council. The expectations of the world changed, but so did the expectations of the theologians. The Council had over four hundred *periti*, most of whom merited their title; and they became aware, perhaps for the first time in their theological existence, that they could effect change in the Church. No longer was their task simply to bolster up acquired convictions. They could actually shift the Church: that is to say that finding the Church at point a, they could expect to bring it to point c or d. Naturally this was done in the name of renewal and of going back in order to go forward; but the point is that it ushered in a new, constructive, and sometimes combative role for theologians in the life of the Church. Sometimes this was referred to as their prophetic role. No longer were they to be the conveyor-belt system of the *magisterium*; they were to be the heralds of the new and dynamic element in the Church. They began to argue within the Church for change in the Church.

But their campaign quickly revealed one of the flaws in the Council documents. Wherever the Council faced a difficulty, it had produced a compromising text which simply set the contrasting positions alongside each other. It repeated previous doctrines, and hoped that they would be modified by being set in the context of rediscovered doctrines. Thus the papal prerogatives were reasserted, but it was hoped that the emphasis on collegiality and the 'sense of the faithful' would modify the exercise of the papacy.

The consequences of such ambiguities could be seen in the theology which flourished in the immediate aftermath of the Council. Many theologians busied themselves in commenting upon and exploiting 'the new openings' offered to them by the Council. It was the era of the great commentaries and congresses on 'the theology of Vatican II'. But already some of the cracks were beginning to appear. What theologians stressed in their reading of Vatican II was not always what pastors stressed in theirs. Here is one representative witness from 1968: 'The Pope is constantly warning us that all sorts of things are being said in the name of Vatican II which are not to be found in that Council's Acta. This is perfectly true. Nevertheless Vatican II made – and made dramatically – a generic decision which opened the door to all the forces now disturbing the peace of the Church. For Vatican II decided to accord full and decisive weight to the existential principle in theology' (Sebastian Moore, in *Authority in a Changing Church*, edited by J. Dalrymple, p. 1). What the 'existential principle' meant was not altogether clear, and one of the 'new breed' of lay theologians had analysed with devastating accuracy some of its weaknesses: '"Existential", "dynamic" and "living" are preferable on any reckoning to "essentialist", "static" and "dead", but it is possible to forget that while we Catholics were plodding around in the wilderness of sacrament-as-thing and Latin in the liturgy, the world had latched on to the language we have recently discovered and absorbed it naturally into its thinking. We didn't have to *tell* intelligent, rational humanists that life is a dynamic flexible affair or that society should be a living organic community' (Terry Eagleton, 'The Language of Renewal', in *New Blackfriars*, September 1965, pp. 18–25). But what was obvious to Terry Eagleton caused alarm to pastors who thought of the Council as a point of arrival. The majority of theologians took it as a point of departure. Misunderstanding and collision were therefore, in the end, unavoidable.

It is symptomatic that Karl Rahner, master to so many, should have thought that the most significant teachings of the Council were those which had not appeared central at the time of drafting. He laid great stress, for example, on the assertion that the Church was truly present in the local church, and found in it confirmation of his theory that the Church of the future would be a 'diaspora' Church, scattered in small groups in a largely secularized world. Other theologians, like Johannes Baptist Metz, emphasized the Church as 'the sacrament of hope' in a way which suggested that numbers were of little account. Missionary zeal felt threatened by such theories. The men sweating in the frontline did not always appreciate the efforts of theologians working in comfortable academic surroundings. Another gap opened up. A text that was particularly welcome to theologians – it was addressed to them – was that which spoke of 'an order or "hierarchy" of truths', which vary in their relationship to the foundation of Christian faith (*On Ecumenism*, 11). This idea found its way into the Council documents thanks to a speech by Archbishop Pangrazio, but he had been influenced by Lukas Vischer, an observer from the World Council of Churches. It was a boon to theologians since much of their work consists precisely in the ordering or articulation of Christian faith. It was commonly felt that Catholics had not always distinguished the trivial from the important, the rosary from the Incarnation, and in the attempt to re-order the expression of faith, theologians tended to give a low place to narrowly 'Catholic' features, especially those of cultural origin. Ecumenical discussion in which they engaged confirmed this trend. It was not that they set out to 'water down' the faith, though they were accused of this; it was simply that the ecumenical experience taught them to deal with the most fundamental questions of Christian faith in a post-Christian age.

After the heady days of the Council and the prospect of influence which it offered, from 1968 a certain disenchantment seems to have set in. It is true that theologians were honoured by the setting up of the International Theological Commission, but it was a nominated body, and despite its competence and bulky reports, little attention has been paid to it. Its work on ministry was largely ignored by the 1971 Synod, and in 1972 the Commission devoted itself to the study of the idea of 'pluralism', which is more one of the conditions for the practice of theology than a matter of its content. Its wordy document on the subject was published a year later, and there was no great rush at the bookstalls. Its 1974 study, *Catholic Teaching and Apostolic Succession*, deserved more attention than anyone was prepared to give it. Karl Rahner resigned from the Commission partly on grounds of (as he claimed) old age, and partly because it was 'stewing in its own juice'. 'It sets itself problems,' he said in an interview in *Herder Korrespondenz*, 'speaks about them in a more or less praiseworthy way, but nothing else happens' (February 1974, p. 90).

Other, less official groups of theologians had been organizing themselves in the meantime. The multi-language review *Concilium*, by 1975 exactly ten years old, was an important forum for post-conciliar progressive views. At a congress held in Brussels in 1970 it celebrated the first five years of its existence with a ringing statement on the need for freedom of research and expression. Theologians can fulfil their service to the Church 'only if they have the freedom to debate and pursue theological issues among themselves'. It might seem odd that they found it necessary to assert the right to talk to each other. But many pastors imagined that theologians went about shocking the simple faithful in a thoroughly irresponsible way. Cardinal Heenan's remarks are typical of this attitude: 'It is a form of pastoral sadism to disturb simple faith. Those close to God are untroubled by the winds of academic controversy . . . A man with the soul of a pastor never indulges in the pastime of shocking the pious' (*Council and Clergy*, p. 85). The *Concilium* theologians would have rejected that garbled account of what they were doing. They believed on the contrary that theology could not be done in isolation from people and their real needs and problems: 'Hence, only Christian communities involved in the life of the contemporary world and taking active responsibility within their society can fashion the theology of the future.' Not that they wanted to sever their links with Rome and the teaching authority: they were at the service of the same Christian message preached by the *magisterium* and wanted to remain in constant dialogue with it. But they objected to underhand methods of dealing with theologians, and expressed the hope that 'in all cases due process that respects human rights and Christian freedom should be observed'. Ivan Illich was one maverick theologian who had been subjected to methods judged inquisitorial and odious. He later went on to disturb the medical and educational establishments with his pronouncements.

The increasingly committed and frustrated attitude of theologians appeared in a statement signed by thirty-three professors of theology from all over the world. It was dated 17 March 1972, and called *Against an Attitude of Resignation in the Church*. Its starting-point was the crisis of credibility from which the Church was suffering: 'The credibility of the Catholic Church, which was perhaps at its highest point in five hundred years at the beginning of the pontificate of Pope Paul VI, has declined, to such an extent as to cause anxiety. Many are suffering because of the Church. Resignation grows.' In attempting to explain this situation, they blamed not individuals but rather 'the ecclesiastical system' itself. Bishops were still chosen for their conformity, and the numerous intermediary bodies which had been set up did little to modify the style of authority in the Church which was still characterized by 'princely absolutism'. They noted the contrast between what the Church demands from others and what it is prepared to concede in its own life: the Church preaches freedom, justice and accessibility to others, but only 'as long as it does not cost the Church anything'. Trifling secondary matters receive great attention, while clear priorities and 'ideas that look to the future' are ignored. There was a contrast between 'interest in Jesus Christ and disinterest in the Church'. Faced with this catalogue of woe, they looked for some 'third way' between revolution and resignation.

They committed themselves to speak out where need be, to accept their own share of responsibility for the state of affairs, to work with others ('One member of the community approaching the parish priest counts for nothing; five are an annoyance; fifty will change the situation') and to seek for provisional solutions by 'persistent loyal pressure from below'. Despite its polemical and aggressive tone, the document was more of a *cri de cœur*, an appeal from the heart, than a theological landmine. The thirty-three did not want to usurp the function of leadership in the Church, nor

were they advocating the settling of doctrinal questions by democratic procedures: their whole effort was directed towards trying to
ensure that the minimum conditions for the credibility of the
Christian message would exist within the Church. They promised
unremitting struggle: 'In the renewal of the Church, the worst
temptation or the gravest alibi is the thought that nothing has
meaning any longer, that there is no hope of success, and so that
departure is best: outer or inner emigration.' Such declarations of
'loyal opposition' would have been impossible for Catholic theologians in 1955 – they would have lost their jobs – and were unnecessary in 1965.

But in one respect theologians could not complain. 'Pluralism'
has become a fact of theological life. There is a greater diversity in
theology than ever before, and the differences go beyond the earlier
disputes between theological 'schools' who disagreed but within a
large and stated framework of agreement. Neo-Thomism has
ceased to be a unifying factor, and one of the reasons for the differences in theology is that theologians have such varied philosophical
backgrounds. Karl Rahner, for example, addressed himself to the
version of 'modern man' which he found in Heidegger's 'being-
for-death'. But other theologians had a totally different portrait of
'modern man'. Many American theologians had to 'work through'
Rahner before discovering a voice of their own and addressing the
contemporary American who seems less death-haunted and more
technologically aware. The Latin Americans, on the other hand,
were more concerned to speak to the oppressed peoples of their
continent. The more theology was rooted in the local cultural
situation, the more diverse it was likely to be.

But one constant was the desire to justify political commitment.
Thus, Johannes Baptist Metz elaborated what he called 'a new
political theology'. It was based first on the conviction that Christians had to restore the social dimensions of hope, which they had
erroneously turned into a matter of private consolation. One hopes
not just for oneself, but for the world. Next, in Jesus is proclaimed
the dominion of God as 'the liberating power of love unreserved'.
Jesus sets aside the 'dominion of men' and embraces the insignifi-
cant, the poor, the oppressed. The role of the Church is to be an

'institution for the creative criticism of society', and its message is therefore 'dangerous', subversive, disrupting, disturbing. This further means that the Church, or Christians, can never identify with any given form of society, since to do so would be to declare that the Kingdom had already arrived in its fullness; but that offends against the 'eschatological proviso', and every form of society can be subjected to criticism in the cause of greater justice and closer brotherhood.

But it has to be admitted that the 'radicalism' of Metz remained rather notional. He gestures towards the market-place without appearing to spend much time there. The same can be said of Jürgen Moltmann, whose 'theology of hope' provided a Protestant complement to the work of Metz. The contribution of Christian faith to society is to be a source of eschatological unrest in a society which dreams the mistaken dream of technological perfection, and, once again, hope is seen not as an individual affair, but rather as 'the expectation of the shalom of the Kingdom of God . . . of the new heaven and the new earth' (*Hope and Planning*, p. 124). But one can read the complete works of Moltmann without ever discovering a precise political option on a controverted question.

For that one has to leave Germany and reflect on the trauma that the war in Vietnam was for the United States. Metz and Moltmann are cashed. Instead of declaring in the abstract that Christians, armed with their 'eschatological proviso', should criticize all societies, the anti-war protestors drew conclusions from it. The Berrigan case was not that the war was a monstrous injustice into which America had accidentally strayed, but rather that it was the result of the American ethos. The war, it was suggested, was possible, indeed 'normal', because a society had been created in which power, competition, violence, death and pre-emptive strikes were the normal though unexamined categories of thought and action. Here is Dan Berrigan: 'Suddenly for all of us, the American scene was no longer a good scene. It was, in fact, an immoral scene, corrupted by a useless and wasting war abroad, and a growing putrefying racism at home. Ours was a scene that moral men could not continue to approve of if they were to deserve the name of men' (*No Bars to Manhood*, p. 40). What *kind* of judgement is this?

Does it still belong to 'theology'? Most certainly, would say those who agree with Jean-Pierre Jossua, OP, professor at Le Saulchoir. At the *Concilium* congress in Brussels, he maintained that theology was not a specialized activity confined to those who possess some scientific competence, 'but simply the activity of any true Christian who reflects on his faith and is qualified by the fact that he belongs to the People of God through baptism'. That leaves the field wide open. Jossua did not shrink from the conclusion that the idea of a professional theologian, a specialist in God, is blasphemous. Here the theologian disappears into the crowd.

But some continued to accept their 'leading role', and the most serious and substantial attempt to turn the theologian into an activist was found in the work of Gustavo Gutiérrez, *A Theology of Liberation*. Without denying the traditional functions of theology such as wisdom and rational articulation, Gutiérrez claims that he offers 'not so much a new theme for reflection as a new way to do theology'. It becomes a critical reflection on what is happening, in his case in the Latin-American situation, but a critical reflection which 'tries to be part of the process through which the world is transformed'. The debt to Marx is frankly and fully acknowledged. Hitherto, Gutiérrez is in effect saying, theologians have contemplated the world; the point is, to change it. Many familiar themes are brought in to reinforce this project – the stress on the *anawim* or 'poor' in the Bible, the function of Jesus as liberator, the notion of 'operative charity' in the New Testament, the idea of the Church as the sacrament of human history – and all are brought into relation with the sociological data. At this point the theologian is not so much down in the market-place as away in the hills with the guerrillas.

Thus the factors for diversity are built into the theological enterprise itself. Tell me what you read, and I'll tell you what you are. In the case of the contemporary theologian, the maxim needs to be rephrased slightly: tell me with whom he is in dialogue, and I'll tell you who he is. And he can be in dialogue with a different philosophical tradition, with a different projection of 'modern man', with an intractable local situation, or with all three at once in various combinations. Further, any serious attempt to work in these new areas involves an inter-disciplinary study. Theology reveals itself not so much as a single discipline, but as a cluster of sub-disciplines. It has always been recognized that professional theology needed to work through history, linguistics, semantics and philosophy; but now the claims of psychology and particularly sociology have also been recognized. This is another reason for the diversity of theology and its increasingly critical attitude.

One example of the effect of the study of sociology can be found in the work of Gregory Baum. He holds that the task of theologians is to exercise a critical role in the Church, and that their purpose is to stop faith declining into ideology. For example, he attempts to explain why the Church, despite proclaiming love as the highest value, could nevertheless treat the Jewish people with bias and prejudice throughout so many centuries. The key to understanding this puzzle is, he suggests, the fact that the Church was unwittingly subject to ideology: 'Ideology, in the sense in which the term is used in the sociology of knowledge, refers to the set of teachings or symbols unconsciously generated by a society to protect itself against others, legitimate its power, and defend its privileges . . . We have come to realize that woven into the language we use, the teachings we propose, and the institutions in which we live, may well be trends that aim at protecting and promoting the power we hold as a group and keeping those under our power in their position of subjugation' (The Cardinal Bea Memorial Lecture, in *The Month*, June 1972). Here the theologian becomes a sort of therapist, constantly alert to the 'hidden story' and the 'hidden agenda' which may be operative. There is implied the view that theologians of the past have often indulged in rationalizations; that is, they found reasons for what they wanted to believe on other grounds. But once the theologian, after Marx and Freud, has woken up to the possibility of ideological influences, one of his functions will be to unmask them, and let faith stand out clear and cleansed of ideological interferences. 'It is God's word', adds Baum, 'which redeems us from ideology.'

This is an explosive theme, but Baum is not alone in developing it. Magnus Löhrer, for example, holds that the function of theology is not so much to propound doctrines as to reflect critically on the doctrines that are put forward in the Church. The Protestant theologian Gerhard Ebeling has been influential with his idea that theology has a critical duty with regard to the corruptions of Christianity. Pastors whose 'theology' was completed more than two decades ago are bewildered by this concept of theology which does not correspond to what they remembered. Theology was supposed to establish and confirm the Church's known teachings. While Protestant theologians had no difficulty in admitting the existence of corruptions within the Church, both in its life and doctrine, Catholics found it more difficult. Moral corruption might be admitted – so long as it was placed conveniently far away in the past with the Renaissance popes – but corruption could not extend to doctrine, for that would involve the supremely difficult admission that the Church had been mistaken. It is difficult not to agree with Hans Küng at least in this: 'creeping infallibility' illegitimately tends to spread over the whole of Catholic teaching and casts its shadow, even when it is not specifically invoked. Such thoughts distressed the Roman Curia, accustomed to thinking of theologians as the tame creatures described at the start of this chapter, and it responded with administrative measures.

Küng had long been regarded as a man to watch, but it took a long time to assemble the case against him. But in 1975 he gained the distinction of being the first theologian since the Council to be 'admonished' by the Sacred Congregation for the Doctrine of Faith (formerly known as the Holy Office). On 15 February it published a declaration which listed three doctrinal errors to be found in Küng's work: on infallibility, on the nature of the Church's teaching authority (*magisterium*), and on the possibility of any baptized person validly consecrating the Eucharist. There was a sense of barrel-scraping about this list, since the third 'error' (said to be contrary not only to Vatican II but to the Fourth Lateran Council) was detected in *The Church*, a work first published in 1967. Eight years had been required to take action. In any case Küng had merely said that the question of a non-ordained person celebrating the Eucharist in an emergency was 'at least debatable', which is not a very heinous suggestion. However, the Congregation's dilatoriness was presented as a demonstration of its patience. It had waited all this time, its letters unanswered, with infinite forbearance, until finally it spoke out, as, alas, it had to do. The reason for the condemnation was said to be 'so that there should be no doubt about the doctrine that the Catholic Church professes, and so that the faith of Christians be not obfuscated in any way'. It is fair comment that theologians can judge Küng's view for themselves, and that the 'ordinary faithful' would not have been aware of Küng's dissenting ideas but for the admonition. It was hard to see who exactly had been 'obfuscated'.

In any case the picture of the Sacred Congregation as the very model of patience, staying its hand until the good of the Church compelled it reluctantly to speak, does not bear close examination. The dossier on Küng went back a long way, and one of the reasons why he refused to enter into discussion with the Congregation was the refusal of his request to see the files inherited from the Holy Office. The Congregation was thus able to present Küng as a most unreasonable person, who refused the face-to-face dialogue which it ardently desired to have with him. His answer was that he had not refused dialogue, but simply insisted on having a legal advisor present at any meeting. He also objected to the presumption that guilt existed until innocence could be proved. Furthermore, the notion of the Congregation wearily bestirring itself to administer a mild rebuke – and it congratulated itself on not taking disciplinary action – was incompatible with the long and careful preparation in depth of the attack on Küng. He had stuck his head above the parapet. Someone had determined to get him.

The ground was well prepared. After Küng had refused to attend a 'trial' (as he saw it) in 1971, a document was prepared called *Mysterium Ecclesiae* which came out on 5 July 1973. The need or usefulness of such a document appeared obscure at the time, but it made sense as a remote preparation for the attack on Küng. The tactic was simple: write a document which contradicts Küng, and then point out that Küng contradicts the document. The next step was to enlist the support, expressed in another statement, of the German bishops. They obliged and Küng was cornered. In his reply he turned in the only direction left to him: 'My concern as a theologian and pastor is . . . to give a convincing Christian answer to the pressing questions of modern man, and the reactions of countless people confirm me in this task.' This was the crucial point, and it is one that the bureaucratic mind can never comprehend: theologians ask questions, not because they are wrongheaded or playing to some admiring gallery of the media, but simply because *they are asked questions*. They do not invent the questions. Many others shared Küng's difficulty with the notion of 'infallible *statements*' which are nevertheless uttered in history and so time-conditioned in some way. Real problems cannot be banished by the airy wave of an authoritarian wand. And he had attempted to express *in another way* the substance of the doctrine. His attempt had not been intellectually refuted. It had simply met with flat rejection.

The episode has wider significance in that it represented an attempt to return to the earlier concept of what a theologian was. He was the apologist for known truths. The German bishops were quite clear about this. The function of theology 'is to show if and how a truth of faith or a theological statement is grounded in scripture and the tradition of the Church'. Granted that the theologian can never cut loose from the Christian community, but has he no other tasks of inquiry and dialogue? If theologians paid heed to the warnings of the German bishops and the Sacred Congregation, there would be an end to open-ended inquiry in theological questions, and instead of operating on the frontiers of faith, in contact with new disciplines and the unavoidable problems of modern man, theology would once more be conducted from deep within the hinterland of faith, safely but irrelevantly. But this is not likely to happen, because the questions will not go away and theologians' habits cannot be changed by decree.

There is, finally, a deep irony and a welcome novelty in the conclusion of this phase of the Küng case. The irony is that the charism or special gift of infallibility which is being defended so vigorously is not of much practical help. No one expects it actually to be exercised. It is like a rusty weapon, reassuring as a reminder of the past, but not very useful. Infallibility was not claimed for the Second Vatican Council. Nor was *Humanae Vitae* endowed with its prestigious cover. If we have managed to get along without it, it could be that part of the reason is the one suggested by Küng: we simply cannot ascribe to language that kind of property. But that is a further step which remains to be taken. The welcome change in this affair was that no one publicly at any time impugned Küng's sincerity or suggested that his right to teach should be withdrawn. He was asked to refrain from teaching these particular doctrines. That was all. It was the mildest form of rebuke compatible with saying anything at all. When the sword of Damocles actually fell, after hovering for eight years, it turned out to be made of rubber. The theologians of 1955 would have rubbed their eyes in welcome astonishment.

Chapter 8

Ecumenism Is for Everyone

There is so much tokenism and nominal support for such things as ecumenical projects . . . that for many Christians Church leaders and bureaucracies are fast losing their credibility. We urge a sharp examination of what has been called each denomination's 'sovereignty' or 'empire-building'

report presented to the
Church Leaders' Conference, Birmingham, 1972,
quoted in David L. Edwards,
The British Churches Turn to the Future, p. 51.

The theologians and pastors of the future Church will be ecumenically minded, not because they are more virtuous than their predecessors but simply because they are being educated in an ecumenical setting. They do not have to be told to take other Christians and their theologians seriously. They already do. Bishops will emerge from among them before long. Ecumenism in the last decade has frequently had to suffer at the hands of men formed in quite different habits of thought. The battle raged within them between an old, half-remembered theology with its instinctive responses and the newer attitudes which the Council imposed. The balance tilted, now this way, now that. As a result ecumenism in the last decade has swung between high hopes and sad disappointment. There have also been periods of profound boredom since in no other area of Christian life have so many pious clichés been uttered and so much all-encompassing good will been expressed.

The decree *On Ecumenism*, approved on 20 November 1964, set Catholics firmly on the ecumenical road. It provided a charter for ecumenism, not as an optional extra or a theologian's hobby, but as the concern of all Christians. Yet the decree came down from the

Vatican in clouds of thunder and lightning: the Council's text was modified 'by higher authority' at the last moment, and the changes on which the Pope insisted all seemed to strengthen the Roman Catholic position and to weaken the ecumenical case. For many this provided the scenario which was to be repeated time and time again throughout the next decade: power-hungry Pope – or his Roman servants – hold in check the ecumenical enthusiasm of the Christian people. Manifestly, however, this simple-minded account does not do justice to the complexity of the situation. It is as false as the alternative scenario in which it is the Catholic theologians who make all the concessions and chip away at the substance of faith, while their Protestant partners in dialogue complacently welcome their conversion to the principles of the Reformation.

What is certain is that when it came to deal with ecumenism, the Council set down admirable principles which released expectations and unleashed hopes which then began to look menacing. They were cut down to size either by doctrinal niggling or by plain delaying tactics. At first sight the admirable principles sound like the most crashing of banalities, but when set in context they are seen to contain dynamite. Thus, for example, to attribute the ecumenical movement to the Holy Spirit may not seem a particularly bold assertion; and indeed it is the ordinary manner in which Christians declare their belief that something is good and of God. Yet one has only to compare the decree *On Ecumenism* with the encyclical letter, *Mortalium Animos*, published on 6 January 1928, to measure the distance that had been covered in less than forty years. Pope Pius XI spoke ironically of the various Christian assemblies which had been meeting after the First World War. 'Congresses and meetings are arranged,' he wrote, 'attended by a large concourse of hearers, where all without distinction, unbelievers as well as every kind of Christian, even those who have unhappily rejected Christ and denied his divine nature or mission, are invited to join in the discussion.' The principal charge against such meetings was that they led to the peril of 'indifferentism', the notion that it did not really matter what you believed. Assemblies of this kind, continued Pope Pius XI, were a snare and a trap which 'under the appearance of good' could only threaten Catholics.

Satan himself was, of course, well skilled in exploiting the 'appearance of good' for his own nefarious ends. Catholics must resist ecumenical blandishments. Not that the aspiration to church unity was an empty hope: it could be met, but only on condition that other Christians were prepared to submit to Rome.

It is chastening to reread *Mortalium Animos*. First to remind oneself how deeply its sentiments impressed themselves on the minds of those who were young at the time – like the seventy-year-old bishops and cardinals of today – and secondly to realize the depth of the change which has come over the Roman Catholic Church. It also gives one a chance to ruminate on the inefficacy of encyclical letters. If they were as powerful as they are sometimes alleged to be, the nascent ecumenical movement would have been strangled at birth.

But it survived lustily to move from the Catholic shadows to the full light of Vatican II. Against the background of previous utterances, to say that ecumenism was the work of the Holy Spirit was no mere pious cliché: it was a dramatic reversal. Moreover, such a declaration about the ecumenical movement cast reflected light on the nature of the Church – the Roman Catholic Church – itself: for if the quest for unity is to be attributed to the Holy Spirit, then it is the Holy Spirit who is presented as the source and origin of the Church's unity. But then one has enunciated a far-reaching principle: to assert the primacy of the Spirit implies that the unity of the Church cannot be made to depend *in the first place* on structure or organization or church order, be it papacy or episcopacy or whatever, but on the Holy Spirit transforming hearts from within. 'God's love', says St Paul, 'has been poured into our hearts through the Holy Spirit which has been given to us' (Romans 5:5). Of course, to claim that structure and organization are secondary and relativized is not the same as saying that they can be ignored or dispensed with. The assertion of the primacy of the Holy Spirit is not incompatible with holding that papacy or episcopacy are important and have a role to play. But the historic forms in which they have been handed down, and their cultural accretions, are not an absolute. The vision of a Church animated by the Holy Spirit led to thinking of it as a communion, a *communio*, rather than an organization. This was something in which all Christians could share. It would perhaps be unfair to apply to the ecumenical movement what Péguy said of the Reformation: '*Tout commence en mystique, et finit en politique.*' But there can be no doubt that the high and extravagant hopes of the immediate post-conciliar period soon gave way to the more sobering business of committees and reports. It was not always easy to see the ecumenical wood for the institutional trees. One of the problems was that the precise goal of ecumenical work remained distressingly vague.

This was not a question which needed to be raised in 1965 since the delight of discovering other Christians and the surprise at finding a large measure of agreement kept everyone busy. But sooner or later the question of the ultimate goal had to be raised. It was not a popular question among ecumenists, who feared either that it was unanswerable or that the answer would prove uncomfortable; so hoping against hope, they did not ask to see the distant scene, one step enough for them. Cardinal Willebrands, who succeeded Cardinal Bea as president of the Secretariat for Christian Unity, liked to explain that since unity is not a matter of human organization but rather 'a gift from God, something that belongs to the mystery of the Church', no one could predict what the next milestones along the road to reunion would be. But to embark on a journey, one needs to have some idea, however vague, of the goal.

There were in fact three broad options, three 'models' of possible unity. The first continued to envisage the simple 'return' of other Christians to the Roman Catholic Church. This view remained strong and, given its deep roots in tradition, no one should have been surprised; and even Vatican II had not completely undermined it since it had repeated the doctrine of 'the one, true Church' compared with which other 'ecclesial bodies and Churches' exhibited various kinds of structural inadequacy or doctrinal imperfection. From this point of view, ecumenism could mean little more than increased friendliness, growing tolerance and ever more contacts, but it had no doctrinal implications. No one proposed to budge. Those who held this opinion tended to lie low during the early part of the period because their views were unfashionable, but they emerged later to complain of betrayal or confusion.

At the other extreme lay the shimmering horizon of some kind of 'World Church Federation'. The very expression is ghastly and makes one squirm at the idea of such a vast, amorphous jelly-like grouping. It would have to build on the World Council of Churches, although the WCC has always insisted that it is not a 'Church' and does not aspire to be one. Nevertheless, in the absence of anything else, it offers a model for a future federation in which, while each Church would retain its own tradition and traditions, there would be a common statement of faith and common action. Few ecumenists actually advocate this kind of vast federation. It would be too huge. It would be an organizational and administrative colossus. And there is no guarantee that such a super-structure would bring anyone nearer to the knowledge of Christ.

Most ecumenists in the 1960s favoured a midway solution in which a renewed (some would say 'reformed') Roman Catholic Church had come far enough to be acceptable to other Christians, while the other Christian bodies would have re-examined their doctrines and found that they were not incompatible with the values which Catholic doctrines were trying to express. This involved the recognition by both sides that theological positions had not been frozen for all time at the Reformation. The polemical situation had distorted their picture of each other, and the understanding of terms like 'ministry' and 'Eucharist' was far from static. A theological statement is never uttered in abstraction: it answers a particular question that has been raised in a Christian tradition, it may contain muddied elements of outworn ideology which need to be abandoned, but in intention it sets out to express and defend a Christian value. Luther's 'justification by faith alone' was designed to stress the initiative and primacy of God in the work of redemption, while the Catholic reply stressed that man really did co-operate with his salvation. Discovering the values behind the doctrines was best done bilaterally between Churches, and this approach proved to be more profitable than more grandiose and all-embracing schemes.

This midway solution was the one demanded by the logic of the Council. For it had recognized the status of other Christian communities as *Churches*: that is, it went beyond the assertion that individuals in them had responded faithfully to Christ and declared that in other Christian communions there was a genuine *collective* response to Christian revelation. And although it was perfectly true that statements about 'the one, true Church' were retained, they were set in a totally different context which modified their meaning. Secondly, the decree *On Ecumenism* recognized different levels of 'communion' with Rome, and this involved the possibility, at least in theory, of gradual stepping-stones to unity. It spoke of 'obstacles to perfect ecclesiastical communion' (4), which implied the existence of some kind of 'imperfect communion' – and Pope Paul used the phrase 'almost total communion' to describe relations with the Orthodox Church. The third decisive new element in the ecumenical situation was the admission that it demanded not only a change of heart or conversion, but also the possibility of change of structures. This was indicated by saying that the Church is summoned to 'continual reformation', 'as she goes her pilgrim way' (6), and the invitation to make changes wherever there have been 'deficiencies in conduct'. Reform was envisaged in discipline, in doctrinal formulations and in *disciplina ecclesiastica*, i.e. the exercise of church government (cf. René Beaupère, 'What Sort of Unity?', in *One in Christ*, 1974, no. 3). On the pilgrim way, then, everyone would have something to contribute and something to unlearn.

This 'model' provides a yardstick for judging the success or failure of the ecumenical movement. There have been loud protestations of failure which have laid the blame on recalcitrant elements in the Roman Curia. In 1972, August Hasler, having first prudently resigned from the Secretariat for Christian Unity, wrote a resounding article on the failure of ecumenism. This is how it began: 'The ecumenical movement between the Roman Catholic Church and other Churches has come to a halt: there is no progress on intercommunion; the legislation on mixed marriages remains unsatisfactory; the evangelical Churches have given up hope of the discussion on the validity of their ministry ever getting anywhere; and the entry of the Roman Catholic Church into the World Council of Churches seems more unlikely than it did three years ago' ('Rome Closes the Door to Ecumenism', in *Evangelische Kommentare,* April 1972).

Of the four criteria proposed by Hasler, the last can be excluded as irrelevant. It became increasingly clear that membership of the WCC was largely a non-issue: Roman Catholic entry would pose insuperable problems – for it would be on either a world-wide or a national basis, and in either case the WCC would be swamped and find its balance gravely disturbed; conversely, non-membership did not prevent collaboration, which was in fact steadily pursued, despite setbacks like the blow administered to SODEPAX in 1972. SODEPAX was a liaison body between the WCC and the Pontifical Commission for Justice and Peace intended to encourage combined work for peace and development. It proved too adventurous and radical and was reduced in importance. Despite such upsets on the international level, there are twenty-two examples of Catholic membership of national councils of Churches; and even in England and Wales, where the bishops rejected membership of the BCC in spring 1974 for fear that the moral positions of the Catholic Church would be diluted, there was a 75% membership on the local level.

Mixed marriages, however, remained a permanent irritant, despite the Catholic attempt to modify the impact of the 'promises' by shifting them from the non-Catholic to the Catholic partner. Some thought that dishonesty had been substituted for imperialism. And what happened where a lax or easy-going Catholic married a devout Protestant? In practice solutions varied from region to region, or sometimes from priest to priest. The hazards of geography determined whether the promise to bring up the children as Catholics was regarded as a make-or-break issue, or as a positive opportunity to develop the idea of an 'ecumenical marriage' lived out by those who experienced in their daily lives both the pain of divisions and the hope of reconciliation. Hasler's other two criteria interlock; for recognition of the validity of the Eucharist of other Christians entailed a recognition of the validity of their ministry – only a valid ministry could effect a valid Eucharist. If ministry was the chief doctrinal question which theologians concentrated on, intercommunion was the principal practical question which caused controversy and heartbreak.

On the Catholic side, the demand for intercommunion flowed quite naturally from the conciliar teaching and the new emphasis on the importance of the local church. The Council had said that sharing in the Eucharist could not be used 'indiscriminately' as a *means* to unity, since it was the expression of unity already achieved: 'The fact that it should signify unity generally rules out common worship. Yet the gaining of a needed grace sometimes commends it' (8). This cryptic text nevertheless seemed to leave the door ajar. Full communion clearly remained the ideal and the goal, but did this mean that occasional intercommunion could be permitted as a step towards it, a kind of foretaste of the eventual unity that was glimpsed some way ahead? To ask this question, said Avery Dulles, was rather like asking whether an engaged couple could have intercourse before marriage: they were doing no more than anticipate what they firmly believed would be theirs by right in the not so distant future. But, added Dulles sagely, he did not wish to complicate one emotional issue by another that is even more emotionally charged.

In the post-conciliar period many Christians began to take the law into their own hands. It was not simply that they were chafing at the restraints placed upon them or that they were disobedient merely to cause annoyance to their church authorities. They reasoned that in their work together they had already arrived at a sufficient degree of unity in faith for it to require expression in a common liturgy. They contrasted the 'abstract' type of unity so often found in Catholic parishes on a Sunday morning, with the 'existentialist' experience of unity which they had found in their work together. They believed that they were pioneers of future unity.

Examples can be given from a wide variety of sources. At Venhuizen in the diocese of Haarlem in Holland, the Catholic and Protestant parishes had together celebrated a 'week of peace' and at its conclusion they celebrated a common Eucharist (5 October 1967). One cannot say that permission was refused, because it had never been asked. The Bishop of Haarlem, not for the last time, was placed on the spot and forced to choose between offending the local people or offending Rome. Bishop Zwartkruis made his choice: after deploring the manner in which it had been done, he conceded that there could be exceptional situations in which 'the local communities on their own level might have attained a degree of unity which their Churches generally had not yet attained'.

In Paris the following Pentecost there was another instance of spectacular intercommunion – or, more precisely, of 'co-celebration'. The French had been deeply stirred by 'the events of May', which had briefly claimed to 'put the imagination in power'. Methods of direct action had proved politically effective: in the enthusiasm and effervescence, they began to spill over into the Church. This was the mood in which the Pentecost celebration took place in an apartment in the rue de Vaugirard. There were present seven Protestant pastors, along with eight Catholic priests and a number of well-known laymen. The philosopher, Paul Ricoeur, introduced the eucharistic prayer. This was no hole-in-corner affair, but a consciously chosen 'prophetic gesture' which the participants did not intend as a regular occurrence. They explained their action in a letter sent both to the archbishop of Paris, Archbishop Marty, and to Pastor Westphal, president of the French Protestant Federation: 'Aware of our deep communion in the faith, we have been led to celebrate in a common sign the unity that has come from our numerous meetings with students and workers . . . We do not intend by this act to cut ourselves off from our respective communities. We take account of the fact that the real *de facto* unity of Christians today cuts across denominational barriers: the events that we have together lived through have done more for our progress towards unity than the theological discussions we have taken part in.' Brisk controversy broke out. A special number of the review *Christianisme Social* was entirely devoted to the affair, but it was halted by the French bishops even though it had already reached proof stage. Archbishop Marty wrote an article encouragingly called 'We understand, but we do not approve', which earned him a letter of commendation from Cardinal Bea. But more significant for the future was the letter received by the Dominican, Père le Guillou, who had fiercely attacked the co-celebration: it praised his stand, and was signed on behalf of Pope Paul by the newly arrived 'Substitute' at the Secretariat of State, Mgr Giovanni Benelli (28 June 1968).

Meanwhile the World Council of Churches was holding its fourth assembly at Uppsala. For the first time ever a Roman Catholic speaker, Fr Roberto Tucci, addressed the assembly. But the event which attracted most attention took place on Sunday 7 July, when the Swedish Reformed Church invited all participants to an 'open Eucharist' in the cathedral of Uppsala. Although the official Vatican delegation abstained, a number of Catholics received communion, among them a Swedish Dominican, Fr Tengström, who could not remain either invisible or anonymous. Such was the atmosphere that even an Orthodox bishop – and the Orthodox are most opposed to the idea of intercommunion – also joined in, to the embarrassment of his superiors.

One more instance is worth mentioning to illustrate that the spontaneous drive towards intercommunion was not simply a 'European' phenomenon. The Latin-American bishops held their decisive meeting at Medellin. On the final evening, and with the consent of Cardinal Samoré, who was present as the representative of the Vatican, they allowed the six Protestant observers who had shared in their work to receive communion. The observers offered this explanation: 'We have been present each day at the eucharistic celebration. We have increasingly suffered at being unable to carry to completion our sharing in the communion of faith that we have lived so intensely ... We confess that the Eucharist is the effective sign and pledge of Christ in person ... the sacrament of the body and blood of Christ, the sacrament of his real presence.' This profession of faith undercut the objection that what had happened at Medellin was merely the result of enthusiasm. One of the Vatican conditions for intercommunion was precisely that there should be a declaration of eucharistic faith, without which, it was argued, to receive communion would be, if not meaningless, then at least ambiguous.

On all sides, then, and from different levels of the Church, there was a ground-swell towards intercommunion. Seen from the point of view of the central authority, this runaway movement represented a grave danger. Every infraction of the current discipline constituted a precedent which others could quote and exploit. If unchecked, a massive movement might grow. The papal reaction after Medellin was swift, sharp and vigorous. On 18 September 1968 Pope Paul deplored 'acts of intercommunion which are contrary to the correct ecumenical line', a somewhat cold-waterish observation. And in his address to the Secretariat for Christian Unity on 13 November he developed his objections at greater length. He referred to 'recent events' which had come to his notice, and said that 'these initiatives, far from helping ecumenism, check and halt its progress'. The fundamental mistake the enthusiasts had made was according to Pope Paul 'to overlook the essential links which exist between the mystery of the Eucharist and the mystery of the Church, and so to prejudice an agreement which is not yet realized'. Yet the Pope claimed to understand the aspirations which had led to the desire for intercommunion. 'This impatience contains', he added, 'a positive aspect: no one can deny that it could be a sign of the love of Christ.' 'But', he concluded sadly, 'it is an unenlightened zeal.'

But already the Secretariat for Christian Unity had published a 'note' setting down the conditions in which intercommunion might be possible. Two of them were familiar: the separated brother seeking communion should be spiritually well-disposed and should himself spontaneously ask for communion; and secondly, he should share the eucharistic faith of the Catholic Church. But it was the third condition which virtually put an end to the hope of official intercommunion 'in our time': supposing that the first two conditions were fulfilled, communion could only be given if there were no minister of the would-be communicant's own Church available. This was to make intercommunion an unlikely event except in remote places. At the Birmingham Church Leaders' Conference in 1972 Cardinal Heenan, asked about intercommunion, replied that he could only conceive of it 'in the most exceptional circumstances – maybe in a concentration camp'. This led Canon Bernard Pawley of St Paul's Cathedral to remark: 'It seems, then, that we should all pray for a multiplication of concentration camps.' The Vatican ruling went clean contrary to the experiences of local unity on which the demand for intercommunion had been based. It placed narrow juridical limits on what had been a profound aspiration welling up from below. It turned a Christian demand into a piece of casuistry. It halted a movement which the Council had initiated.

However, intercommunion did not stop altogether as a result of the hard-hitting Roman reaction. Instead it became discreet. It went underground. For that reason it is hard to document, but one well-informed witness, writing in 1975, remarked: 'Even five years ago, this [intercommunion] was something we associated with wild Dutchmen and obviously disintegrated Americans. Now . . . it is increasingly common at home' ('Ecumenism in England since the Council', in *The Month*, March 1975, p. 74). Thus another gap opened up between theory and practice, between official, institutional ecumenism and the organic reconciliation of Christians on the local level.

Meanwhile, patient theologians were trying to close the gap and providing the groundwork for the future, even if their progress seemed – to themselves as much as to anyone else – lamentably snail-like. Relations between the Roman Catholic Church and the Anglican Communion moved steadily, if not headily, forward. They may be studied as an exemplary instance and a cautionary tale.

It is important to note that from the outset it was the Anglican Communion, and not simply the narrower Church of England, which engaged in dialogue. This was one of the wisest decisions of Dr Michael Ramsey, Archbishop of Canterbury from 1962 to 1974, who realized that a dialogue confined simply to English Anglicans and Roman Catholics would inevitably carry a greater burden of prejudice and would run into difficulties. Cardinal Bea, nothing if not wily, knew that too; but he was also aware that any attempt to eliminate English Catholics from the discussion would be an injustice as well as a mistake. Although English Catholics, because of their history of persecution, might be inherently suspicious of Anglicans, they were even more mistrustful of foreigners who claimed to understand Anglicans better than they did themselves. It is perfectly true that strangers, especially if inclined to interpret the world in clear-cut Cartesian categories, could be hard-pressed to understand the many-faceted, non-committal Englishness of the Church of England. For their part, Anglicans had tended to show more enthusiasm for meeting continental Catholics than the English variety. Cardinal Heenan has described, with fair accuracy, the outlook of his fellow bishops: 'Traditional interference by continental Catholics made the bishops wary of the activities of Cardinal Bea. Few of the bishops are instinctive ecumenists. The more sturdy their English stock the harder it was to persuade them that ecumenism is not a betrayal of their Catholic forefathers' (*A Crown of Thorns*, p. 320). Those of sturdy Irish stock had much the same approach. And in explaining the attitude of his fellow bishops, Cardinal Heenan reveals something of himself as he had been: 'It was theologically and psychologically almost impossible to persuade such men to approach Protestants without any intention of converting them' (ibid., pp. 320–1).

For these reasons it was wise of Dr Ramsey, when he went to the Vatican in March 1966, to present himself not so much as the Archbishop of Canterbury but rather as president of the world-wide Anglican Communion. His visit made a great contrast with that of his predecessor to Pope John, historic though it had been. There was nothing apologetic about the Ramsey visit. He was received not in the private setting of the papal library, but in the awesome, humbling splendour of the Sistine Chapel. The papal greeting matched the occasion. 'By your coming', said Pope Paul, 'you rebuild a bridge, a bridge which for centuries has lain fallen between the Church of Rome and Canterbury.' The image was an ancient one, and one of the Pope's titles, *Pontifex*, means bridge-builder. It was completed by the image of the house with an ever-open door: 'Your steps do not resound in a strange house: they bring you to a home which, for ever valid reasons, you can call your own.' But the most emphatic passage was that in which the Pope spoke of 'the long and sorrowful history which this hour intends to bring to an end'.

The Pope's words and even more the Common Declaration published the next day, 24 March 1966, liquidated the polemical past, consigning it 'to the hands of the God of mercy'. The emphasis was to be on hope and the unpredictable future which likewise lay in

the hands of God. Yet it proved easier to declare the past banished
than to overcome its inheritance, especially when the canonization
of forty English and Welsh martyrs was announced for 25 October
1970. The 'cause' had been hanging fire for generations. The known
opposition of Cardinal Bea, who was rumoured to have given
assurances to Canterbury, prompted the English bishops to work
even harder for its realization. Some Anglicans were upset at this
rekindling of memories from a time of bitterness and hatred, and
thought that canonization was a peculiarly Roman Catholic way of
glorifying exclusively Catholic heroes. They swallowed their hurt.
The British Council of Churches contrived to put out a generous
statement in which it expressed the view that the proposed canonization would do no harm to ecumenical relations provided it were
conducted in a spirit of common repentance rather than exclusivist
triumphalism. Their desire was not realized in the way they quite
expected, but in compensation they heard Pope Paul give an
address in which he not only reasserted his commitment to ecumenism but broke new ground: 'May the blood of these martyrs',
he said, 'be able to heal the great wound inflicted on God's Church
by reason of the separation of the Anglican Church from the
Catholic Church . . . Their devotion to their country gives us the
assurance that on the day when – God willing – the unity of faith
and life is restored, no offence will be inflicted on the honour and
sovereignty of a great country such as England. There will be no
seeking to lessen the legitimate prestige and usage proper to the
Anglican Church when the Roman Catholic Church – this humble
"servant of the servants of God" – is able to embrace firmly her
ever-beloved sister in the one authentic communion of the family
of Christ: a communion of origin and faith, a communion of priesthood and rule, a communion of the saints in the freedom and love
of the spirit of Jesus' (25 October 1970). This passage was added
by Pope Paul personally very late on the previous evening. Those
who had worked on the speech were taken by surprise by it, and the
Secretariat for Christian Unity was delighted. Even if it was not
altogether clear, it hinted at a vision of realized unity according to
what was sometimes called the 'Uniate' model. Like the Copts or
the Armenians, the Anglican Communion would retain its own

rites and discipline. That seemed to be the implication of saying that this 'sister Church' would retain its legitimate 'prestige and usage(s)'.

Earlier the same year Cardinal Willebrands had developed similar ideas in a sermon at Great St Mary's, the university church of Cambridge. He spoke of a *typos* of Church which existed 'where there is a long coherent tradition, commanding men's love and loyalty, creating and sustaining a harmonious and organic whole of complementary elements, each of which strengthens and supports the other' (*The Tablet*, 24 January 1970). It was not exactly a local or a particular Church, as defined by Vatican II, nor was it primarily a diocese or a national Church (though it might coincide with one), it was a *typos*. When liturgy went into the vernacular, theologians began to speak Greek, but the Anglican Communion was prepared to recognize itself as a *typos* and these ideas launched the serious work of theological dialogue between the two Churches.

Already, the Joint Preparatory Commission, set up as a result of Dr Ramsey's visit to Rome, had made some concrete proposals for 'the second stage of our growing together' such as joint use of churches, shared facilities in theological education, and co-operation in the revision of liturgical texts. The chrysalis of the Joint Preparatory Commission was transformed into the Anglican/Roman Catholic International Commission (ARCIC), and in his Cambridge sermon Cardinal Willebrands expressed the hope that the Anglican and Catholic Churches might 'expect to see in the none too distant future a vision of that unity in truth given us in Christ. I would go so far as to hope that a limited period, say five years, might allow them to give, conscientiously and loyally, this service they are qualified to give to the Churches' (*The Tablet*, 24 January 1970).

Cardinal Willebrands gave the theologians five years. That was in 1970. The five years are up. In 1975 they met at St Stephen's House, Oxford, to tackle the toughest of their problems: the understanding of authority in the Church. In their discussion on ministry they had provided themselves with a lever with which (or so some of them thought) they could manage to lift the boulder of papal authority. The minister's function is one of 'oversight' or *episcope* (the Pauline word from which 'bishop' is derived). That means that he has to co-ordinate the life and mission of the community, discern the work of the Spirit in it and the world, and symbolize the unity of the flock. But these, in essence, have been the traditional tasks of the papacy in the Western Church. The Lambeth Conference of 1968 had agreed that the papacy might be regarded as 'having a primacy of love, implying both honour and service, in a renewed and reunited Church'. There was a beginning of convergence.

The 'Agreed Statement' on the Eucharist (7 September 1971) is another example of the process of perceiving Christian values behind apparently divisive doctrinal statements. In the words of Dean Henry Chadwick, the aim of the Commission had been 'to outflank the Maginot Line of sterile controversy' and to try to express the authentic faith of Christians today. However, there was no question of whittling down anything considered essential by either side. It was a matter of insight rather than compromise. The pivot of the Agreed Statement is the idea of the Eucharist as a memorial (*anamnesis*) which is something more than a mere recalling of a past event: 'Christ instituted the Eucharist as a memorial of the totality of God's reconciling action in him. In the eucharistic prayer the Church continues to make a perpetual memorial of Christ's death, and his members, united with God and one another, give thanks for all his mercies, entreat the benefits of his passion on behalf of the whole Church, participate in these benefits and enter into the movement of his self-offering.' This emphasis was designed to do justice to the Reformation insistence that the Eucharist is not a *repetition* of the passion and resurrection of Christ. But at the same time the Commission tried to do justice to the Catholic emphasis on the realism of Christ's presence, which does not depend on the faith of the individual: 'The sacramental body and blood of the Saviour are present as an offering to the believer awaiting his welcome. When this offering is met by faith, a life-giving encounter results. Through faith Christ's presence – which does not depend on the individual's faith in order to be the Lord's real gift of himself to his Church – becomes no longer just a presence *for* the believer, but also a presence *with* him.' Some Catholics were upset that the term 'transubstantiation' was relegated to an obscure footnote, but even the Council of Trent described it as 'the most satisfactory' (*aptissime*) way of speaking of the Eucharist (Dz. 1652). Other ways are possible.

On the Eucharist the Commission had reached 'substantial agreement', while the agreement on ministry was described as 'full'. This distinction was made by Bishop Alan Clark, Roman Catholic co-chairman of the Commission, who addressed the Anglican Synod on 7 November 1974. He was not only rapturously received but rapturously anticipated, being given a standing ovation not only after his speech but, remarkably, before it. This was despite the fact that on the two outstanding practical questions which emerged from the discussion – intercommunion and the validity of the Anglican ministry – he could bring them little comfort. On intercommunion he said: 'We suffer a nagging temptation to rush to *institutionalize* the degree of agreement we have actually reached . . . The problem arises when, without care, we urge – to take one example – a degree of sacramental sharing which is not supported by this degree of agreement. It is one thing to ask for greater eucharistic hospitality: it is another to request general intercommunion.' The Bishop showed similar caution in dealing with Anglican orders, declared 'absolutely null and utterly void' by Leo XIII's bull *Apostolicae Curae* in 1896. 'It would be inhuman of you', he conceded, 'not to ask the question', but having asked it, he did not stay for an answer and invited the Synod to be content with 'the sober words of our conclusion', which said that it remained unsolved. 'Nevertheless', the report on ministry concluded, 'we consider that our consensus, on questions where agreement is indispensable for unity, offers a positive contribution to the reconciliation of our Churches and of their ministries.'

One speaker at the Anglican Synod remarked that the agreements on Eucharist and ministry were among the most important ecumenical achievements not only in Britain but in the whole world. But there were many others. The Catholic/Methodist Joint Commission did not have to overcome the handicap of Reformation controversy, and was able to concentrate more on the heritage of spirituality found in the two Churches. It describes the Church as

catholic, 'knowing how to express what is universal in the Christian
message of God's love for all'; *evangelical*, 'reaching out effectively
to share this good news by word and life in community'; and
reformed, 'willing to engage in self-criticism'. The common ground
is sought in meeting the needs of contemporary man for contem-
plation, compassion and community. This approach through
'spirituality' has been praised as more likely to engage ordinary
people than the theological discussions which have characterized
Anglican/Catholic relations; but that is to set up an abusive opposition between spirituality and theology. A further point needs to be
noted. Discussions between Churches are not like diplomatic
negotiations between states, in which to draw near to one group is
to risk estrangement from another; on the contrary, to draw close to
another Church *in Christ*, is to draw nearer to all other Christians.

The details of ecumenical discussion seem laborious to the out-
sider, who may feel it is rather like moving deckchairs about the
Titanic while the ship prepares to founder. A decade after the
Council the ecumenical movement seems to have entered a state of
suspended animation. The Roman Catholic Church is poised for
action on the local level, but hesitates because of Vatican coolness.
But this is not the only reason for marking time. Ecumenical
advance is checked by many factors: the weight of history which
has conditioned psychological responses and in some cases a class
structure, the reluctance of institutions to let go what they have
long cherished, a genuine concern for the integrity of Christian
doctrine. A concern for the fullness of Christian doctrine is entirely
legitimate, and it has sometimes been presented as the characteristically Roman Catholic contribution, along with the need for
visible unity, to the ecumenical symphony. But it should never be
allowed to act as an alibi for foot-dragging. There is much more
doctrinal agreement than is sometimes supposed, though the eye
must be washed clean to perceive it. *The Common Catechism* (first
published in German in 1973 and in English in 1975) revealed a
remarkable measure of doctrinal agreement between Protestants
and Catholics, so much so that the editors could say that 'the
statements which can be made in common are quantitatively and
qualitatively more important than any contradictions' (p. x).

The hope for ecumenism is that it should cease to be introverted. Christians can progress when, instead of gazing wonderingly into each other's eyes and raking over the dead ashes of the past, they confront together the massive fact of unbelief in the modern world. To accept that God intervened in the course of human history in the person of Jesus Christ is a sufficiently startling faith to mark off those who hold it from those who do not or cannot. The following of Christ involves, on the personal and institutional level, a death to self and to pride, and in this way the hope of resurrection, both personal and institutional, is born. It is not easy. A canon of Westminster Cathedral had the habit of blocking every ecumenical suggestion with the remark: 'We mustn't try to run before we can walk.' He received the answer: 'My dear Canon, no one is asking you to run, nor even to walk – all that is asked of you is that you should be seen to be placing one foot in front of the other.'

Chapter 9

Dialogue with Humanism in a Secular World

> It is a tide which has turned only once in human
> history . . . There is presumably a calendar date – a
> moment – when the onus of proof passed from the
> atheist to the believer, when quite suddenly, secretly,
> the noes had it
>
> 'GEORGE MOORE',
> in *Jumpers* by Tom Stoppard, p. 25.

It has been said that a problem is not acknowledged to exist in
Rome until a body has been set up to deal with it. Ecumenism
began in earnest when Pope John set up the Secretariat for Christian Unity and put Cardinal Bea in charge of it. In a similar way the
setting-up of the Secretariat for Non-believers in April 1965 marked
the official recognition that unbelief existed and was a cause for
worry. Something had happened which it was hard to label, and
which yet gave grounds for disquiet. Was it the point made by the
character in Tom Stoppard's play quoted above? Was it to be attributed to the onward march of secularization, and what did that
mean? Or should humanism be made the scapegoat?

No one knew the answers to these questions, and indeed they
could not be prescribed in advance. '*Usus docebit*,' said Pope Paul
to Cardinal König who was the president of this new body, 'you
will learn from experience.' One of the things quickly learned was
that some 'unbelievers' did not care to be addressed in this way: to
say of a man that he 'believes in nothing' is not very complimen-
tary to him, since he can perfectly well believe in truth and goodness and justice without referring them to God as their source; but
in that case it is inaccurate as well as insulting to call him an 'unbeliever'. No satisfactory solution was found to this problem, and

all the alternative suggestions were more appalling or misleading than the original – the 'Secretariat for the Study of Contemporary Ideologies' being one of the deservedly unsuccessful candidates. In practice, and apart from Marxists, the 'unbeliever' came to mean the contemporary humanist who disclaimed any explicit religious faith or was agnostic about it.

The Council had an ambivalent attitude towards the humanist atheist. On the one hand it noted the existence of a modern form of humanism 'in which man is defined first of all by his responsibility toward his brothers and toward history' (*On the Church in the Modern World*, 55). That was certainly not a hostile statement, and if it really did define the essence of the humanist position, then there would clearly be an overlap with Christianity, and dialogue could devote itself to exploring the common ground. More significantly still, the Council's treatment of humanism came in its section on culture, man's humanization of nature and society, and not in the section on atheism, as might have been expected; that suggested that humanism was not necessarily atheistic, but only accidentally so.

But on the other hand the Council also spoke of the need to find 'remedies' for atheism. Here the atheist was seen as a sick man, and the conciliar doctors gathered eagerly round his bedside, discussing in anxious tones what the diagnosis should be and the prescriptions for a cure. One well-disposed atheist became indignant at this procedure, and complained that he did not feel particularly ill, that the doctors just went on talking and would not let him get a word in edgeways (Francis Jeanson, 'Un athée devant *Gaudium et Spes*', in *L'Eglise dans le Monde de ce Temps*, edited by Yves Congar and M. Peuchmaurd, vol. 3, pp. 155–65). A strange dialogue, indeed, in which one of the partners has to confess his sickness before dialogue can begin.

This ambivalence was to remain, and it was built into the situation: for the humanist could be seen either positively or negatively, as someone who made an assertion or a denial. In so far as he affirmed human values, there was convergence and grounds for dialogue; in so far as he denied God, there was a parting of the ways. The Secretariat's work was based on the possibility of convergence. But Pope Paul's interventions on the theme of humanism were numerous and they stressed the divergence. In *Populorum Progressio* he quoted Henri de Lubac: 'There is no doubt that man can organize the world without God, but in the last analysis he can only organize it against man. Exclusive humanism is an inhuman humanism' (42). In his 1969 Christmas message Pope Paul said: 'There is no such thing as a true humanism without Christ.' Not unaware that humanist sensitivities were bruised by these rough remarks, he returned to the theme in his 1973 Christmas message and envisaged the humanist as a sort of superman, engaged on building 'a cosmic utopia in which man becomes his own God'.

All of which would have been enough to stifle the dialogue at birth, were it not for the fact that there were, as usual, some subtle qualifications to be noted. In his very first encyclical Pope Paul had spoken of the need to 'probe the mind of the contemporary atheist in an effort to understand the reasons for his mental turmoil' (*Ecclesiam Suam*, 104), and the setting up of the Secretariat was a further declaration of intent. The Society of Jesus, with its wide range of intellectual ability and experience, was also enlisted in this enterprise. Though the Jesuits were invited to 'stand in the path of atheism' ('*ut atheismo obsistant*') on 7 May 1965, the context clearly excluded a crusade. Moreover, the Pope's presentation of atheism owed a great deal to one of his French mentors, Henri de Lubac, and in particular to his book *The Drama of Atheist Humanism*. This admirable work, however, is a study of the pretentious all-encompassing anti-theist thinkers of the nineteenth century. Manifestly the prospects for dialogue with Prometheus were unpromising, and the modern humanist was more likely to be a diffident and modest man pushing a bicycle and trying to help mankind than a hero stealing fire from the gods. Finally, Pope Paul had left himself a loophole by speaking of 'some forms of contemporary humanism', which left open the possibility that there might be other and less unacceptable forms. Such casuistry may be laborious, but it is the only way to understand how it was that Pope Paul did not undermine by one series of statements the dialogue that he was encouraging by another.

It was by no means certain that humanists would respond favourably to the invitation to dialogue. Most humanism is implicit, unformulated, and above all unorganized. There is no body of doctrine commanding general assent and only the sketchiest account of a tradition. But among those humanists who were organized it was possible to distinguish two attitudes which may be called the 'tough-minded' and the 'tender-minded'. The tough-minded humanists not only rejected religion, but thought that it was a harmful mistake, a cruel deception, and that it was therefore perverting, warping, truncating and to be fought. They were not interested in dialogue, not because, as in Pope Paul's image, they were busily engaged on building some cosmic utopia, but because they were still rooted in nineteenth-century attitudes. In Britain this strand was represented by the National Secular Society, whose members sometimes seemed to be so obsessed with the God they rejected that their plight evoked sympathy. These descendants of the bearded prophets of the nineteenth century felt that they had nothing to learn from superstition. Polemics and hostility remained the order of the day, and the whiff of grapeshot hung heavily in the air.

With the tender-minded humanists the situation was different, and here it was possible to emerge from the trenches. Though convinced that religion was mistaken and misguided, they did not believe that it necessarily and always had warping and harmful effects; it could express and embody *values* which made sense to the humanist, even if he rejected the historical and ideological synthesis in which they were embroiled. These values provided a basis for dialogue. Thus the Secretariat for Non-believers was able to hold joint meetings with the International Humanist and Ethical Association in Holland in 1965 and 1966 and later in Brussels, 2–4 October 1972 (the papers of this meeting were later published in *A Catholic/Humanist Dialogue*, edited by Paul Kurtz and Albert Dondeyne). These meetings made it clear that the common ground among humanists was the notion of 'ethical autonomy', and that God was rejected because he appeared to infringe that autonomy. At the same time the humanists were anxious to stress that their position was not simply Christianity less its dogma. So J. P. van den Prag insisted that 'the humanist is not a Christian stripped of his

Christian expectations and attitudes: he has a different approach', though he did not find it easy to express the difference. A characteristic Catholic claim was made by Antoine Vergote: 'I wonder if it is not harder for the unbeliever to grasp what belief is than for the believer to understand humanism. For the believer often has a questioning attitude, being a scientist or a philosopher as well, and he faces conflicts of belief and humanism within himself every day' (ibid., p. 87). The humanist tended to suppose that all questions were resolved in advance and from on high for the believer, and was gratified to learn that this was not so.

The ground rules for these exchanges had been laid down, on the Catholic side, in a document which never received the attention it merited. It should have been read by all those who thought that hobnobbing with humanists was a matter of making ruinous concessions. The Secretariat for Non-believers published its Directory in October 1968 (it was dated 28 August). It dealt seriously with the objections which could be raised against dialogue. Roman documents frequently catalogue objections to show an awareness of the problems; but the questions remain unanswered. The Directory was novel. It listed the objections, and answered them with honesty.

It might be said, first of all, that to embark upon dialogue implies an attitude of perpetual quest and the rejection of any idea of absolute truth. One cannot be always seeking and never arriving. The answer of the Directory is to turn the objection. No dialogue at all is possible unless 'one has confidence in human intelligence and admits that it is capable of attaining truth, at least to some extent'. Moreover, dialogue is a basic human need, since it is born 'of the moral duty that everyone has to search for the truth in all things, and especially in religious matters'. This was a useful reminder that 'dialogue' was not some esoteric activity engaged upon only by remote intellectuals, but was a part of what it means to be human. Like M. Jourdain discovering that he had been speaking prose all his life, many people began to realize that they had been engaging in dialogue without knowing it. Conviction was not imperilled by dialogue, though prejudice – an attitude, say the psychologists, characterized by rigidity, obstinacy and wrongness – was threatened. Through dialogue there is a dissipation of prejudice and the growth of understanding.

So far, so good. But the objection can be more sharply formulated, for in traditional theological categories the 'truths of faith' fell into a different category from ordinary truths, and so could not be put on the same footing. The answer of the Directory revealed an important switch of attitude. The truths of faith are of course different, it concedes, 'and in so far as they are revealed by God, they are in themselves absolute and perfect, but they are always inadequately grasped by the believer who can always grow in his understanding of them'. The attribute of 'perfection' lay not in the formulation, but in the source, which meant that it was likely to escape the rigours of dialogue by its inaccessibility. Moreover, not everything which Christians have come to believe derives from revelation. Sorting out the cultural accretions will enable Christians to discover what is essential and so to 'examine still more the signs of the times in the light of the Gospel'. Furthermore, Christians are constantly impelled to seek out the grounds of their faith and to try to justify it, and should know in any case that 'faith does not provide pat answers to all problems'. That leaves a wide field of unanswered questions which can be tackled in common.

The second objection was the gravest of all: how can there be a dialogue when there is an immanentist view of truth, where truth is seen as dependent upon man's freedom and no view of truth is admitted which transcends man? This was a portrait of what David Jenkins had called post-Copernican man, for whom 'truth is relative and it becomes truth as it is discovered, established, and put to the test, articulated and used as the basis for further discovery, further relative but relevant truth. You cannot "go beyond" the knowledge you have save by building on what you have got in strict continuity with it' ('Whither the Doctrine of God Now?', in *A Reader in Contemporary Theology*, edited by J. Bowden and J. Richmond, p. 164). There appears to be a yawning gap between this view of truth and what has usually been taken to be the Christian position. The Secretariat rightly noted that the first task would be to hammer out criteria of truth which might be acceptable to both sides, but blithefully conceded that 'even if that is not possible, one should not therefore conclude that dialogue is a waste of time, since it is useful to establish the limits beyond which one cannot go'. It is certainly useful to determine limits, but even more important to identify them clearly. The Directory added that, in any case, 'it is not necessary that dialogue should be established on all sides and at any price'.

There were a few places where progress was made beyond dialogue towards active co-operation. In Britain the Social Morality Council was founded in 1969 'to foster mutual understanding between religious believers and non-believers, and to undertake joint studies of major social issues in the light of ethical values'. Two reports have been issued. The first, presented in March 1970, was concerned with the tricky issue of *Moral and Religious Education* and the second, published early in 1974, with *The Future of Broadcasting*. In both cases it was difficult to distinguish the contributions of the different groups. The broadcasting report, for example, warned of the danger of viewing people under one aspect alone, 'as consumers, employers or citizens, householders, electors, party members, etc.', rather than as 'whole human beings' (p. 27), and noted: 'By morality we mean the good of the whole person, not merely the puritanical sexual mores which are often wished upon the broadcasters.' However, such fraternization was not always welcome. After the appearance of *Humanist Manifesto II* in 1973, *The Catholic Herald* produced the following stylistically fascinating piece of vituperation: 'Unfortunately quite a lot of Christians, including prominent Catholics, have been making fools of themselves recently slobbering over humanists and plunging into co-operation in a way that is very helpful to humanism but in no way advances the cause of Christianity. The humanists have welcomed the efforts of these well-meaning mugs, since they (the humanists) need us more than we need them' ('Humanists and Their Doctrines of Death', in *The Catholic Herald*, 9 September 1973). Bishop Christopher Butler had been president of the Social Morality Council, and he may have been one of the misguided mugs in mind. It would strengthen his conviction that this dialogue was 'the Cinderella of ecumenism' and destined to remain by the hearth, and at the same time prove the truth of the Directory's sagacious remark that public dialogue might 'disturb the faith of an audience that was not sufficiently prepared'. But this was no excuse for inaction, since 'the risk of such challenges and pressures to faith is inevitable in a pluralistic society such as ours'.

Whatever excellent principles the Secretariat might lay down – and in October 1968, two months after *Humanae Vitae*, commentators clutched desperately at straws rather than bid farewell to 'the spirit of Vatican II' – the real dialogue with unbelievers was not one for which rules could be prescribed. For one thing, it took place in the minds and hearts of believers before it was transferred to the 'others'. The line of demarcation between the Church and the world ran through the heart of the believer. Many candid Christians agreed with John Robinson, at that time Bishop of Woolwich, who had written in *Honest to God*: 'Not infrequently as I watch or listen to a broadcast discussion between a humanist and a Christian, I catch myself realizing that most of my sympathies are on the humanist's side' (*Honest to God*, p. 8). Such perceptions are more likely to be found among pastors or theologians who worked on the frontiers of faith and spent much of their time with post-Christians. On the frontier it was self-evident that faith had to *commend itself*, and that it could not be commended by simple assertion, however sincere, still less by raising the voice, evoking hell-fire or thumping the table. Thus there developed a new way of presenting Christian faith which grew out of the continual conversation with the humanism that is diffused throughout Western society. And this extra-curricular dialogue was to prove more important in itself and for the self-understanding of faith than the official formal dialogues we have mentioned.

The effect on theology was considerable as theologians tried to wrestle with the humanist's searching questions. Theology, one might say, was stood on its head. Classical treatises followed the order God-Christ-Church-world, and in this scheme the primacy and sovereignty of God appeared with the utmost clarity, manifesting themselves in Christ and then through the Church until, in the end, they reached the 'world'. Here the 'world' was seen as the object of the divine action and the recipient of divine gifts. The

attempt to expound the Christian faith in the light of the humanist's questions involved a reversal of perspective, as though one
were now looking down the other end of the telescope.

The new starting-point was 'the world' and human experience.
The overriding conviction was that God was at work in the world
and that his saving grace could not be confined exclusively to institutional channels. Theology thus had the task of discerning God's
veiled presence in the world, a presence that is focused in Christ
whom the Church proclaims. But what the Church proclaims makes
sense only as an answer to a question that has really been asked.
Instead of being seen as the initiator, the *fons et origo* placed at the
start of the process, God was rather seen as the goal, bringing fulfilment, the 'absolute future' who goes beyond all human expectations and yet satisfies them at the deepest level. The claim was
often made that this approach 'from below' meant the abandonment of a static view of the world in which an ordered cosmos
wheeled round again and again, and its replacement by a dynamic
attitude which saw man as involved in history and as creating his
future.

So presentations of the Christian faith ceased to be the take-it-
or-leave-it exposition of a perfect scheme, worked out in advance,
and became rather a series of tentative explorations which tried to
'make sense' of ordinary human experience. It was here that the
humanist or the half-believer might have a sense of inadequacy or a
glimpse of mystery. One can put it most simply by saying that a
descending method in which God was posited at the start gave way to
an *ascending method* in which God might be discovered at the end.
Christian faith began to be understood as a form of *human self-
understanding*. The claim was not made that God wanted men to be
this or do that because it was his will. The claim was rather that
until men discovered God there would be something incomplete
about their experience and lacking to their fulfilment. Christianity
became the best way to be human. As Ladislaus Boros, one of the
most influential spiritual writers of the period, put it: 'In the
thornbush of the human endeavour to become a real man, the flame
of the absolute burns' (*Meeting God in Man*, p. viii). What this
grandiosely asserts is that in order to discover God man does not

have to turn away from human experience but rather to penetrate it more deeply.

Much of the spiritual writing of the decade was based on these ideas. A characteristic, if rather barbarous, vocabulary was developed. Thus Karl Rahner popularized if he did not actually coin the term 'anonymous Christians' and the slogan 'anthropology is theology'. Both were closely related to contemporary man's capacity to embrace Christianity. 'Anonymous Christians' involved the idea that people could express Christian values in their lives without themselves being aware of the fact. All grace is grace of Christ, and all men are in the realm of grace. They are therefore implicitly related to Christ, even though they may not know it and perhaps would hotly deny it if it were put to them. Rahner's theory might be described as an attempt to recover on the swings of the implicit what had been lost on the roundabouts of the explicit; as practising Christians declined in numbers, the ranks of the anonymous Christians grew. But it was a serious contemporary attempt to tackle the age-old problem of 'the virtue of the pagans' and 'the salvation of the unbeliever'. It also implied a pastoral and a missionary method in which the values actually perceived or held by people would be the starting-point.

'Anthropology is theology' led in the same direction. It meant that a complete study of man in all his dimensions involved the recognition that he moved in a sphere of 'mystery' which he could later identify and name as 'God'. Man is defined by his openness to transcendence, and therefore any shutting out of the divine dimension truncates him, leaves him orphan-like and bereft in a world of partial meanings. To Anglo-Saxons this may have seemed all very *a priori*, as indeed it was since Rahner was concerned with stating the fundamental conditions which governed all human thought and action. But these ideas had important practical consequences, for, if there were any truth in them, they ought to be verifiable in ordinary human experience. In simpler terms: man's thirst for the absolute ought to be traceable in his everyday experiences, in the sense of wonder that accompanies love or trust or the discovery of community or in the protest against the radical absurdity of death. Many writers of the period, such as Boros, Gregory Baum and

Rosemary Haughton, set themselves the task of unveiling God's incognitos in the midst of ordinary existence.

These ideas began to affect religious education. They fitted in harmoniously enough with modern educational methods, which preferred the method of discovery to that of didactic handing down from above. Faith was not a matter of collecting and learning a series of pre-packaged truths, but a quest for God that unfolds with life and is never done. Discussion of human situations replaced abstract doctrine. Of course this did not happen everywhere, nor was it always consistently pursued. But it happened often enough to worry parents and, eventually, bishops. Rumours of what was alleged to be taught in schools filtered through, distorted in the telling. Although the objections to the new catechetical methods tended to focus, with wearisome insistence, on the existence of Adam and Eve and of angels and devils – thus revealing a Catholic version of fundamentalism – the real point at issue was one of method and starting-point. The catechists, like the theologians, had started in the thick of human experience. The objection was that they had got stuck there. The reply was that there was no alternative if they were to interest and engage the children of today. An impasse was reached. The question raised by the catechists – 'What shall we say to the children?' – became almost identical with the question raised by theologians – 'What shall we say to post-Copernican man?' This hazardous enterprise was fatally prone to misinterpretation, and misinterpreted it was.

Ethics was as much a minefield as catechetics. Yet if 'ethical autonomy' was the defining note of humanism, theologians could be expected to challenge humanists on this ground as well. The process was illustrated in the work of Enda McDonagh, Professor of Moral Theology at St Patrick's College, Maynooth, a venerable institution once regarded as a bastion of Celtic Jansenism. In an early book called *Invitation and Response* he followed the traditional method and took Christian revelation as his starting-point. But then in 1975 he published *Gift and Call*, which reverses this procedure and starts from generally available moral experience. McDonagh sees moral experience as imposing an obligation or, as he prefers to say, expressing a 'call': it is inter-personal, social, in a given time and place, and unconditional. Other-centredness becomes the criterion of morality. However, other people are not simply a demand made upon us; they also represent a gift, an enrichment, an experience of uniqueness. It is through mutual recognition that men and women live out morality and reach fulfilment: the call is also a gift. Having completed his analysis, McDonagh 'confronts' it with Christianity, while maintaining that he could have compared it with, say, Buddhism, and he finds in the Gospel the same call-gift pattern he discovered in moral experience. Whatever one thinks of the success of this operation, it is very typical of the way theology begins to occupy the ground which had previously been thought to be the humanist's domain. This kind of 'verification from below', provided it is done without fixing and manipulation, is the form that commending faith is likely to take today.

However, this method should not be confused with the habit of making Modern Man the universal norm. German theologians in particular had a way of drawing an identi-kit portrait of modern man, who appeared as a sort of technological Prometheus, securely confident in his mastery of the universe, without the childish fantasies of earlier periods. Johannes Baptist Metz declared that 'modern man' had lost interest in the past as he strained towards the ever-perfectible future. The authors of *The Common Catechism* quote sociological witnesses to the effect that 'man is no longer concerned with meaning and is content simply to make everything function properly' (p. 52). Theologies were devised to cope with this abstraction. But an equally plausible account of modern man could be given in which he appeared far more afraid of the scientific forces he had unleashed, far more vulnerable to meaninglessness, and anxious to preserve something from the past before it was too late. The Modern Man of the theologians was sometimes a fictional character.

Behind the question of Modern Man lay the graver question of secularization. Was Modern Man spontaneously secular-minded? The humanist, after all, was the product of the process of secularization. He welcomed it and thought it inevitable. It suggested to him that the decline and eventual disappearance of Christianity was merely a matter of waiting. History was against it. Theologians had two main strategies for dealing with this problem. The first was to suggest, following Friedrich Gogarten and Harvey Cox, that the Judaeo-Christian revelation, far from being the enemy of secularization, was actually its cause. In the ancient world every tree and stream had its nymph or dryad, but the doctrine of creation, by distinguishing God clearly from the world he had created, established the world in its legitimate autonomy. Great Pan was dead. The nymphs and dryads have departed. 'Secondary causes' can be studied and investigated in their own order. Science becomes possible. The second strategy was to distinguish between secularization as a process and secularism as the theory which accounted for it; theologians could accept the process while rejecting the explanation proposed and offering an alternative one of their own. Secularization became the process by which man took charge of the universe, not as the enemy of God but as the responsible steward of creation.

Since secularization was defined as a transition from one way of looking at the world to another, the crucial problem lay in the account given of the base-line of the argument. From what was secularization a departure? As David Martin pointed out, sociologists tended to begin with a fairy-tale view of the Middle Ages in which 'once upon a time there was a sexually frustrated hermit who lived on bread and water' (*The Religious and the Secular*, p. 31). In other words, if certain features of thirteenth-century religion such as the temporal power of the Church, realism in philosophy, and extreme asceticism are taken as the definition of religion, any departure from that pattern will be 'secularization'. But there are alternative definitions which disrupt that neat pattern. By 1973 the review *Concilium* had challenged the assumption that 'sacred' and 'secular' could be so conveniently divided and refused to accept the equation of the 'secular' with the 'modern' and the 'progressive'.

The Secretariat for Non-believers was increasingly concerned with such problems. At its third plenary session in March 1974 an attempt was made to determine the changes which had taken place since its foundation in 1965. Cardinal König referred to an audience with Pope Paul on 6 April 1972 when the scope of the Secretariat was significantly widened. No longer was it to be limited to the study of atheism and to dialogue with unbelievers. It was now to embrace 'a consideration of and contact between the main currents of contemporary thought and the Church' and the factors which influence the religiosity of contemporary man: industrialization, urbanization, and the impact of the mass media. In other words, its work was beginning to be seen rather as an arm in the pastoral work of the Church and to include an investigation into the reasons why faith had become difficult. This was precisely the question which had been preoccupying theologians. One can say that the principal effect of the diffused humanism of the period was to make Christians ask themselves probing questions and try to produce a new rationale for their faith. Humanism stimulated the internal debate within Christianity. The humanist was the hidden interlocutor in theological discussion.

Chapter 10

Learning from Marxists

'To create is to unite', Teilhard never tires of telling
us: and this too is the Marxian hope – to unite in an
ordered whole in which each shall play his allotted
part

R. C. ZAEHNER
*Dialectical Christianity and
Christian Materialism*, p. 81.

The dialogue with humanism left untouched the most aggressive,
powerful and obvious enemy of Christianity: Communism. In the
time of Pope Pius XII it seemed self-evident that the Church and
world Communism were and would continue to be locked together
in implacable hostility. Where Communists had power, the Church
was persecuted. Cardinals were thrown into jail and drugged into
signing faked confessions of their anti-State activities. Cardinal
Mindszenty, the tough Hungarian who refused to submit, was the
symbol of heroic resistance to the godless persecutors who could
break the body, distract the mind grievously, but not touch the
inner spirit. On the day he came out of prison in 1956, Pius XII
issued no less than three messages of support. Communist persecution was met by Catholic denunciation. There seemed to be no way
out of the impasse. Yet by 1974 this same Cardinal Mindszenty,
the hero of the 1950s, had been lured out of the American Embassy
in Budapest and unceremoniously dismissed from his post as
Primate of Hungary and Archbishop of Esztergom. He had fallen
victim to *détente* and his *Memoirs*, published in 1975, record his
bewilderment as he went off into 'complete and total exile'. He
died a few months later. The hero had become an embarrassment,
the martyr an obstacle.

How had this remarkable transformation, not to say volte-face,
come about? Any answer has to distinguish two aspects, the political

or pastoral and the ideological. In the first place the Vatican, from the time of Pope John, began to look for some kind of truce or accommodation with Communism in those countries where it held power. Over sixty million Catholics lived in Eastern Europe. The collapse of the Hungarian uprising of 1956 and the impotence of the West to do anything other than utter pious lamentations made it clear that Communism had come to stay and that therefore dreams of restoration had little immediate future. The Church had 'dealt with' obnoxious regimes before. The exchange of insults and invective had not proved very profitable. Perhaps dialogue would succeed where recriminations had failed. *Détente* could be tried. Pope John's last encyclical, *Pacem in Terris*, which came to be regarded as his 'testament', embodied the new approach. He made two distinctions. The first was shattering in its simplicity, far-reaching in its implications. One can distinguish, he noted, between 'the error and the man who errs', reprove the erroneous or false teaching while respecting the man who propounds it. The distinction was at least as old as St Augustine, but in the excitement of the cold war it had been lost sight of. Pope John's second distinction was harder to fathom.

He distinguished between 'a false philosophy' about man and the world, and 'the economic, social, cultural and political programmes' which issued from it (*Pacem in Terris*, 159). What exactly he had in mind is not easy to determine. The link between theory and praxis in Marxism is allegedly such that one cannot drive a wedge between them, and this is one of the originalities of Marxism. On the other hand, it was difficult to deny that Pope John had an insight into something of fundamental importance: the denunciation of Stalinism at the Twentieth Party Congress had opened the way to forgotten notions such as Togliatti's theory of 'different roads to socialism'. But if there were really to be 'different roads to socialism', then might not part of the explanation be that proposed by Pope John? Communists go on repeating the same slogans, he said in effect, 'but the programme cannot avoid being influenced to a certain extent by the changing conditions in which it has to operate' (ibid., 159). The new policy of the Vatican might help to encourage welcome change. Pope John could say all this because, instead of condemning Communism lock, stock and barrel, he was prepared to detect in it positive elements. *Pacem in Terris* went on: 'Besides, who can deny the possible existence of good and commendable elements in these programmes, elements which do indeed conform to the dictates of right reason, and are an expression of man's lawful aspirations?' Pope John wanted to help to create conditions in which the 'good and commendable elements' could grow and flourish, but he also had a deep conviction that any Manichaean view which divided the world into black and white was mistaken. God wanted the salvation of all men. His grace was at work in them all. Cautiously, he began to find out what this might mean in practical terms. The results will be examined in the next chapter, devoted to the *Ostpolitik* of the Vatican.

Besides a change in practical policy towards Eastern Europe, Pope John had provided the theoretical framework for dialogue with Marxists. Pope Paul VI took this inheritance and developed it still further. By speaking of 'good and commendable elements', his predecessor had invited theologians to discover what they were, and Pope Paul put some content into this enterprise by noting how frequently 'atheists' had borrowed Christian language: 'They are quick to make use of sentiments and expressions found in our Gospel, referring to the brotherhood of man, mutual aid, and human compassion' (*Ecclesiam Suam*, 105). There is a hint here of Marxism considered as a secularized form of Christianity, and of the Chestertonian idea of heresy as 'Christian ideas gone mad'. That, at least, was a possible interpretation of Pope Paul's conclusion: 'Shall we not one day be able to lead them back to the Christian sources of these moral values?' And until that distant day, dialogue can help to remove misunderstandings. It is true that Pope Paul laid down stringent conditions: dialogue requires clarity, absence of arrogance, trust and prudence. It also requires that the other side should wish to enter into dialogue, and doubts on this score led Pope Paul later to issue warnings about ambiguity. Nevertheless, the unprecedented dialogue with Marxists could begin.

In the decade that followed it has seesawed to and fro. At the risk of simplification, one can distinguish three broad stages. First came the semi-official dialogues between Christians and Marxists held under the auspices of the Paulusgesellschaft in Central Europe. The Russian invasion of Czechoslovakia in 1968 put an end to these exchanges. Meanwhile, the flame so abruptly extinguished in Prague had developed its own independent life in Latin America, particularly in Chile with the movement called Christians for Socialism. In the third stage the Latin-American model began to flow back to Europe and to influence Christians there, particularly in 'Latin' countries. We will examine the three stages in turn to understand how 'dialogue' led, patchily and imperceptibly, to a form of critical convergence.

The Paulusgesellschaft was a society of German Catholics, mostly scientists and theologians, who were interested in a contemporary expression of faith. Their patron, St Paul, had been 'all things to all men', was ready to dispute with the Greeks in the market-place, and had a vision of the whole of creation groaning towards its liberation in Christ. They believed, therefore, that theology was best conducted in dialogue, and that only in this way could the separation of theology from everyday life – one of the causes of secularization – be overcome. If it is true that modern man needs faith in his quest for wholeness, then it is also true that traditional faith needs modern man in its search for a common language. (In the book *Gott in Welt*, volume II, the founder and president of the Paulusgesellschaft, Dr Erich Kellner, explained its aims and spirit, pp. 724–55.) Though the society by no means confined its activity to dialogue with Marxists, there were three successive meetings with Marxists, at Salzburg in 1965, Chiemsee in 1966 and finally at Marienbad in 1967. On the Communist side, one of the leading figures was Roger Garaudy, whose book, *From Anathema to Dialogue*, published in French in 1965, embodies in its title the first lesson that was learned. Garaudy based the imperative need for dialogue on the requirements of survival in the atomic era: 'The future of man cannot be constructed either without believers or against them. Neither can it be constructed against Communists or without them' (*From Anathema to Dialogue*, p. 26). Dialogue had become possible, he argued, because both partners were being driven to scrape off the barnacles of myth and dogmatism and to rediscover what was basic in their own philosophies.

More precisely, Garaudy distinguished three new historical conditions which made dialogue both possible and necessary. The first was the ending of the colonial era and the development of national liberation movements. To these the Council had responded by emphasizing the legitimate diversity of local cultures, the importance and equality of the 'young churches', and admitted that the Western 'model' of Christianity was not normative for the rest of the world. Marxists had reacted in a similar way, admitting the principle of 'different roads to socialism' in the developing countries and recognizing that they could no longer be 'provincial' (i.e. European) in their outlook.

The second factor was the continued existence and stability of socialist states where the Church was gradually learning to distinguish what was essential in her message and what not, while abandoning the dream of the restoration of the political *status quo ante*. Co-existence was a daily feature of the Church's life in Eastern Europe. Moreover, although the Council reasserted the importance of private property, it set this doctrine in the context of the right of everyone 'to have a share of earthly goods sufficient for oneself and one's family' (*On the Church in the Modern World*, 69), which at least provided an opening for a more benevolent view of socialism. Meanwhile the socialist countries had been learning the hard way that control of all the means of production did not put an end to all alienations, and that a rigidly planned economy could lead to new alienations between the Party and the workers, the leaders and the people.

Garaudy's third point was the most important. The progress of science, he claimed, was leading both Christians and Marxists to ask themselves searching questions. He noted the Council's teaching on the autonomy and values of science, and paid tribute to Teilhard de Chardin who had discovered 'the point of fusion between science and faith', combined 'the most lucid intelligence with the purest faith' and so presented 'the strongest challenge of faith to the unbeliever'. From Paul Ricoeur he borrowed the distinction between religion and faith: 'religion is the alienation of faith', faith gone wrong, and religion must die so that faith can stand out purified. But the progress of science has called into question Marxist dogmatism and materialism, and much of the allegedly 'scientific' thinking of Marxism has been crude mechanistic scientism; but mechanistic scientism is the alienation of science just as religion is the alienation of faith. For all these reasons, the time was ripe for dialogue.

But beyond these comparable experiences of change and renewal lay the fundamental question of atheism and Marx's attitude to religion. Was not this opposition insuperable? Garaudy made a distinction. For the Marxist, religion can be either the reflection of real distress which provides an ideology to justify the distress; in which case it is 'opium for the people' and a method of keeping the proletariat quiet. Or it can be a protest against distress, and a protest which leads to change. Hence the Marxist should not speak of religion in general but should examine what in each case it actually does. To assert that religion always and everywhere turns people away from 'this world', said Garaudy, is contrary to experience and to history. The Council had recognized the autonomy of the profane, laid down its conditions – pluralism and religious liberty – and provided fresh motives for commitment in this world and incentives for building a better world. Marxism, he claimed, had taught Christians to commit themselves politically, to reject all speculation on 'ends' which refuses to discuss the means of their realization. Much Christian discourse on 'the dignity of man' omitted to say how this value was to be put into practice. Meanwhile Marxism has much to learn from Christianity, and in Communist states men will continue to ask questions about the meaning of existence. For the Marxist the important feature of Christianity is its stress on the need of conversion and perpetual reconversion, which means that it is opposed to pessimism and passive fatalism.

There could be no doubt about Garaudy's sincerity: it was to earn him expulsion from the French Communist Party in 1972. The Party particularly resented the implication that Marxists had anything to learn from Christians, and strongly objected to his habit of placing the Communist Party – liberated and unalienated as it was thought to be – on the same level as the Catholic Church, which was still deeply alienated and unliberated. But in the years

1965 to 1967 Garaudy was not a Marxist lone ranger and the Christian theologians who joined in the dialogue took him seriously enough. But they did not try to make a synthesis. Instead, they began to develop a 'political theology' in response to the Marxist challenge. It was in this dialogue that Johannes Baptist Metz defined the Church as 'an institution for the creative criticism of society' and as 'the sacrament of hope for all mankind', embodying, however imperfectly, its aspirations towards greater justice and brotherhood. But the Church could not begin to fulfil this mission if it confined itself to a contemplative attitude: 'The city of God at the end of time is already being established', said Metz, 'and as we move towards it in hope we build it up, not just as spectators but as co-workers in a future whose animating power is God himself.' Both 'political theology' and 'the theology of hope' were born out of this dialogue with Marxism. Karl Rahner too developed a theology of hope, but confessed that he was never happy with the term 'political theology'.

However, there was another and quite distinct form of response on the Christian side. Both Metz and Rahner had attempted to re-express Christian faith in the light of legitimate Marxist questions. Giulio Girardi, at that time professor at the Salesianum in Rome, had a better grasp of Marxism and was able to put a series of pointed questions to the Marxists. Girardi described the phenomenon of 'rigid' or 'dogmatic' Marxism, which he defined by a series of contrasts: base and superstructure, institution and person, history and the individual, class and humanity. Wherever the first limb of these antinomies was preferred, he argued, then inevitably the State or the Party would dominate and the individual person would be subordinated to it. And it was this type of Marxist 'integrism' which had been practised and proclaimed by the Communist Party. But there was an alternative, and Marxism could be rescued from these degraded forms. A return to the young Marx helped. If man, for example, is the agent of history, then the community as a whole should be the subject of power, since so long as power remains concentrated in the hands of a small group, abuses are bound to occur. Girardi concluded with an invitation: 'A regime which the people did not freely accept would not be a truly Marxist regime. Marxists should be prepared to run the risk of liberty . . . It is time to offer an adult form of Marxism to an adult humanity.'

Girardi challenged Marxists on their own ground and found that they failed in the light of their own principles. This attitude was found among the 'New Catholic Left' and helps to explain the apparent paradox of those who called themselves 'Christian Marxists'. The 'Marxism' of Frères du Monde, a group which gathered round the Franciscans in Toulouse, and of Slant in Britain, was never the orthodoxy of the Communist Party but a revised version of 'Marxism with a human face'. Hostile critics, who were numerous, failed to realize that this approach, far from leading them into the arms of the Communist Party, estranged them from it. But the 'Catholic Marxists' were not always very lucid in explaining their position, and sometimes their would-be synthesis remained an unappetizing salad in which, said Theo Westow, 'they are wildly trying out the combinations, hoping they will hit on the right one – some day' (letter to *The Tablet*, 13 September 1969).

More important was the response to Girardi on the Communist side. The proof that he was not knocking on a locked door was provided at Marienbad in 1967. Even though Novotny, who showed not the slightest inclination to trust the people and remained an impenitent Stalinist, was still in power in Czechoslovakia, the ideas put forward by Girardi were the echo of inner-Marxist discussions among Italian Communists and, more importantly, among the Czechs. Philosophers like Milan Machoveč and Milan Pruha felt the need to learn from other philosophical views, refused to subordinate science to ideology and made a plea for tolerance. Their Communist establishment critics dismissed them as 'revisionists', i.e. heretics, but they helped to provide the intellectual context which made the Dubček regime, the most hopeful development within Communism since the war, possible. Looking back on the Marienbad meeting a year later, Dr Erika Kadlecova, a sociologist who briefly became Minister of Cults in the Dubček regime, noted: 'There were many complaints at Marienbad about the powerlessness of intellectuals who can make fine speeches but have no power to put them into effect. That is both true and false. Of course they do not have armies and prisons, they can neither make promises nor pronounce bans. But they can create a spiritual atmosphere in which change is possible' ('Die Gespräche in Marienbad', in *Dialog*, 1968, no. 1, pp. 101–9). With hindsight, Dr Kadlecova's words acquired a tragic ring. The Christian-Marxist dialogue had contributed to the changed intellectual atmosphere which made Dubček possible, and it could not therefore be dismissed as 'two old aunts talking about problems that interest no one else' (as Jürgen Moltmann is reported to have said). But then power asserted itself, the Czech experiment was halted, those who had tanks and prisons made use of them, the Czech philosophers lost their jobs, and this phase of dialogue came to a sudden end. Those who had been sceptical all along could say, 'We told you so', but such wisdom after the event overlooked the very real change which had been glimpsed as a promise for the future.

The Russian invasion of Czechoslovakia was not the only important event of 1968. In the autumn of that year the Latin-American bishops held their second plenary meeting at Medellin in Colombia. This assembly was for Latin America what the Council had been for the rest of the Church. For Archbishop Pironio of Mar del Plata, later to become president of CELAM, Medellin was 'a sort of new Pentecost, bringing a new spirit, a new mentality' and, quite explicitly 'the rediscovery of a Latin-American consciousness' which would no longer be dependent on Europe's culture and America's finance. 'We have faith in God, in man, and in the values and future of Latin America', the bishops declared. They committed the Church to *integral* human development – an expression borrowed from *Populorum Progressio* of 1967 but traceable further back to Jacques Maritain – and it involved the realization that 'pastoral work' which did not take into account all the dimensions of political and social life was doomed to failure. However, their key concept was not development, which by this time was considered to have paternalistic overtones, but *liberación*. By their statements at Medellin, the Latin-American bishops encouraged theologians like Gustavo Gutiérrez and Juan Segundo who had already been developing a 'theology of liberation'.

This did not mean that the bishops of Latin America had suddenly discovered that they were Marxists, though any expression of dissatisfaction with the political and social *status quo* could lead to such accusations. But it did mean that when the theologians tried to put some content into the condemnation of the unjust *structures* of society, they found themselves using Marxist categories because none other were available. Marxism provided the conceptual tools for analysis. A typical statement comes from Juan Luis Segundo, a Uraguayan Jesuit, whose five volumes, *A Theology for Artisans of a New Humanity*, are a kind of *summa* of liberation theology, covering everything from the sacraments to social action. Segundo is quite clear that an 'option for socialism' is necessary in the Latin-American situation, and he defines socialism as 'a political regime in which the ownership of the means of production is removed from individuals and handed over to higher institutions whose concern is the common good'. And he rejects capitalism, by which he means 'a political regime in which the ownership of the goods of production is open to economic competition' (*Concilium*, June 1974, p. 115). However, he insists that the choice is not between society as it exists in the USA or in the Soviet Union: the Latin-American option is taken in the light of the special sociopolitical conditions of peoples who live on the margin of the great economic empires. Where injustice is 'built into the structures of society', the remedy for it can only be on the level of those structures.

Such an analysis would have been false to itself if it remained on the theoretical level. It found practical expression, for example, in the movement of Christians for Socialism in Chile. It became a matter of practical politics after Allende's victory in the presidential elections of 1970, the only instance of Communism coming to power 'by legal and democratic means'. The movement held a national congress at Santiago in April 1972. 280 people took part, including 113 priests and 42 nuns. Its manifesto was one of the most striking products of the movement. Its crucial choice is that the Church should be on the side of the oppressed. The older social teaching of the Church – including that of Pope John – condemned the class-war and held out the ideal of harmonious co-operation between complementary groups in society. This comforting idea was criticized by Christians for Socialism as being simply a mask for the defence of the *status quo*, with the Church in fact blessing the privileged and the oppressors. *Interclassismo* was to be replaced by a class choice, the choice of the oppressed. That would mean conflict.

Christians for Socialism spread to Argentina, Peru, Mexico and Central America, and there is now the beginnings of an international movement with groups at work in Italy, Spain and France. Their relationship with the 'official Church' has been uneasy, but they do not intend to break with it. In Europe they have been to a great extent 'marginalized', that is pushed into a corner and ignored. Fr Gonzalo Arroyo, SJ, one of the founders of the movement, who was expelled from Chile after the military *coup* of September 1973, explained the relationship to the Church in an interview: 'We aim at a Church in solidarity with the interests and struggles of the workers, but without breaking with the present Church. If we want to gather together and form a group as Christians inserted in the heart of the organized proletariat, it is firstly to cultivate our faith, to make our hope more dynamic, and to develop our theology' (*Dialog*, 1974, no. 3; English translation in *New Blackfriars*, November 1974). At this point it is clear that we are way beyond dialogue, and it might seem that Marxism has been swallowed whole and uncritically. But Arroyo makes a by now traditional distinction. The aim of Christians for Socialism, he explains, is to demonstrate 'that the Christian faith can and must become more and more at home in a socialist option, *even if it cannot be enclosed within that option*'. Much depends on the viability of that distinction. There are many cross-currents, but most Christians for Socialism hold that Marxism cannot be identified with the Communist Party, which they regard as sectarian and monolithic. But they accept its analysis of society.

It is difficult to give any statistics to measure the importance of the movement. The Santiago text was produced by a group numbering just over 200; a comparable group held a congress at Avila, Spain, in January 1973. On the other hand, at the congress held in Bologna, Italy, in September 1973, some 400 were expected while over 2000 actually arrived. There are reasons for taking the

Italian Christians for Socialism seriously, especially in view of the strength of the Italian Communist Party and its avowed desire to reach an 'historic compromise', by which odd expression is meant a *rapprochement* with the left-wing of the Christian Democrats. The Christian Democrats will resist this process for as long as they can, but they have been increasingly dispirited as they have seen the rug of 'Christian social doctrine' systematically removed from beneath their feet. The decline of Christian social doctrine meant the creation of a vacuum which Christians for Socialism has endeavoured to fill.

This is a point of crucial importance, for if Christians for Socialism are a clear example of 'the runaway Church', the movement was set in motion by the actions of the *magisterium*. The first encyclical of Pope Paul spoke of 'dialogue'. In 1967, in *Populorum Progressio*, he stated that 'development was the new name for peace', and prophetically pointed out that the North-South struggle between the developed and the underdeveloped world would be more important in the latter half of the century than any East-West confrontation. But the final abandonment of the attempt to formulate a complete social doctrine, which could provide an alternative blueprint for society to that of Marxism, was expressed in *Octogesima Adveniens* of 14 May 1971. Pope Paul was quite explicit: 'In view of the varied situations in the world, it is difficult to give one teaching to cover them all or to offer a solution which has universal value. *This is not our intention or even our mission*' (4). The task which the papacy felt unable and incompetent to fulfil is entrusted to 'the Christian communities' scattered throughout the world, which have to diagnose their own situations in the critical light of the Gospel. The result will evidently be a 'pluralism of options' (50). There is, moreover, a long passage on 'the historical development of socialisms' – the plural is important (30 et seq.). Pope Paul distinguished four aspects: continual struggle against domination and exploitation, the exercise of political power in a single-party state, an ideology based on historical materialism and the denial of transcendence, and finally a scientific approach to social and political realities (33). He concedes that the latter, despite its one-sidedness, can offer 'an instrument of analysis' which some find useful. Christians for Socialism could well feel encouraged and legitimated by the Letter to Cardinal Roy, since they claim to be discriminating in their Marxism, usually accepting the scientific analysis and the struggle against exploitation, while rejecting the one-party state and the denial of transcendence.

The *Wall Street Journal* had called *Populorum Progressio* 'souped-up Marxism'. But *Octogesima Adveniens* goes much further than *Populorum Progressio*, which may explain why the status of an encyclical was withheld from it and it was officially described simply as 'a Letter to Cardinal Roy' in his role as president of the International Justice and Peace Commission. The Pope's reluctance to place the full weight of his authority behind the document may be explained by last-minute anxieties about its radical nature. For it seemed discriminating and gentle in its discussion of 'socialisms' while being tough and uncompromising in its rejection of 'the ideology of liberalism', which it defined as 'the erroneous assertion of the autonomy of the individual in his activity, his motivations and the exercise of his liberty' (35). No doubt the pontifical intention was to declare a plague on both ideological houses and invite Catholics to exercise the keenest critical discernment when presented with any vision of a political utopia, but the marked contrast between the plain statement on liberalism and the nuances on socialism was striking and significant. The effect of disengaging the Church as such from precise political options was to enable Christians to commit themselves politically as individuals in new ways. Catholic action became the action of Catholics. The taboo on socialism was broken. This may turn out to be one of the most decisive choices of the pontificate, especially in those countries where there is a sizeable majority of Catholics. And it is too late to ring alarm bells once the movement has begun.

That has not stopped them from ringing out. The case of Giulio Girardi is exemplary. At Chiemsee in 1966, as we have seen, he had called for 'an adult form of Marxism' for 'an adult humanity'. By 1974 he was beginning to formulate the problem in quite different terms. He wrote: 'If it is true that a Christian can be a revolutionary, one still has to explain why a revolutionary should be a Christian. The question is no longer whether Christianity is compatible with Marxism, but whether it is not superfluous once Marxism is accepted. One no longer asks whether Christianity is a hindrance to the revolution, but whether it can contribute something to it' ('Nouveauté chrétienne et nouveauté du monde', in *Lumière et Vie*, 1974, no. 116, p. 99). Girardi was already banned from teaching at the Salesianum in Rome and the Institut Catholique in Paris. The final blow came from Lumen Vitae, the catechetical institute in Brussels. The most severe measures were taken, involving the appointment of a new principal and a cooling-off period in which the institute would not take any more students for a year. The provincial of the Jesuits of southern Belgium, Fr Simon Decloux, said that Girardi had been teaching an unacceptable mixture of Marxism and Christianity. In a speech at Lumen Vitae he explained: 'To my mind the thought of Fr Girardi . . . is incompatible with the requirements of Catholic theology. Not because Fr Girardi declares himself to be a "revolutionary", but because the dialectical way in which he develops his political positions and relates them to his interpretation of Christian faith puts in jeopardy the possibility of a theology based on scripture, the living tradition and the *magisterium* of the Church, not to mention a concept of the Church's unity which transcends the diversity of political options.' The Provincial conceded that Girardi had not been formally teaching 'theology', but that did not let him off the hook, 'since his way of understanding the relationship of Christian faith to politics not only undermines the foundations of one kind of theology, but undermines the foundation of any Catholic theology'. The Council of the Centre had 'almost unanimously' supported Girardi's right to teach, but the Provincial bravely risked unpopularity in going against their decision, believing that the limits of pluralism had not only been reached but traversed. He had considered intermediate solutions, such as inviting Girardi to confine himself to an objective course on Marxism, but after listening to the cassette recordings of his lectures, he had realized that the distinction was not one which Girardi either could or would want to respect. So he had to go. Sadly. With due compensation. But inevitably.

With Roger Garaudy dismissed from the Communist Party and a cloud of heavy disapproval looming over Giulio Girardi, one phase of Christian-Marxist dialogue has come to an end. The heroes of the sixties have almost exchanged roles, with Garaudy announcing in 1975 his conversion to a form of Christianity and Girardi agonizing over the specifically Christian contribution to the revolution. One might be tempted to conclude that the whole enterprise of Christian-Marxist dialogue was a massive failure and write its obituary. The risk of dialogue had always been that at some stage the ideas being expressed and exchanged would collide with the interests of the institutions represented, and when this happened the institutions would call a halt. There were enough Catholics, mistrustful from the start, who welcomed any evidence of failure and preferred clearly identifiable battle lines to the fuzziness of dialogue. They talked of Christian-Marxist dialogue as a 'Trojan horse' within the Church, and advanced the theory of a gigantic conspiracy to explain the 'penetration' of the Church by Marxism. What they overlooked was that if certain 'Marxist' ideas began to invade the Church, they were modified in the process and helped it to abandon its 'idealistic' stance in political affairs, as we shall see in chapter 12. Conversely, the Christian-Marxist dialogue has also had an effect on Marxists, though it is harder to detect since the Communist Party exercises a tighter control on its members than does the Church.

The crucial unanswered question was whether Marxism will remain a total ideology, claiming to possess the single, exclusive key to the meaning of the universe, and necessarily implying materialism, or whether it could become a way of organizing society which leaves open wider philosophical questions. It was the question posed by Pope John in 1963. If the word 'prophetic' means anything, it is appropriate here. The fitful dialogue of the last decade is important in keeping open the options for an unknown future.

Chapter 11

The Vatican's Ostpolitik

With regard to civil society, be a witness to Christ and
his Church, which considers with great respect everything which is true, right and good in the institutions,
however diverse, which mankind has created and
continues to create . . .

ARCHBISHOP AGOSTINO CASAROLI
in a sermon preached at Olomouc,
Czechoslovakia, 4 March 1973.

In the previous chapter we saw the principles, derived from the
encyclical letters of Pope John, which provided the theoretical
justification for cautious dialogue and collaboration with Marxists.
'Marxist' is of course a looser term than 'Communist', and there
are many claimants to the title and the heritage. But in terms of
world power, it is the Communist Party which actually holds power
and can influence the lives of millions, including the 60,000,000
Roman Catholics living in Soviet Russia and Eastern Europe. It is
also the Communist Party which is on the doorstep of the Vatican,
polling a steadily increasing number of votes in Italy. When Pope
John in 1963 received Alexis Adjoubei, Khrushchev's son-in-law,
the right-wing press alleged that he had thereby lost a million votes
to the Christian Democrats. The 'Italian factor' is a persistent
element in Vatican policies. Pope Pius XII had a recurrent night-
mare in which he saw the red flag flying over the Campodoglio,
and through Catholic Action, Catholic Trades Unions and the
Christian Democrats he did everything in his power to prevent it
coming to pass. Pope John's policy represented a new departure.

However, Pope Paul, in his first encyclical, did not accept this
account. He claimed that the Holy See had not changed, but rather
that the Communists had changed. 'We are driven', wrote the
Pope, 'to repudiate such ideologies as deny God and oppress the

Church' (*Ecclesiam Suam*, 101). So much is obvious. But the Pope added a nuance, a characteristic interrogation: 'Yet is it really so much we who condemn them? One might say that it is rather they and their politicians who are clearly repudiating us, and for doctrinaire reasons subjecting us to violent oppression' (ibid.). The Church's voice was 'more the complaint of a victim than the sentence of a judge'. In this way Pope Paul was able to assert continuity with the positions of Pope Pius XII. The same theory of continuity was sketched out in the most complete statement of the Vatican's *Ostpolitik*, which is found in a lecture given by Archbishop Agostino Casaroli in February 1972 ('La Santa Sede e l'Europa', text in *Civiltà Cattolica*, 19 February 1972). The Church, Casaroli maintained, was waiting all the time with outstretched arms, ready to welcome any modification of the harshness or rigidity of the Communist line.

Archbishop Casaroli is a diplomat. Since Pope John first dispatched him to Vienna in 1961 to head the Vatican delegation at a United Nations conference on diplomatic relations, he has been increasingly identified with the carrying out of the Vatican's *Ostpolitik*. Clearly the term will not mean the same as, say, the *Ostpolitik* of West Germany. The Vatican has no trade to offer, no technical know-how, no weapons to lay down – though Casaroli did go to Moscow in February 1971 to add his signature to the Treaty on the Non-proliferation of Nuclear Weapons. It was a symbolic gesture. The Vatican's *Ostpolitik* is a subtler and more intangible affair. It has two aims and works on two levels. It hopes to improve the lot of Catholics living under Communism and to contribute something to peace and *détente* on the wider international scene. It has a pastoral and a world-political objective.

The situation of Catholics in Eastern Europe varies from country to country. Poland has a population of 33 million, 95% of whom are baptized Catholics – a figure that is actually higher than before the war, when there were Jews and Orthodox to be taken into account. Of Hungary's 11 million 60% are Catholic, and Slovakia is predominantly Catholic. There are significant minorities elsewhere. Within the Soviet Union itself 95% of the 3 million Lithuanians are Catholic, and there are said to be about 3 million former Eastern-rite Catholics in Belorussia and the Ukraine. The structure of the Roman Catholic Church meant that they owed allegiance to a head outside their own countries, the Pope; and this unique situation brought down on them additional harassment and persecution, and at the same time made them look to the distant papacy as their champion. This is the basis of the *Ostpolitik*. An international Church has a duty to be concerned about the fate and freedom of its members wherever they are and to do what it can to negotiate greater freedom for them.

But that is far from being the only aim of the Vatican's *Ostpolitik*. Its diplomatic service is not large, consisting of 36 nuncios, 36 pronuncios, 16 apostolic delegates and one chargé d'affaires. Casaroli has been at the head of the Council for the Public Affairs of the Church since it was reorganized in 1967. The general aim of Vatican diplomacy was defined in Archbishop Inigo Cardinale's classic work as 'the art and science of fostering good relations between Church and State'. The Vatican diplomatic service takes itself very seriously indeed, and endeavours to contribute to peace, reconciliation and *détente* in the international field. In the speech on his feast day in 1973 Pope Paul declared that the nations 'find in the Holy See an authority which comes from its history no less than from its nature'. He went on to be a little more specific: they find, he said, 'a direction, a moral inspiration that all, however confusedly, feel should animate and guide the life of the nations and their dealings with each other'. And the way to achieve this, he added, was not simply by preaching to the nations, but 'by participating, as a member with full rights, although having particular characteristics of its own, in the life of the international community'.

These large claims can be seen at work in the Vatican's dealings with Eastern Europe. Communist top officials have flocked to Rome. The durable Russian Foreign Minister, Gromyko, has been three times, in 1966, 1970 and 1974. In 1967 it was the turn of the President of the Supreme Soviet, Mr Podgorny, whose meeting with the Pope took the unusual form of a working session sitting round a table. Popes do not usually receive in that way. President Tito of Yugoslavia even paid a state visit in 1971. Mr Ceausescu of Rumania called in 1973. Contacts with Polish officials have been frequent in the move towards what Mr Gierek calls 'normalization' and they have now been placed on a regular footing. The Communist leaders have not been seeking conversion, and whether they take the Vatican at its own evaluation may be doubted. Lenin's question, 'Who-whom?', is always relevant in any diplomatic situation, but in this case it admits of no easy answer. The communiqués that are issued are of remarkable banality. Leaks are slightly more revealing. During the meeting with Ceausescu, the Pope kept trying to bring the conversation round to the fate of the suppressed Uniates of Rumania, but each time Ceausescu dodged the question and observed that 'twenty-five years have elapsed' or talked of the need for 'peace and collaboration'.

A little more light is cast on these abstruse conversations if one looks at the exchange visits. Casaroli is a much-travelled man, and this has led Italian journalists to speak of him as 'the Henry Kissinger of the Vatican'. 1971 found him in Moscow for the first visit of an official Vatican representative since the October Revolution. After fifty-three years of hostility and recriminations, said Mgr Casaroli on his return, 'we have put an end to monologue and opened a dialogue'. The subject of the dialogue was 'peace', a word so tarnished that it has become almost useless. Casaroli distinguished two possible approaches, parallel action and co-operation. By 'parallel action' he meant a situation in which the Holy See and the Soviet Union each work separately but for the same goal, peace. He suggested as an example that certain Arab countries were receptive to the influence of both the Holy See and Russia, and so in such a case each would reinforce the action of the other. As for co-operation, he instanced 'the on-going action for disarmament and the project for a European security conference' (Katholische Nachrichten Agentur, 16 March 1971). Meanwhile the plan for a European security conference stumbled forwards and the Holy See has been taking part in it, the first time it has participated in a major international conference since the Congress of Vienna.

Casaroli made a speech at its opening meeting in Helsinki in July 1973, tucked in between Dom Mintoff of Malta and the Dutch

Foreign Minister. He gallantly recognized that many of the problems facing the conference lay beyond the competence of the Holy See and adopted an attitude of 'respectful discretion'. In the main he lent his support to the Russian theses on the recognition of frontiers, territorial integrity, and non-intervention in the internal affairs of other countries. He twice used the give-away phrase, 'despite the diversity of political systems', which in the context is diplomatic shorthand for the acknowledgement of the *status quo*. The nearest he came to controversy was to denounce the inadequacies of *Realpolitik* and to utter the following warning: 'The flouting of fundamental human rights will lead, sooner or later, somewhere in Europe, to grave internal disturbances which, in spite of the principle of non-intervention, will threaten equally the peace of other countries.' He could hardly have said less at a time when Solzhenitsyn and other dissidents were taking calculated risks and detailing 'the flouting of fundamental human rights'. Casaroli's speech owed more to the diplomatic art than to Christian conviction.

It is precisely this diplomatic caution which has aroused the wrath of the exiles. They cannot forget the past. At the Council the Slovak Bishop Rusnak spoke movingly of the terrible sufferings undergone by his Church, and how the whole diocese of Presov in Slovakia, which counted more than 300,000 people, was declared inexistent by a stroke of the pen. At the 1971 Synod Cardinal Slipyi, who had been extricated from his prison camp by Pope John in 1963, spoke of the destruction of the Ukrainian Catholic Church in 1948, a catastrophe described by Patriarch Pimen of Moscow as 'one of the most glorious events in the life of the Orthodox Church'. With rather more accuracy an Anglican expert on Russia, Michael Bourdeaux, called it 'the most dishonorable act perpetrated by the Russian Orthodox Church in modern times' (cf. *The Tablet*, 13 March 1971, p. 264). Cardinal Slipyi indeed has been heard to murmur that he 'prefers a Russian prison to so-called Roman freedom'. What the exiles fear is that the goals of peace and *détente*, splendid though they may be, are to be achieved above the heads and at the expense of Catholics living under Communism. Should Casaroli be talking so coolly to the perse-

cutors of the Church? Is there a shady bargain, an obnoxious deal?
What does he offer in exchange for the minimal concessions he is
sometimes able to extract? Is not the final embrace of Catholicism
and Communism an obscene insult to the martyrs?

Casaroli is not unaware of these objections. He knows that the
Vatican's *Ostpolitik* is said to be naïve, dangerous, fruitless and
based on an impossible quest for compromise. The mistrust of the
exiles is the cross he has to bear. He attempted, not very successfully, to counter their charges in the lecture already referred to.
'Dialogue', he patiently explained, 'does not and cannot mean the
abandonment of those who have struggled and suffered for the
Church; on the contrary, its aim is to help them, and it is based on
their capacity to sacrifice themselves for a higher cause, that of the
Church and their country' ('La Santa Sede e l'Europa', in *Civiltà
Cattolica*, 19 February 1972, p. 372). He went on: 'In a certain
sense, dialogue is a homage paid to those who through their
fidelity enabled the Church to survive and to convince others to
open a dialogue with her.' This was equivalent to saying that the
blood of martyrs is the seed of dialogue: those who narrowly
escaped martyrdom remain unconvinced and regard the con-
nivance with power as highly suspicious.

But it is by no means certain that the Christians who actually
live under Communist regimes share the views of the exiles. They
have, in varying degrees, 'come to terms' with regimes which give
a frightening appearance of permanence. When Casaroli goes
among them, their response is more ambivalent. They recognize
the complexity of his task, and they know the rules of the game.
Casaroli is a diplomat, but he is also a bishop, and in March 1973
he donned his mitre to consecrate three new bishops at Nitra in
Slovakia. 'Great is this day', he declared in Latin which was immediately translated, 'for the Catholic Church in Slovakia, great
is this day for the whole of Slovakia and for the entire Catholic
Church.' Crowds lined the streets to the ancient cathedral which
forms part of a complex of buildings including a ninth-century
castle. The bells pealed out, a most unusual event for a Communist
country. The next day he was at Olomouc in Moravia for another
episcopal ordination, but this time his rhetoric was more restrained.

Rather than dwell on the man who was being appointed, he spoke at length of one of his predecessors, Archbishop Stoja, who even though he lived long before Vatican II had embodied its ideals of simplicity and service. He was known locally as '*Taticek* Stoja' – 'Pope Stoja' – and had died in 1923 with a reputation for great holiness. It was here that Casaroli spoke the words placed at the head of this chapter. He exhorted the new bishop to acknowledge 'everything which is true, right and good in the institutions, however diverse, which mankind has created and continues to create'.

Among the diverse institutions which mankind has created is the Czech Communist Party, which has devoted itself systematically and thoroughly to the elimination of the Catholic Church. Priests had been jailed. Orders of monks were disbanded. Nuns lived in 'concentration convents' and were allowed to do only the disagreeable tasks that no one else wanted to do. Above all, for years eleven out of the thirteen dioceses of Czechoslovakia had been without a bishop. This was because the Vatican would not accept the assortment of puppets and stooges – men like Plojhar and Stehlik – who had been proposed by the Party. But now in 1973 the bells rang out, and in two days there were four more bishops. 'Great is this day', as Casaroli said. But was it?

An analysis of the significance of these episcopal ordinations will reveal the delicate tightrope which Casaroli has to tread. There were concessions on both sides. The new bishop at Olomouc, Mgr Vrana, had been president of the government-sponsored 'Peace Priests' movement (*Pacem in Terris*) which could be relied upon to give enthusiastic and uncritical support to the regime. That was why it existed. Among its less pleasant activities was that of suggesting stiffer penalties for priests who had 'offended against the State', a vague and hold-all crime. The appointment of Vrana seemed like an insult to the men whose hands had been hardened in prison. However, a condition of his appointment was that he should renounce all contact with the despicable movement. The balance tilted Casaroli's way. Moreover, the appointment of Vrana was conditional on his good behaviour, since it was qualified '*ad nutum Sanctae Sedis*', which is to say that it could be revoked at any moment. To reinforce the point, Mgr Trochta, a worthy man who had long suffered in prison, was made a cardinal. Casaroli's diplomatic victory might seem complete. It had merely the flaw that neither loyal Catholics nor Communist officials had much esteem for the man he had ordained bishop.

In this example one senses the extreme complexity of Casaroli's task. It is easy to tax him with naïveté and to blame him for being weak where he should be strong, but he has few bargaining counters. He is aware that he might be duped. On his return from Czechoslovakia he tried to defend himself. In Catholic theology, the bishop is the cornerstone of the Church, and without a bishop there can be, in the long run, no Church at all. 'The Holy See', he explained, 'never appoints a bishop unless it is convinced of his fidelity and good will.' He added with characteristic understatement: 'Given the concrete circumstances of the various countries, there is always a risk involved. But it is a risk that must be taken.'

The problem arises because Communist governments have ignored the developments noted in the last chapter and remain faithful to Marx in refusing to regard religion as a private matter: it is an alienation of capitalism, destined to disappear. Even Vitězslav Gardavský, a relatively sophisticated Czech philosopher who had taken part in the dialogue at Marienbad, committed himself to the revealing idea that 'a world without God would be easier to control' (*God Is Not Yet Dead*, p. 153). If religion is to be tolerated for an interim period, then at least the State must have a monopoly of it. It may be allowed to continue, but only if it is rigorously controlled. No institution or organization deriving from any other source than the State has the right to exist. But the Roman Catholic Church is precisely such an institution, and this explains the special venom of Catholic-Communist relations. But it also explains why Communists are ready to talk to the Vatican. By habit and experience, they suppose that the masses will follow the lead given them from on high. So they troop to the Vatican, believing that it is worth enlisting in the cause of world peace and *détente* in Europe. They assume that it can deliver what they want. And at this point Casaroli doffs his mitre once more and becomes a diplomat, punctilious and agreement-minded. For he has to offer that most precious of diplomatic commodities: recognition.

The 'recovered territories' of western Poland had always been the thorn in the flesh of Vatican-Polish relations. The Vatican refused to appoint Polish bishops, giving as its official reason the fact that there had been no peace treaty confirming the new post-war frontiers. But once the treaties between Bonn and Moscow and Bonn and Warsaw had been signed, this technical difficulty was removed. The Vatican then appointed Polish bishops on 28 June 1972. A certain fussiness about international law is characteristic of Vatican diplomacy. It is not in a hurry. 'We think in centuries here' is a favourite saying. In this case, neither was the Polish government in a hurry. It was not until 15 October 1972 that the Catholic weekly, *Tygodnik Powszechny*, was allowed by the censors to report and comment on the event.

Another piece of tidying up was the *de facto* recognition of the German Democratic Republic. After negotiations with Herr Werner Lamberz, Secretary of the East German Central Committee, in January 1973, apostolic administrators were named on 23 July for the three dioceses which had till then been humiliatingly dependent on West Germany. The West German government was upset. It conceded the right of the Vatican to make such appointments, but felt that it should have been consulted. This is another instance of the diplomatic tightrope Casaroli has to tread.

Beyond the basic step of 'recognition' lies the further horizon of 'diplomatic relations'. They exist so far only with Yugoslavia, and were set up at a time when the country was out of favour with Moscow and looking for anything that would bind its disparate religions and nationalities together. The 'protocol' or agreement recognizes the socialist nature of the Yugoslav state but concedes to the Vatican jurisdiction 'in matters of a spiritual, ecclesiastical and religious character'. This concession, however, was limited by the clause 'in so far as they are not opposed to the internal order of the Socialistic Federative Republic of Yugoslavia'. And the Church promised to lend a hand in dealing with 'political terrorism or similar criminal forms of violence'. The 'protocol' was welcomed when it was signed. Franc Franic, Bishop of Split, said that 'it could signify a new era in the life of the Church'. But it has been severely criticized subsequently.

'It gives the Church freedom,' said one Croatian priest, 'but it is the freedom of the sacristy.' Another remarked that 'the *modus vivendi* is in fact a slow form of death'. He meant that the Church's voluntary acceptance of abstention in political matters condemned it to silence, and therefore irrelevance, on social and political questions. Others complained that the agreement was negotiated above the heads of the Yugoslav bishops and thought that, just possibly, they might have secured a better deal for themselves. Once more Casaroli has been compared to Henry Kissinger. As he moves rapidly from country to country, stitching together agreements, others are left to live with the situation and to pick up the pieces. Some system of checking whether agreements are fulfilled is needed. But Casaroli is modest in his claims: 'Diplomatic relations have not solved all problems, but experience shows that they can have positive results.' They are not a magic wand. Nor are diplomatic relations on the Yugoslav pattern the goal everywhere. 'The form that relations take', said Casaroli, 'is secondary: what matters is that there should be relations.' Needless to say, recognition by the Vatican does not mean approval. Like the British government, the Vatican is prepared to deal with whoever happens to be in power. The principle was stated as long ago as 1929 by Pope Pius XI: 'Where there is a question of saving souls, we feel the courage to treat with the devil in person.' He was thinking of Mussolini, but the principle has a wider application, provided the spoon is long enough.

In every respect Poland is a special case. The Polish Catholic Church is by far the strongest in Eastern Europe, both statistically and institutionally. It has always claimed to embody the 'soul' of the nation and shared the terrible fate of Poland during the war: seven thousand priests were in prison and concentration camps, and two thousand of them perished. It has greater freedom in publications than elsewhere. Uniquely in Eastern Europe, it has its own university in Lublin. It has a tough-minded hierarchy led by the formidable Cardinal Wyszinski who has already outlasted two First Secretaries. From time to time he issues thunderbolts directed at the third, Gierek. He always wants to know the cash-value of Gierek's policy of 'normalization'.

Moreover, Wyszinski is an old fox who has suffered at the hands of Rome. Pius XII once showed his disapproval by keeping him waiting in Rome for a week before granting an audience. At a press conference in Rome during the Council in 1963, irritated by repeated questions on 'the Church of silence', Wyszinski snapped back tartly: 'Is there a Church of silence? I think I can speak my mind. But here in Rome, one finds a Church of the deaf.' He believes that a strong line is the only way to extract concessions from his government, and that he knows the situation better than the officials in Rome. But the legend of Polish doctrinal orthodoxy is such that, as Bishop Rubin, a Pole working in Rome, confided: 'Rome needs Poland more than Poland needs Rome.'

The Vatican has tried to respect Polish sensitivity. Mgr Bronislaw Dabrowski, secretary of the Polish Episcopal Conference, has usually been on hand during or shortly after any negotiations with the government. The Polish government has tried to secure diplomatic relations because it believes that it could more easily deal with a Vatican diplomat in Warsaw than the obstinate Polish bishops. The tactic of Wyszinski is equally plain: it is to prevent such a move, on the not unreasonable grounds that he has dealt with the government himself with relative success. When Solzhenitsyn addressed an open letter to Patriarch Pimen in Lent 1971, he contrasted the timidity of the leaders of the Orthodox Church, who boldly denounced injustice everywhere in the world while remaining silent about Russia, with the courageous outspokenness of the Polish bishops. It was sweet music to the ears of Cardinal Wyszinski and an unexpected vindication of his policy. The contrast between Wyszinski and Casaroli is between the man on the battlements who rather relishes the whiff of gunpowder, and the diplomat who is cautious and tries to circumvent conflict. Wyszinski exhorts his troops to do battle steadfastly, while suspecting that Casaroli has let down the drawbridge marked 'dialogue'. Wyszinski lectures the Polish government, Casaroli negotiates with it.

The impact of the Council in Eastern Europe was not what it was elsewhere. At the Council itself the few bishops from Eastern Europe who were allowed to come enjoyed great prestige as confessors of the faith. But on most issues they sided with the conservatives and so lost much of their influence. Philippe Levillain summed up their dilemma: 'By definition a minority at the Council, divided among themselves, often misunderstood, the bishops of Eastern Europe were torn between the need to think of the universal Church and a natural tendency to scale down the purpose of the Council to the demands of their own situation' (in *Documentation sur l'Europe Centrale*, 1973, no. 2). Their problems redoubled when they went home from the Council. They had to introduce a number of changes, of which liturgical change was only the symbol: but this was particularly difficult in countries where the tradition was one of popular manifestations of piety – processions, pilgrimages, Marian devotion – and where tradition was valued precisely because it was a link with the past that had managed to survive even Communism. They felt that much that they had cherished was being swept away, ironically through Dutch and French influence. Seen from Eastern Europe, the Dutch and the French, though they had never been short of ideas, had experienced declining religious practice and shown only feeble resistance to secularization. 'We want', said Cardinal Wyszinski, addressing a congress of Polish theologians in 1971, 'a Polish theology for Poles, written from the standpoint of the East for a community living in the East.' It was his way of warding off dangerous foreign influences.

The bishops of Eastern Europe found something else when they returned home from the Council. Because of the emphasis laid by the Council on ideas like 'dialogue' and 'openness' and its reassertion of the relative autonomy of the secular, the Party was provided with a splendid propaganda weapon which it did not hesitate to use. It could contrast unfavourably the local bishops as die-hard traditionalists with the open-minded Vatican. There were endless articles on Pope John's love of peace. The town council of Wroclaw erected a massive statue of him. But such transparent propaganda moves had less and less effect and gradually the bishops of Eastern Europe felt strong enough to express a grudgingly realistic acceptance of the *status quo*. Here, for example, is the delicately formulated reply of the Polish bishops to the government's offer of 'normalization': 'The Polish Catholic Church and the episcopate understand that after the Second World War the social, economic and political conditions of our country were changed. The Church, an intrinsic part of the nation for a thousand years, wants to serve the nation in these new conditions . . . The Church in Poland, which is served by the episcopate, does not want to create a political opposition, nor does it seek to mobilize social forces to fight against the system established in the constitution. The episcopate has not assumed and does not wish to assume the role of political leadership' ('How Normalization Should Be Understood', 21 June 1971).

This text hardly reveals any great enthusiasm for the building of socialism. It is more like a reluctant admission that the bad weather has come to stay. But it does indicate the beginnings of a more active form of co-existence. One of Mgr Casaroli's main aims in his journeys throughout Eastern Europe has been to assure governments that the Church on the highest level has no desire to bring them tumbling down and, equally importantly, to look for candidates for the episcopacy who will support this line without forfeiting the confidence of the local church. That does not necessarily mean docile and pliant bishops, but men who are prepared to accept that they live under socialism and that it is not of the devil. However, the example of Hungary suggests that even when these conditions have been met, all is not well, since the bishops are hedged in by government-appointed vicar-generals and chancellors. The balance remains precarious. The *quid pro quo* does not always yield results. The theory is that in exchange for assurances of loyalty, Mgr Casaroli can ask for certain basic rights for the Church. He has in view especially freedom of assembly, freedom of publication, the right to work among children and students. It is characteristic of the Vatican style not to speak so much of religious liberty as of basic human rights, of which religious freedom is an aspect. In all this Casaroli is following the traditional Vatican policy: if you cannot secure the *bene esse* of the Church, then strive at least to lay solid foundations for its *esse*. Beyond both lies the promised land of the *plene esse*. In other words, it is better that the Church should exist even under constraints than that it should not exist at all: and at the same time you strive to inch forwards and gain some palpable concessions. The difficulty lies in guaranteeing them.

Any assessment of the Vatican's *Ostpolitik* has to be provisional. It depends to a great extent on the estimate one forms of Russian intentions. Why do the Communist leaders go to the Vatican? Religion has a place in Soviet foreign policy, but it is a minor place. The representatives of the Orthodox Church travel from conference to conference, uttering soothing words of peace, trying to win the support of foreign public opinion and demonstrating that religious freedom exists. William C. Fletcher concluded that 'any *rapprochement* with the Vatican offers considerable benefits to the Soviet State in its continuing problem of maintaining control in its own domains' (*Religion and Soviet Foreign Policy, 1945–1970*, p. 106). This is undoubtedly part of the answer. When the Lithuanians complain to the Soviet authorities, they can be rudely reminded that they need not look to the Vatican for support.

If that were the whole story, the Vatican's *Ostpolitik* could be written off as a discreditable failure. The reverse of the coin is that the Vatican has a certain diplomatic weight. Pope Paul has done little to offend Communist governments and much to commend himself to them: he was critical of the war in Vietnam, he has committed himself to the development of the third world, and he has supported *détente* and the European Conference on Security and Co-operation. He cannot be described, as was Pius XII, as 'the Pope of the Atlantic Alliance'. In exchange the Vatican has won some concessions, especially outside Soviet Russia. And even if social control is the principal motivation in Communist eyes, it is a two-edged weapon, since anything which contributes to the survival of religion in Communist countries sets up a visible and permanent contradiction between the theory, which asserts that it ought to have disappeared, and the practice, which permits it to continue. Throughout the fastidious detail of negotiations, Casaroli's concern is with the long-term. He wagers on youth and the future: 'It is my conviction that the human element – man's instinctive need for freedom and religion – will eventually triumph as the sense of truth imposes itself.' He likes to quote Leonardo da Vinci's maxim: '*Non si volge colui che a stella è fisso*' ('He does not alter whose gaze is fixed on a star').

One can admire Casaroli's tenacity of purpose and long-term vision. But at the same time the Vatican's *Ostpolitik* has been pursued wholly on the diplomatic level. It represents a significant change in the Church's approach to a question that vitally affects the future. Yet the fact remains that there is no system in the Vatican for evaluating this or any other policy, no forum in which questions can be asked, no system of accountability except before God. The rest of the Church looks passively on. Criticism is condemned to take the form of polemics. Even though the content of the Vatican's *Ostpolitik* builds on the insights of the Council, its style is pre-conciliar. This may make it an apt instrument for dealing with Communist governments which act first and explain, if at all, afterwards.

Chapter 12

Taking Politics Seriously

What the world expects from Christians . . . is that
they set themselves free from abstraction and look at
the blood-stained face of history in our own times

ALBERT CAMUS
address to the French Dominicans in Paris, 1948.

No one should have been surprised at the growing involvement of
the Church in politics: and in that sentence 'Church' is to be taken
as widely as possible. It means the hierarchy, local groups and
individuals. Once more the principle that words cannot be lightly
uttered was verified. Words commit the speaker more than he
knows. The Council had plainly if platitudinously stated: 'If the
demands of justice and equity are to be satisfied, vigorous efforts
must be made . . . to remove as quickly as possible the immense
economic inequalities which now exist' (*On the Church in the
Modern World*, 66).

But just how quickly and vigorously ought one to set about the
task? Camilo Torres, the Colombian priest turned revolutionary,
showed his vigour by going off to the hills to join the guerrillas. He
was shot and became a folk-hero for Latin America. It was with
him in mind that Che Guevara had said: 'If Christians dared to
give a thorough-going revolutionary witness, the Latin-American
revolution would be invincible.' But on the same continent, no one
could dispute that the commitment of Dom Helder Camara
Pessoa, Archbishop of Olinde and Recife in north-east Brazil, has
been equally vigorous, even though he has insisted on a Ghandi-
like 'revolution without violence'. But even those in less extreme
situations than Camilo Torres and Helder Camara began to speak
of the urgent need for 'justice and peace', which became the
Catholic euphemism for politics.

For there remained something slightly sordid and hand-dirtying about 'politics'. It needed rescuing. On the right, the faded cliché that 'the Church ought not to interfere in politics' was occasionally heard. In practice the maxim meant either a consolidation of the *status quo* or the anti-clerical assertion that priests should not use their special position of influence to advocate particular courses of political action. Of course they had always done so, in one way or another, especially in Latin America. Moreover, priests had never been afraid to be patriots, whether they were Hungarian or Polish or Irish. And Don Camillo in his Italian village could rout the Communist mayor with impunity because, after all, anti-Communism was not so much politics as the defence of the faith. A special licence was given to be anti-Communist. But despite these exceptions, it was generally held that the priest's task of embodying and promoting the unity of the community was incompatible with partisan and divisive political options. The political priest might be applauded by half his congregation and denounced by the other half. Safety lay in silence which never touched on dangerous questions or in spirituality which hovered above them.

When early in 1974 Fr Michael Connolly, a Wolverhampton priest, praised an IRA bank robber who had died on hunger strike, he was dismissed from his parish and addressed in these terms by Dr Dwyer, Archbishop of Birmingham: 'A priest must speak words of peace and reconciliation. Your actions can only foment bitterness and division.' The Archbishop was much praised in England for his stand, though the Irish were less enthusiastic. But he had only followed a sound enough tradition and echoed the conventional wisdom: the priest stands above the heat and dust of the mêlée. Yet elsewhere this conventional wisdom had been undermined and the tradition lay in ruins.

The Council had dealt them a series of severe blows. It became difficult to argue, for example, that because the mission of the Church was 'spiritual' and its ultimate destination 'eschatological', a Christian can virtuously choose to ignore this temporary home and devote himself exclusively to prayer and penance. Throughout the conciliar texts there is a sustained attempt to reject the Marxist charge of alienation, to reject, that is, the idea that because

Christians assert the existence of a coming kingdom in which compensating justice and mercy will be done, they can neglect the claims of this world. The rejection was based on two principal considerations. The first was that man has a duty to 'transform the earth' and 'that the triumphs of the human race are a sign of God's greatness and the flowering of his own mysterious design' (*On the Church in the Modern World*, 34). This was one of the conciliar passages in which the optimistic influence of Teilhard de Chardin could be seen. But more fundamentally still, if creation impels men to master the earth, redemption should make them aware of their common destiny and their interdependence. If all men are brothers in Christ, then the split between faith and everyday life will be a serious error, and 'the Christian who neglects his temporal duties neglects his duties towards his neighbour . . . and jeopardizes his eternal salvation' (ibid., 43). That removed the last loophole for anyone who wished to opt out.

But as the Christian, thus exhorted, arrived panting on the political scene – or rather as he began to concern himself with justice and peace – what did he have to say? He spoke at first of man and his dignity, and the Council made the notion of 'human dignity' – man seen as free, responsible, rational, social, collaborative – the norm of judgement. Where human dignity was trampled upon, the oppressors were to be denounced. The fact that modern men were becoming increasingly aware of their human dignity was said to be 'a sign of the times' and therefore in some sense a coded message from the Holy Spirit. For the Holy Spirit 'brooded over this development' and 'the ferment of the Gospel' was at work in the demand for dignity (*On the Church in the Modern World*, 26). The difficulty lay in attempting to realize this concept of human dignity. It could remain a vague rhetorical device which made one bursting to fight, but without indicating where precisely the enemy lay. We saw in chapter 10 how *Octogesima Adveniens* left detailed political options to the local churches and marked an 'opening to the left'. And increasingly the social and secular meaning of the liturgy began to be emphasized.

It was the renewal of an ancient patristic theme: Christ comes to us wearing two disguises, the Eucharist and the poor. It had never wholly disappeared from the Christian tradition. Léon Bloy used to say that those who exploited the poor struck again the wounded face of Christ. But now the theme was radicalized and given a social dimension. An editorial in *New Blackfriars*, for example, commented: 'Unless we recognize Christ in the tortured prisoners of Vietnam, it is idle to pretend that we recognize him in the sacraments of the Church' (*New Blackfriars*, October 1965, p. 58). Some went further. Not only would it be idle, it would be blasphemous. But who were these tortured prisoners of Vietnam? Not much familiarity with the literature was needed to know immediately that it was not the American prisoners in North Vietnam whom Christians were being urged to identify with Christ, but those held in jail in the South. This led to complaints on the right about 'selective indignation', but by now a semantic shift had occurred which transformed 'being committed' into 'being committed on the left'. New coinages confirmed the trend. 'Conscientization', Paolo Freire's tongue-twisting term for prodding people into an awareness of the injustice which surrounded them, reinforced the movement away from resignation and towards protest.

A powerful agent in the change of mentalities was the International Justice and Peace Commission. It owed its existence to one of the rare speeches made by a layman at the Council. On 5 November 1965, Mr James Norris, at that time president of the International Committee on Migration, spoke of the ever-widening gap between rich and poor nations and the Christian responsibility to work for change in the social order. He concluded: 'This aim will only be achieved if, in each country, a group of men of good will are firmly organized, well-informed and courageous, and prepared to consider poverty in the world as one of the great central concerns of our times and constantly support the policies of aid, exchange and technical education that will reduce the growing gulf between rich and poor.' Just over a year later the International Justice and Peace Commission was set up by the *motu proprio*, *Catholicam Christi Ecclesiam* (6 January 1967).

In an address to the Commission later that year, Pope Paul compared it to a weathercock placed on the top of a church 'as a symbol of watchfulness', and said that it would have the task of 'keeping the eye of the Church alert, her heart open and her hand outstretched for the work of love she is called upon to give to the world' (21 April 1973). The strength of the Commission has been that it brought lay competence into the service of the Church – Lady Jackson, better known as Barbara Ward, has been a prominent and eloquent member of it from the start – and that it provided the Roman Curia and local hierarchies with an alternative source of information and judgement on political events. The information was not always welcome and the judgements were not always shared. The hunger and thirst for justice frequently found itself at odds with what 'diplomatic considerations' seemed to require. Mgr Benelli indulgently called the Commission 'the *enfant terrible* of the Roman Curia'. That was a polite way of saying it could be awkward.

In 1970, for example, the Commission received eye-witness accounts of torture on Brazilian prisoners. The Dominican Frei Betto appealed from his cell: 'The Church is the only hope for us prisoners because it is the only Brazilian institution not under the control of the military. Its mission is to defend and promote human dignity. The time has come for the bishops to say, before it is too late: "Put an end to the tortures and injustices perpetrated by the regime."' The Brazilian bishops were divided on what attitude to adopt, though there had already been protests from some of their commissions. In October 1970 Cardinal Roy, president of the International Justice and Peace Commission, denounced the use of torture in Brazil. For a week events tumbled over each other. First the Central Commission of the Brazilian Bishops accused the government of hindering the free activity of the Church and said clearly, 'One cannot reply to the terrorism of subversion with the terrorism of suppression' (16 October 1970). The text was published in *Osservatore Romano* four days later with a supporting editorial (19–20 October 1970). Cardinal Rossi, Archbishop of São Paulo and head of the Brazilian hierarchy, was received in audience by Pope Paul, along with Mgr Ivo Lorscheider whom the Episcopal Conference had made responsible for dealing with the prisoners. At his Wednesday audience, Pope Paul

declared that 'torture, that is to say cruel and inhuman methods by
which the police extract confessions from the lips of prisoners, is to
be condemned absolutely' (21 October). No country was mentioned
by name, and though the allusion to Brazil was transparent, it could
never be proved.

While the Pope was speaking Cardinal Rossi arrived back in
Brazil, where he explained that Pope Paul knew perfectly well that
there was no religious persecution in Brazil, and that he appreciated
'the efforts shown by the President of the Brazilian republic to lead
Brazil along the path of development, while fighting against
subversion and trying to stem the intense international campaign
of calumny so unjustly being conducted against Brazil'. Having
crossed the wires, Cardinal Rossi proceeded to trip over them.
The very next day he was removed from his post in São Paulo and
it was revealed that he was urgently needed to head the Congregation for the Evangelization of Peoples in Rome. The sudden and
unexpected promotion of Cardinal Rossi removed him from
Brazil for good. It is difficult to interpret unambiguously this
complicated diplomatic fandango, but it cannot be denied that the
International Justice and Peace Commission had acted as a catalyst.

Its intervention had proved both timely and embarrassing. After
1970 the Commission tried to be 'more positive' and to concentrate
on what was piously called 'constructive work' rather than mere
denunciation. Two resolutions at its 1970 assembly laid down the
main lines of its policy for the 1970s: 'In the affluent world,
emphasis should be laid upon the Christian duty of transforming the
world and of changing power structures for a more just world
order, in keeping with the spirit of the Gospel. In developing
regions, the stress will be upon the action of these nations to help
themselves, and of their integration to maximize their influence on
the world scene.' The influence of the Commission as a pressure
and interest group within the Church's central administration has
been far from negligible. Its existence helped to put 'Justice in the
World' on the agenda of the 1971 Synod, alongside the more
inward-looking theme of 'Priestly Ministry'. But there have
been disappointments and upsets. As we have seen, the links
with the equivalent WCC body were loosened in 1972, when the

Joint Committee on Society, Development and Peace, known as SODEPAX, was reduced in importance. Fr George Dunne, who had been secretary of SODEPAX, was thanked for his trouble, given a pontifical medal, and little more was heard from the Joint Committee. An official survey on the state of ecumenism presented by the RC/WCC Joint Working Group noted that one Justice and Peace representative had ruefully said: 'Any action which seems liable to upset the established order is regarded as bad and, therefore, to be eliminated by measures or decrees, whether at international or local level' (*One in Christ*, 1975, no. 1, p. 46).

The same complaints have been heard on the local level. Richard Dowden, in a letter to the chairman of the England and Wales Commission, Bishop Gerald Mahon, described its work as 'tired and aimless', and remarked that on most issues 'the criterion of action is not "What is a just and Christian response to this situation?" but rather "What will the bishops think of us if we say this?" ' (quoted in *The Times*, 18 February 1975). The difficulty of ever taking a vigorous stand is heightened when one recalls that the advisors to the Commission in England and Wales cover most of the political spectrum, which means that the likelihood of agreement on controverted questions is remote. A further onslaught came from another member of the Commission, Jonathan Power, who wrote in a letter to *The Catholic Herald*: 'Most scandalous of all has been the attitude towards Ireland. An attempt to set up an ecumenical office . . . was blocked by the bishops with the meek acquiescence of the Commission, despite the fact that funds were available from an independent source' (14 February 1975). In reply to these charges Bishop Mahon protested that it was not so much that the bishops did not listen to the advice given, but that they did not always accept it. And he truthfully remarked that the Commission could already claim some success in educating the Catholic community 'to the challenges of the Gospel in a world so violently divided between the haves and the have-nots' (*The Tablet*, 15 March 1975, p. 270). In the midseventies the emphasis of the Commission has more and more shifted, on the local and the international level, towards the less controversial cause of feeding the hungry. Pope Paul's words to the World Food Conference in September 1974 provided the new slogan: 'Hunger no more.'

However, the move from the dangerously political to the safely humanitarian can never be complete, firstly because the food situation is itself embroiled in political and economic questions, and secondly because individual national situations have developed in such a way that local churches find themselves leading the opposition. Those regimes which confidently expected the Church to go on producing loyal and docile citizens who would invariably be on the side of law, order and the establishment have been disconcerted time and time again. One of the most striking examples is Spain, where the bishops – with the exception of the Basques – once blessed General Franco's crusade. This policy has long been abandoned. The Asamblea of the Spanish Bishops meeting in Madrid in September 1971 surprised everyone by its radicalism: it even surprised its participants, who had a feeling of making up for lost time. It recommended the disengagement of the Church from the State and resolutely placed the Church on the side of the poor, the under-privileged, the weak. It wanted to become 'the voice of those who have no voice'. The Church, said Mgr Echarren, Auxiliary Bishop of Madrid, must strive to regain the confidence of the poor, even if that meant losing the confidence of those classes which had traditionally supported the Church. The whole movement of renewal culminated in the Church's commitment on the side of those who advocated change, and 'against the establishment' ('Spain on the Move', Michael J. Walsh, in *The Month*, June 1972, p. 163). This switching of alliances would be merely opportunistic unless it were based on fidelity to the Gospel. The Spanish bishops claimed that it was and the war of attrition grinds on, with harassment and censorship from the police and eloquent protests from the Church. One of the difficulties in the long-drawn-out renegotiation of the Vatican's concordat with Spain is that it contains a clause which would, it is alleged, confine the clergy to the sacristy. The Spanish clergy has not been in the least confined there in the last five years. In November 1974, for example, the Archbishop of Barcelona, supported the striking car workers and said that 'capitalists should accept new forms of worker participation'. Bishops have not only not feared to speak out, they have feared not to speak out.

In country after country the Church moved from acquiescence to critical challenge. One of President Park Chung's most articulate opponents in Korea has been Bishop Daniel Chi Hok Sun, who was imprisoned in August 1974. Released after the referendum, he was greeted by several hundred demonstrators bearing banners inscribed 'Three cheers for the anti-dictatorship hero'. Shaken, President Park Chung dispatched his Foreign Minister to the Vatican. He returned claiming that he had received assurances that the Church and especially priests 'should not intrude in the domestic affairs, including the politics, of another nation'. Some missionaries were expelled, but the Church has remained the focus of opposition. Cardinal Kim of Seoul remarked at the 1974 Synod that the Church, which in the past had always been swift to defend her institutions when they were attacked, should now show comparable zeal when it came to defending basic human rights. He saw the denunciation of injustice as part of the work of preaching the Gospel.

In December 1974 Bishop Chi Hok Sun managed to smuggle out a letter to Archbishop Jaime Sin of Manila in the Philippines. The letter addressed an appeal to President Ford 'as a man seeking peace, a concerned Christian and a world statesman . . . to help this man of singular courage'. Archbishop Sin seized the opportunity to launch an attack on the injustice of his own President Marcos' martial law regulations. 'We cannot jail a man indefinitely', he wrote, 'and still call ourselves Christians.' When President Marcos announced a referendum, the irrepressible Sin observed that 'even Barabbas was able to defeat Christ by means of a referendum'. The heads of the religious orders in the Philippines proposed a complete boycott of the referendum, but the Bishops' Conference refused to endorse this suggestion. The political conflict was reflected in the Church.

In Mexico unrest has flared up spasmodically throughout the decade. Student revolts in October 1968 and June 1971 were bloodily put down. One of the most remarkable documents to come

from the Mexican Church was the confession of guilt published by
Archbishop Almeida of Chihuahua and his clergy. It begins: 'By
our silence we are guilty of not standing clearly on the side of the
marginalized, the poor, those who have no voice. We are guilty
because of the preferential treatment we have given to certain
social classes and because of our complicity with the power
structures. We are guilty because we have failed to be true witnesses and failed to commit ourselves in practice as the Gospel
demands' (29 January 1972). Other Mexican documents tried to
go beyond breast-beating and analysed the situation of 'established
disorder' – a phrase of Emmanuel Mounier that had an enormous
vogue in the period. The provincial of the Jesuits, Fr Enrique
Guttierez del Campo, was among the most precise: 'Mexican
peons have for years fought a battle against the land-owners,
against exploitation by bankers. They have reacted against an
unjust rent system and against the capitalist way their agricultural
and livestock products are put on the market.' The Mexican
Jesuits had the full support of their general, Fr Pedro Arrupe. They
had proved the seriousness of their commitment by closing down
the elite college, the Instituto Patria, previously regarded as the
best school in Mexico City. Their attempts to identify with the
poor led right-wing newspapers to call them, predictably, 'Communists, confederates of Mao and Castro, Moscow-inspired
subversives'.

   To be called such names is now the fate of those who utter
strong opinions on political or racial questions. Of all the world's
bishops, those of Rhodesia are least likely to deserve the label
'crypto-Communist'. Even so, distressed laymen who share Mr Ian
Smith's conviction that he is defending Christianity by maintaining
firm control over the majority of Africans have applied it to their
bishops. Yet they had done little more than recall the basic
principles of Christian social morality. In 1969 they issued a
'Call to Christians' in which they protested against the powers
which the new constitution conceded to the government. 'To
accept such powers', they wrote, 'is morally unjustifiable: it is the
equivalent of signing a blank cheque for government by bureaucratic dictatorship.' As the blank cheque they had correctly

described was filled out, they renewed their protests. The Land
Tenure Act of 1971 (by which the country was to be divided into
white and black areas) was opposed as a limitation on the Church's
freedom 'to deal with all the people, independently of their race,
and to serve them'. The bishops said that they would not operate
the new law, an instance of episcopal civil disobedience. A few
months later they made it clear that they would rather close their
schools than implement racialist measures in them and, after an
attempt at compromise prompted by a visit of Fr Schütte, acting
on behalf of the Congregation for Evangelization, they withdrew
their provisional support and declared that 'the government's
ideology is so incompatible with the Church's teaching that
further negotiations would serve no useful purpose'. The opposition
hardened still more in the spring of 1975 when the Rhodesian
Justice and Peace Commission published a dossier containing
allegations of brutality by the Rhodesian security forces.

The panorama could be pursued almost indefinitely. A complete
account would also have to mention individual exposés like Cosmas
Desmond's story of the 'dumping' of black workers in desolate
villages of South Africa (in *The Discarded People*) and Fr Adrian
Hastings' revelations of massacre at Wiriyamu in Mozambique in
1973 which contributed to the collapse of the regime in Portugal
and to the rapid dismantling of the colonial empire in Africa.

Despite stragglers and timid exceptions, the Church has on the
whole broken with political conformity. Protest and denunciation
became a common literary form for pastoral letters. One can say
either that the Church has at last woken up to an essential dimension of its mission, or that the world's stock of injustice has
suddenly and dramatically increased. The former explanation
seems more likely. The 'theology of liberation', gesturing and
vague though it could be, helped Christians to emerge from
abstractions. It was one thing to make speeches about 'liberation'
and quite another to work effectively for it in precise situations of
oppression. The Latin Americans stressed that if in the Western
world the threat to faith came from unbelief, in the third world it
comes rather from the marginalized non-persons whom the social
order rejects. The Latin-American question was: how can we

speak of God in a sub-human world? Their experience was generalizable at least to the extent that a political morality based on Providence gave way to one based on prophecy. A stress on Providence could lead to the idea of a divine purpose steadily unfolding in human history: the prospect of its inevitable ultimate victory meant that temporary injustice could be borne. The prophetic view judged political situations in the light of Christian hope and denounced injustice wherever it found it.

Prophecy was comfortable neither for the prophet nor for his hearers. The Church was dragged beyond blandness and into controversy. Nowhere was this more clearly seen than in the trauma produced by the Vietnam War in the United States. The conflict was dramatized in the contrasting roles played by two Jesuits, Frs Dan Berrigan and John J. McLaughlin. Berrigan and his brother Philip fought the American involvement in Vietnam with obsessive intensity. It filled their whole horizon. Dan Berrigan was vainly and laughably pursued by the Federal authorities for several months until they caught up with the fugitive and he was given a three-year sentence for destroying draft cards. For Berrigan, life had simplified itself down to the primordial duty of resistance, and it had become the interpretation of the Gospel that counted: 'Resistance to the war-ridden, bloodshot state is the form that human life is called to assume today. It is also the simplest, most logical way of translating the Gospel into an *argot* that will be exact and imaginative at once. It is an occasion of rebirth, and a bloody one at that' (*America Is Hard to Find*, p. 128). Berrigan was convinced that if the Church did not speak out, it would be judged by history exactly as the German Catholic Church had been judged for its failure to condemn Hitler and the concentration camps. But he always stressed the difference: while German Catholics could plausibly claim not to have known what was happening in their country, no American Catholic could seriously plead such inculpable ignorance.

While Dan Berrigan was out on parole, another Jesuit, John J. McLaughlin, was entering the White House as special advisor to President Nixon. He became known as the Administration's 'hired collar' since he appeared ready to bless whatever cause was placed before him. Even when the Watergate flood began to over-whelm the President, McLaughlin remained steadfastly loyal, praising 'the bomber of Hanoi, the invader of Cambodia, the landlord of San Clemente, the man responsible for the whole network of crimes and cover-ups called Watergate, as "the greatest moral leader of the last third of the century" and the model of Christian charity' (*Commonweal*, 14 June 1974). Yet unlike Berrigan, McLaughlin had no trouble with his Jesuit superiors until in autumn 1974 his provincial, Fr Richard Cleary, suggested to him the classic remedy of a week of prayer. McLaughlin was also invited to live in a less ostentatious apartment: with a degree of insensitivity remarkable in someone attuned to political life, he was living in the Watergate building itself.

This striking contrast raises a number of questions about Christian political involvement. Both men were Jesuits. How far does Jesuit pluralism stretch, and are there no limits to it at all? It is one thing to have no particular dogmatic line on political questions, and another to have men holding diametrically opposed positions. Both were priests. If one is prepared to accept the political commitment of Fr X with whom one agrees, ought one not at least to tolerate the activities of Fr Y with whom one does not agree? The 'prophet' is always the man one agrees with, and he is treated with an indulgence not granted to his 'reactionary' opponents. Furthermore, have not these two priests in any case usurped the function of laymen who have a special responsibility for 'the secular'?

Here Berrigan and McLaughlin differed so much in the rationale they provided for their activities that they seem to come from different worlds. For Berrigan it was a relatively simple matter of witnessing to an abominable and unjust oppression: like any prophet he had to speak out and name the injustice. Priest or layman, the duty was the same; the difference was that the priest, because he may be more in the public eye and is an official representative of the Church, makes a more dramatic impact. The peace movement was never unwilling to make use of lived parables and symbolic acts. Berrigan entered into this process which was part prophecy, part public relations. Moreover, he was building on another of the hints of Vatican II which took some time to fructify. Several centuries of Catholic teaching were broken with by the rejection of the statement that, in case of dispute, *the presumption was that the State was right.* By rejecting this presumption the Council removed in principle the veil of disapproval which had been cast over the conscientious objector – though in Italy the law remained unchanged – and provided a legitimation for civil disobedience. The conscientious objector and the civilly disobedient could be heralds of a future morality.

McLaughlin's justification for his political role could hardly proceed along such lines. His starting-point was different. The secular world must not be left unevangelized, and the presence of a priest is part of the process of evangelization: he changes situations by his very presence. To this must be added the traditional Jesuit predilection for working through elites. But from Louis XIV to President Nixon, working through elites could so easily come to mean assimilating their values, tolerating the intolerable and defending the indefensible. Seen in this light, McLaughlin was a hangover from an earlier period, and Berrigan the prophet of the future. Christ is more likely to be found among those hunted by a regime than those who are fêted by it.

Dangerous romanticism, said Andrew Greeley, the priest-sociologist from Chicago, a voluminous writer who was rarely at a loss for words during the decade. As early as 1970 he launched an attack on the Berrigans (in *Church World*, September 1970). According to Greeley, Berrigan was a totalitarian who wanted to imprison everyone within the confines of his exceedingly narrow moral judgements. He was motivated, thought Greeley, by a thorough detestation of the American people and their traditions, and wished to hasten on the destruction of American society. Moreover, in Greeley's view the resistance movement did not even achieve its own objectives: it actually prolonged the war and made its resolution more difficult. It is not easy to provide evidence on one side or another of this dispute, but having examined what evidence is available, Noam Chomsky concluded that although in the short term there were some indications that mass demonstrations and civil disobedience antagonized sections of the population which preferred not to be disturbed, the movement 'had an appreciative effect in bringing many people to examine their complicity and to draw them to the kinds of actions that influenced policy makers' (*For Reasons of State*, p. 291). It prevented the war from sliding into oblivion. An 'invisible war' would not have provoked any reaction. Greeley's suggested alternative – free and open discussion of the issues – would have left things very much as they were. What he dismissed as 'the protesting rabble' anticipated more exactly what would become the mood of the nation by 1975.

It would be quite impossible to deny the increasing 'politicization' of the Church since 1965. Interpretation is more difficult, partly because of the endless diversity of local situations, partly because there was no *one* way of justifying church involvement in politics. The unity of human life, material and spiritual, was one firm starting-point which led to an awakening of the social conscience and the feeling that certain minimum material and economic conditions are needed for the spiritual life to flourish. Man needs bread to live, even if he does not live by bread alone. We have already noted the influence of Marxism: it is not disgraceful to admit that many Christians learned from Marxists a great deal about the analysis of society and how to move from abstract teaching towards practical involvement, from preaching to commitment. That could be done without swallowing the baited hook of 'dialectical materialism', or even nibbling at it. A Christian personalism, which refused to subordinate the human person to state or party, was the best safeguard against that kind of surrender.

It is true that individuals could embark on the political path only to discover that it was a slippery slope which dumped them at the bottom of the hill of faith. For them secularization was not a theory but an experience, as political commitment came to replace a superfluous ethereal message. But just as many found that their faith and their political commitment mutually supported each other. It is also true that on the fashionable left there could be as much cant, self-deception and knavery as on the hide-bound right; the human condition has not yet been transformed. It is true finally that the Church could not be faithful to its vocation if it declined into a social-welfare organization or a political pressure group; the assertion of God as transcendent and Jesus as the Lord is the basis of anything else the Church has to say. But there was no need to contrast and oppose the love of God and the love of man. Karl Rahner had developed systematically what most Christians come to know by experience: the unity of the two loves. He expressed it characteristically in two propositions: that the love of God implies and unfolds into the love of man; and that the love of man implies and opens out into the love of God – if we let it. This helps to explain, on the deepest level, why the Church began to take politics seriously and to discern the face of Christ in what Camus called 'the blood-stained face of history in our own times'.

Chapter 13

Up from the Underground

A dialectical tension between the framework of the
Church and its points of growth seems to be a condition of Christian existence

HERBERT McCABE, OP
in *New Blackfriars*, February 1967.

There is more to the Church than bishops and cardinals. Initiatives
do not always spring from above. So this chapter is concerned with
the little groups that have arisen almost everywhere throughout the
last decade, with the stirrings that have come from the grass-
roots. They are important because they have come about in response
to a need and not a theory. They are important because it is in
small face-to-face communities that people feel at home and at
ease. And they are important as a factor for renewal. In *The Age of
Discontinuity* Peter Drucker pointed out how inflexible and
resistant to change large organizations can be. 'Large organizations
cannot be versatile. A large organization is effective through its
mass rather than its agility. Fleas can jump many times their own
height, but not elephants' (*The Age of Discontinuity*, p. 179). This
helps to explain why, alongside the larger groupings of the diocese
(which never meets) and the parish (in urban areas too big for
personal contacts), small and versatile groups began to proliferate.
They could act as a kind of research institute or experimental
centre alongside the larger body.

The small groups were freer and had more scope than the official
Church. They could try things out and make mistakes. They could
be alarmingly naïve and uncritical. Belonging to a small group could
be an exciting experience, since it involved cocking a snook at the
ecclesiastical authorities. This aspect of 'the underground Church',
as it was briefly known, was summed up in David Lodge's novel,

The British Museum Is Falling Down. He describes a society called the Dollingerites which existed to write outspoken letters to the Catholic press. Their unofficial chaplain was Fr Bill Wildfire, OP, who, 'after a few beers, could be coaxed into questioning the doctrine of Mary's Assumption into heaven . . . It often seemed to Adam that many of the Dollingerites declined to follow the example of their patron mainly because the liberal conscience has a more thrilling existence within the Church than without it' (p. 67).

But the pleasures of bishop-baiting proved short-lived, and the 'little groups' began to correspond to deeper needs. It is difficult to hit on the appropriate vocabulary to describe this rather sprawling phenomenon which has to cover everything from communes to prayer groups, from the politically committed to the politically indifferent, from those who shared everyday life to those who shared a common cause. French and other Latin speakers talked about '*communautés de base*', which translates somewhat clumsily as 'basic communities', an expression that never caught on. '*Communautés de base*' was not merely a neutral descriptive term: it was from these basic cells that the Church or society was to be prodded and goaded into renewal. This conviction was shared by most of the members of 'little groups'. They were the ones who continued to hope in the possibility of the regeneration of the Church and society, however differently they envisaged it. The movement affected religious men and women, and large barracks-like institutions were exchanged for more informal groupings on the commune model in which life was often gratifyingly uncomfortable. Yet despite an immense diversity of life-style and even purpose, the 'little groups' had four general characteristics.

They were *spontaneous*. No one ordered them into existence. They welled up from below in response to some felt need. As 'Catholic Action', the organized attempt to mobilize Catholics for the apostolate by categories, fell into decline, its place was taken by 'little groups'. Their 'spontaneity', furthermore, could be contrasted with the stiffly regulated formality of the 'official Church' or the 'institution'. It was easy to contrast the institution – with its immediate associations of prisons and hospitals – with the free-flowing, open-minded grouping in which the Holy Spirit had elbow-room. In Holland there were a large number of groups. Shalom at Odijk some ten kilometres from Utrecht became celebrated for its *agape*, 'a meal which gives hunger and thirst'. In a number of books Theo Westow developed the idea that the Church itself is not so much an institution as a movement. This admirably caught the spirit of the times and the aspiration of the little groups. They filled a real emotional gap. They needed only a minimum of organization. They were provisional and could disband without too much upset. They claimed no sacred or absolute status.

Secondly, they represented an *alternative* view of the Church or society. The Catholic Renewal Movement in Britain, for example, sprang into existence after *Humanae Vitae*. It was born of a desire to help those priests against whom disciplinary action was being taken. It was neatly known as 'Cardinal Heenan's unwanted baby'. But soon it broadened its scope to include the whole field of renewal and ecumenism. Most movements begin by challenging a system which is out of harmony with their aspirations. They define themselves at first by what they are opposed to.

Thirdly, little groups were *on a human scale*. This may be their most important feature. Modern man can so easily feel lost in the crowd, anonymous in the vast impersonality of city life and unable to affect what happens in the wider world. He needs a place where he can be addressed by name. In the 'little group' the Church 'came home', i.e. was experienced as a vivid and transforming personal reality. But the little group should not be dismissed as a sentimental refuge from the raw toughness of life in the twentieth century, an oasis for malcontents or a haven of repose. Whether concerned primarily with politics or prayer, most groups knew that they came together not to form a pious introverted huddle but for the world. They had a task and a mission. They had to assimilate personally the values of the Gospel and to change the unjust structures of society. Sociological and psychological laws were invoked to suggest that Christian community could in any case best be realized in groups of about thirty people (cf. Michael M. Winter, *Mission or Maintenance?*).

The fourth feature of little groups was that sooner or later they had to raise the question of celebrating the Eucharist. For them the

Eucharist ceased to be a 'churchy' affair and became a much more spontaneous offering of the group's shared work and worries. The desire for the Eucharist could be taken as one test of the religious authenticity of little groups; for the religious spirit is shown where the mystery of God is recognized as something which we cannot give to ourselves, but only receive. That raised, quite naturally, the question of ministry. It is taken for granted that parish priests and university chaplains should be appointed from above and arrive in places with which they are totally unacquainted; but little groups could not bear such impersonality. So they made use of sympathetic monks and friars who were always ready to travel. Sometimes they felt under pressure to appoint their own 'ministers'. The temptation was all the greater in the informal atmosphere of the small group where no vestments distinguished the 'president' and everyone was a brother.

One further generalization may be risked. If little groups can be regarded as experimental bodies alongside the larger organization, a great deal will depend on how the parent body handles them. If authority descends upon them with all the weight it can command, bans and hectors them, dismisses their priests and disapproves of their liturgy, then the 'little groups' will inevitably be pushed into the margin of church life. If they are persecuted, their isolation is reinforced. They are driven still further into opposition, become more radical in the questions they ask and more 'messianic' in their sense of being heralds of the dawning future. When this happens, the traditional roles can be reversed. As Rosemary Radford Ruether put it: 'In a real sense . . . it is the bishops who become the excommunicated, while a thousand flowers bloom in the open fields around their fortress. The people, not the bishops, define the social possibilities which they choose to call Roman Catholicism' ('Continuing Reform after Vatican II', in *The Month*, March 1973, p. 96). But there is a long way to go before that point is reached. Meanwhile, shrewder bishops can follow the alternative policy and welcome the existence of little groups as a step towards the building of real community. This welcoming policy may resemble the 'repressive tolerance' of which Marcuse speaks: the radicals are tamed and domesticated by being put on committees and commissions. Their teeth are drawn. But this is the way their valuable experience can be made available to the rest of the Church.

The phenomenon of '*communautés de base*' was sufficiently important to be considered by the 1974 Synod of Bishops in the context of 'Evangelization', though its final document was little more than a list (*Elenchus*) of the problems to which they give rise. Difficulties of definition were noted – some wanting to include 'house masses' in the concept and others any meeting of Catholic Action. After much argument, the constitutive elements of 'basic communities' were said to be: 'A community of faith, prayer, brotherly love and mission; a sharing in the liturgy of the word and the Eucharist; the witness of life; active involvement in the better ordering of society' (10, 3). This description was not wholly inaccurate, but it was the result of a strangely *a priori* method of work. Instead of looking at what was actually there, the Synod defined '*communautés de base*' in a rather lofty and idealistic way, and then was able to judge existing communities in the light of the definition it had just put forward. Its main concern was that the 'little groups' should be integrated into the life of the parish and the diocese, and that they should be 'rightly ordered and free from any divisiveness'. In other words, the 'little groups' were to be taken over and assimilated. Though some groups might accept this, not all would by any means; and the attempt to impose a pattern on them revealed a misunderstanding of their spontaneous origin and desire for freedom.

The Synod's judgement was greatly influenced by the Italian situation. Far from being integrated, the Italian 'little groups' were a challenging and dissenting thorn in the side of the official Church. The Isolotto case was a prototype of future events. Few had even heard of Isolotto, a small commune on the banks of the river Arno near Florence, but in autumn 1968 it became a national, and then an international, symbol. On the surface it was simply a conflict between a bishop, Cardinal Florit, and a parish priest, Don Enzo Mazzi. Such disputes are banal, and history does not usually dwell on them. What happened at Isolotto was variously interpreted. For some it was another episode in the long Florentine battle for spiritual freedom. Others saw it as an instance of

Catholic-Communist co-operation on the local level, an anticipation of the 'historic compromise'. Again it was seen as a serious attempt to put into practice the teaching of Vatican II as it applied in a working-class milieu. The laypeople of Isolotto wanted to incarnate the Gospel in the factories where they worked, and that meant shared struggles, shared poverty, shared trials. But this solidarity with their fellow workers immediately led to problems with the institution. If 'incarnation' is to be preferred to separation, what would happen to the 'separated' Christian Democratic Party, to the separated Christian trades unions, and all other organizations which wore the 'Catholic label'? At Isolotto they chose solidarity rather than separation.

The affair started innocently enough in September 1968 when priests and members of the parish wrote a letter in support of a group of 'protesting Christians' who were occupying the Duomo in Florence. A few days later Don Mazzi, the parish priest, received a letter from Cardinal Florit expressing grave displeasure. Parish meetings were organized, there were excited newspaper articles, *Osservatore Romano* joined in, and over a hundred priests of the diocese wrote to Cardinal Florit in support of Don Mazzi. As happens in such cases, the precise point at issue was quickly obscured, and the affair seemed to be petering out when on 4 December 1968 Cardinal Florit dismissed Don Mazzi from his post as parish priest. The grounds were that he disapproved of the Isolotto catechism, *Incontro a Christo*, which had been published late in September. Indignation grew. The school-children went on strike. Parish assemblies called for the dismissal of the Cardinal. Cardinal Florit, however, was not a man to refuse what he called a 'paternal dialogue' and he received Don Mazzi with a group of parishioners. Some of their exchanges were recorded and they provide a classic instance of misunderstanding between the claims of the law and the claims, admittedly confused and stammering, of love. A woman said to the Cardinal: 'We want you to be a brother, a true father, according to the Gospel.' She received the rather dismal answer: 'I have to answer for my actions to God and my superiors.' The woman insisted: 'But what about people? What do people mean for you, and the Church which is made up of people?'

The Cardinal missed this opportunity: 'Now you are getting polemical. We are supposed to be having a dialogue. Let's not get polemical.' A little later a layman said: 'We need to work through love: the world has too many laws and too little love.' To this aspiration the Cardinal could only reply, 'It would be a splendid thing if we could rely on love alone, but we are not perfect and so the law is needed.' The law was put into effect. Don Mazzi was dismissed. Seven years later, however, he still presides at the Eucharist in Isolotto, but on the piazza outside the church. His successor as official parish priest presides inside. To understand what happened at Isolotto, wrote Don Mazzi, you have to see it as the dashing of years of effort to implant the Gospel among the working people of Florence (*L'Altra Chiesa in Italia*, p. 300).

Once groups like Isolotto were pushed into opposition, they provided a natural breeding ground for the extreme left and Christians for Socialism. Not only that, but they began to apply their political analysis to the Church itself. Reviews like *Nuovi Tempi* and *COM* came to regard the Church as a power system which made use of the ideology of humility and obedience to maintain the *status quo*. The alliance with the Christian Democratic Party tied the Church to the rich and the powerful. In Italy much of post-conciliar ecclesiastical rhetoric could be flagrantly contradicted by experience: those looking for homes or living in the shanty-towns which surrounded Rome were not likely to appreciate speeches on 'the Church of the poor' since they knew how much property in the city belonged to the Church. The Concordat – originally contracted with Mussolini – seemed to them to subordinate the Church to the State. In exchange for certain privileges, notably tax-exemption, the Church provided chaplains for the army and blessed 'the established disorder'.

This kind of mixed politico-religious analysis has become very widespread in Italy. Arbitrary acts of authority give it new life. In autumn 1974, for example, the parish of the Sacred Heart in the diocese of Acerenza in southern Italy was up in arms over the dismissal of its parish priest, Don Marco Bisceglia. His crime was political commitment. On 6 October 1974 a crowd of over a

thousand gathered in the parish church, thus refuting the assertion
of the diocesan authorities that the group 'did not represent the
parish of the Sacred Heart, the great majority of which was
opposed to its socio-revolutionary activities'. At a Mass celebrated
by Don Marco with twenty concelebrating priests, messages were
read out from other dissident communities. The message from
Giovanni Franzoni, ex-abbot of St Paul's without the Walls, was
typical of their tone. 'The people', he declared, 'must recover the
Church for themselves and abandon those who exploit the Church
in the name of political power and the dominant class.' Such
rhetoric may not make the nations tremble, but it alarms the
Vatican to discover again and again how readily such appeals find
an echo. Don Marco himself explained: 'We are not against the
Church, but we are against those who, instead of serving the poor
and the oppressed, become themselves oppressors in the name of
the Gospel.' And he called for a removal of the 'curse' of depend-
ence under which the Mezzogiorno or south of Italy labours.

In Italy one can see in an extreme form a tendency which is
found more fitfully elsewhere: the growth of an 'alternative' or
'parallel' Church. It strikes the Roman imagination vividly and
colours the judgement of other dissenting movements, from the
abbey of Boquen in France, which has tried to evolve a new form of
mixed community, to the American 'underground Church'. Yet
surprisingly there has not been a major schism or collective
breakaway from the Church in the last decade. There have been
clamorous individual departures, much individual tiptoeing away,
but no group goodbyes. Part of the reason is that the notion of
'leaving the Church' has been drained of much of its meaning. If
Christian faith is recognized as essentially a community affair,
then to cut oneself off from the community is a strange way to
manifest Christian faith. Charles Davis spoke of being a 'dis-
affiliated Christian'. Individuals may have followed him along that
path, but on the whole, groups have not despite finding themselves at odds with authority in the Church. Catholics have been
so frequently exhorted to 'be the Church' or told that they *were*
the Church, that they have come to believe it. And so 'belonging'
to the Church becomes a question of self-description. When the

'frontiers' of the Church are harder to locate, the terms 'inside' and 'outside' lose much of their precision.

Moreover, most of the spontaneous movements and little groups do not require continual reassurance from the 'official Church' in order to feel authentic. They make minimum demands on the hierarchy. The point was made by Fr Herbert McCabe in *New Blackfriars*: 'Nobody in England expects to be guided and encouraged in his Christian life by pastoral letters – it is a matter of gratified astonishment when they have any theological content at all; this is not what we have come to expect of bishops . . . They provide merely an administrative context within which really vital and immediately relevant institutions can exist. That the established hierarchy is also a hindrance to these groups is obvious and only to be expected' (*New Blackfriars*, February 1967). And he went on to speak of the necessary 'dialectical tension between the Church's framework and its points of growth'. The tension quickly manifested itself, for it was after this 'comment' that Fr McCabe was dismissed from his post as editor of *New Blackfriars*; but with a twist of the dialectic he was back, unchastened, within two years. Once the McCabe position is accepted, that to be a Catholic is to be linked 'to areas of Christian truth beyond our own particular experience and ultimately to truths beyond any experience', then episcopal crassness or inadequacy become less dismaying and the sense of belonging less onerous. Of course tensions remain. But there is no other way for the Church to change. Authority ends by sanctioning what it at first deplored. The new is never welcome in advance.

It was argued that dissent in the Church could be creative in the long term; it was only in the short term that it appeared disruptive. This consoling theory depended on the conciliar teaching that the special or 'charismatic' gifts of grace were in principle showered on the whole People of God (*On the Church*, 12), and the task of authority in the Church was to discern the grace that was emerging. It might take time. But the Spirit could strike where he was least expected. He was not tied down. He was, as Cardinal Suenens frequently said, 'the principle of surprise in the Church'. Yet even while the Spirit was being invoked in this way to legiti-

The Runaway Church

mate dissent, another spontaneous movement of a completely different character was beginning to use Spirit-language for quite different ends. There was a reaction against the preoccupying concern with politics and a turning to prayer. If the characteristic song of the 1960s was 'We Shall Overcome', the 1970s began to sing 'Amazing Grace'. The 'charismatic movement' came into existence.

At first the charismatic movement was regarded with extreme suspicion as a form of Catholic revivalism, a dangerous form of that enthusiasm studied by Ronald Knox; but by 1975 it appeared to many to be the most encouraging and hopeful sign to be seen as they anxiously scanned the horizon. Cardinal Suenens had given a blessing to the movement with his book *A New Pentecost?* and Pope Paul made discriminating but favourable references to it at audiences on 17 October 1974 and 19 May 1975. This may seem like a classical operation in the 'taking over' of a spontaneous movement, but there is plenty of evidence that the Catholic charismatics were only too willing to be taken over. They deliberately sought to reconcile charism and institution, inspiration from within and approval from without. They want to be respectable and respected.

But what is the charismatic movement? It denies, first of all, that it is a 'movement', and consequently that it has 'leaders' in any conventional sense. The impact of the Spirit cannot be predicted or organized in this way, and it is the Spirit who impels and sustains the whole work. Still, even charismatics cannot deny that someone has to edit the bulletin and arrange the meetings, and charismatics proudly point to their rapid statistical growth as evidence that the Spirit is really with them. Their first conference at Notre Dame, Indiana, in 1968 gathered 87 people: by 1974 they had assembled 27,000 at Notre Dame, and in the following year over 10,000 were in Rome for the Feast of Pentecost. There are said to be at least 200,000 Catholic charismatics in the USA. This is the spectacular development of something which began very modestly.

In 1967 Kevin Ranaghan, then lecturing in liturgy at Notre Dame, came across a group of friends from Duquesne University who had experienced the outpouring of the Holy Spirit in prayer meetings. 'I felt angry', he explained, 'that good liberal-minded Catholics should slip back into such a fundamentalist approach. Yet it bore fruit in our lives, and the release of the Spirit worked a transformation in us. For six weeks we were kicking and screaming against it, no doubt out of fear of being changed, but then in March 1967 we prayed with them and during that prayer my wife and I enjoyed the almost tangible presence of Jesus in the room.' This was how Kevin Ranaghan looked back on the experience at a press conference in Rome in 1974. It was a disarming presentation of the charismatic movement, and was no doubt intended to be. Ranaghan's account of the 'fruits' of the Spirit was equally reassuring: 'We found a new ability to praise God in prayer, a new love for the scripture and for the Eucharist, a new ability to relate to each other constructively and lovingly, a new power to lead a Christian life in a gutsy kind of way.'

Having discovered the power of the Spirit, they were impelled to think of living in community. In 1971 twenty-nine people agreed to come together, moved by a 'desire to share their lives and live as brothers and sisters'. Thus 'The People of Praise' was founded. They wanted to 'break away from spiritual individualism, because they had been brought to a new understanding of the body of Christ'. By now the South Bend, Indiana, community consists of 138 adults and 160 children – not all under the same roof. In what was perhaps a significant phrase, Ranaghan added that they had found that 'an environment of Christian community provides an alternative to living under pressure in the secular world'. But he emphasized that the type of community life they led was more lay than religious.

Many accusations, fair and unfair, have been levelled at the Catholic charismatics. Dr William Storey, who was himself one of the founders of the movement, has accused its leadership of authoritarianism, criticized its 'manifestation of conscience' procedure, denounced the confusion of liturgical priorities 'in which the celebration of the Eucharist is sometimes ranked below charismatic prayer service', and warned against its scriptural fundamentalism. The more usual charge is that of elitism and exclusivism. Charismatics tend to smile wearily as these accusations are made. Since the experience of the Spirit is self-validating, it is difficult to put it into clumsy words for the benefit of the uninitiated. Trying hard, they say that of course no one has a monopoly of the Holy Spirit: he can be present wherever two or three are gathered together in the name of Christ. Cardinal Suenens goes further and holds that the aim of the movement should be to make itself redundant and disappear as soon as possible: just as the 'liturgical movement' has now flowed into the mainstream of the Church's life and become indistinguishable from it, so the 'charismatic movement' will cease to be a distinct movement and become a *fait accompli*. It will animate the dry bones of the Church's structure, be present everywhere without being identifiable, and fulfil the Council's promise of spiritual renewal.

Whether one accepts the critical or the optimistic account of the charismatic movement, it is clear that this version of Pente-costalism has undergone considerable adaptation to make it acceptable in a Catholic setting. In classical Pentecostalism 'baptism in the Spirit' (sometimes called 'baptism of the Holy Spirit') is the fundamental experience. It is held to be identical with that of the first Christians on the day of Pentecost, and it will usually be confirmed by tangible signs, notably that of *glossolalia* or speaking in tongues. Catholics tend to transform these two doctrines utterly. 'Baptism in the Spirit', so far from being a new and original experience, is presented instead as the ratification of what is already sacramentally given. 'For Catholics', wrote Dorothy Ranaghan, 'this experience is a renewal, making our baptismal initiation as children now concrete and explicit on a mature level. It is in this sense that we speak of baptism in the Holy Spirit' (*As the Spirit Leads Us*, p. 8). The gift of tongues, though forming part of the expectations of someone joining a charismatic group, is not made a criterion for admission. A string of unintelligible syllables, rhythmic but varied: that is how the 'gift of tongues' strikes the outside observer. Cardinal Suenens attempts to show that it is neither miraculous nor pathological, and he links it with the simpler, non-discursive forms of prayer that have been held in honour by the mystics (*A New Pentecost?*, pp. 99–104). He sees the 'gift of tongues' as providing a release from the shyness, inhibitions and defences which surround us when we try to pray with others. 'It helps us', he writes, 'to cross a threshold and, in doing so, attain a new freedom in our surrender to God' (ibid., p. 102).

In this adaptation neo-Pentecostalism is integrated into an older Catholic tradition. It recalls, for example, the spiritual teaching of the French seventeenth-century Jesuit, Louis Lallement, who laid great stress on the Holy Spirit and spoke of the need for a 'second conversion' in maturity. Thus adapted, the Catholic charismatic movement becomes less dangerous and more acceptable. Yet its vitality is undeniable. It can rout its critics by showing that they do not know what they are talking about. But there are reasons for caution. It is possible, with Cardinal Suenens, to interpret the charismatic movement as the revival of a form of prayer which the rationalism of the liturgy has driven out of the Church, and to compare the 'gift of tongues' with the 'gift of tears'. But it is also possible to see more disquieting psychological factors at work in the charismatic movement. Killian McDonnell, OSB, a sympathetic witness, compares it with the hippy movement, T-groups, sensitivity sessions and the Jesus People: 'These movements belong to a post-literary culture which is experience-oriented, unstructured, spontaneous, inward, almost atomistic in its concern for the now at the expense of history, pursuing illumination, dominated by a sense of presence, sure that somewhere there is ultimate worth. To a greater or lesser degree the movement represents a turning back to recapture the original unstructured experience of the meaning of life at a level which, like tongues, is unutterable' ('Catholic Charismatics', in *Commonweal*, 5 May 1972). The temptation of the charismatic movement is to withdraw from the world and create a haven of private consolation. For that reason it cannot be the only harbinger of the future.

Indeed, the two principal groups we have considered in this chapter, the politically minded dissidents and the charismatics, represent two extremes of the Church's life. They need each other more than they are prepared to admit, and each could bring a corrective to the other. At worst the political groups sacrifice the

Kingdom to the world while the charismatics sacrifice the world to the Kingdom. At best the charismatics could bring a dimension of prayer to the political groups, who in turn could prevent the charismatics from becoming a sect which has given up the expectation of changing the world. But one cannot confidently predict that they will actually begin to talk to each other. The extremes illustrate the dangers without exhausting the possibilities. Most small groups are less clear-cut in their positions. They waver between prayer and commitment, the assertion of the transcendent and the claims of the world. In short, they express in concentrated form the confusions and hesitations of committed Christians generally. But are they a pointer to the future?

Karl Rahner is one theologian who has frequently surmised what the future of the Church might be, while at the same time declaring that it is part of Christian faith not to know. He sees the emergence of small groups as the inevitable result of the collapse of Christendom – and by 'Christendom' he means that sociological situation, commoner in parts of mainland Europe than elsewhere, in which almost everyone in a given village or small town shared one faith and one liturgy. That world has disappeared, and in the modern city people come together because they freely choose to, not because social pressures oblige them to. This Rahner calls the 'diaspora' situation. He compares it with the primitive Church in which small groups evangelized the cities of the Roman empire. The move from Christendom to 'diaspora' is welcome in that it means that conventional 'sociological' religion is replaced by personally committed faith. But it also means that the days of the big Christian battalions are probably over, and that the 'little group' will become the more customary Christian unit than the large parish. In that case, the Church would discover a much simpler and more fraternal style. In so far as small groups are already living in this way, they anticipate the future.

Chapter 14

Honest Talk about Marriage

The Encyclical was an attempt both to find a solution
to a moral dilemma and to stem the undermining of
papal authority and to reassert it in the old style. It
failed on both counts . . . A document intended to
restore a position fomented a revolution

NORMAN ST JOHN STEVAS
The Agonizing Choice, pp. 7–8.

When Catholics spoke, without further qualification, of 'the
encyclical', they meant *Humanae Vitae*, published on 29 June 1968.
It was in fact the last encyclical of Pope Paul; after producing them
at a rate of one a year in the first five years of his pontificate, he
abandoned this literary form and showed no inclination to use it
again. As Milton's *Paradise Lost* exhausted the literary genre of the
epic, so *Humanae Vitae* put an end to encyclical letters. For once
the overworked phrase 'bombshell effect' fitted the situation.
Everyone could remember exactly where they were and precisely
what they were doing when the fall-out reached them. Political
parallels abounded. The encyclical came out only a few weeks
before the invasion of Czechoslovakia by Warsaw Pact forces, and
despite the incongruous disproportion between the two events,
there were those who saw them as comparable instances of
repression. Garry Wills used a different comparison: 'With
Humanae Vitae . . . Pope Paul did to his reign what Lyndon
Johnson did with the Vietnam War. From that moment everything
seemed to run downhill' (*Bare Ruined Choirs*, p. 161). What is
certain is that from the autumn of 1968 the Pope's tone became
increasingly pessimistic. Though he tried to be cheerful, gloom
would keep breaking in. He began to see enemies lurking and
dangers threatening on all sides. The incomprehension of the
world was to be expected: the incomprehension of the Church was
his cross.

Yet he had been urged, time and time again, to 'settle' the question. In tactical terms, if no others, Pope Paul's mistake was implicitly to admit the possibility of change and then, just when it was beginning to be widely acceptable, to go counter to it. The essential assertions of the encyclical were that 'every marriage act (*quilibet matrimonii usus*) must remain open to the transmission of life' (11), and that the unitive and procreative aspects of sexual intercourse should not be separated from each other by any artificial intervention (12). They could only be separated 'naturally', i.e. by the rhythm method. This distinction – a modern one, developed largely by Pius XII in his 1951 address to midwives – was not easy to grasp, led to problems of timing, and produced marital tensions. It depended, moreover, on a particular interpretation of 'natural law' theory which linked parts of the body with given functions. The tongue, for instance, was made for truthtelling, and so lying was a misuse of its function and against the 'natural law'. What was wrong with this approach was its biological determinism, its vain attempt to split the human person into components, and its inability to comprehend that acts of intercourse needed to be understood in the light of the general pattern of the relationship.

The encyclical's reassertion of the 'natural law' argument was even more surprising in that it had been abandoned by the Council. In speaking of marriage, the Council had resolutely used personalistic criteria of judgement. It avoided the language of essences and functions. The constitution *On the Church in the Modern World* propounded no new doctrine, but its emphasis was distinctly new. It asserted clearly that marriage was not only good, but was a state of holiness: it is through their marriage, and not in spite of it, that married people work out their divine vocation; marriage is an enterprise of love, 'merging the human with the divine' (49). It followed, therefore, that sexuality in marriage was not a concession grudgingly made to the power of *eros*, nor simply the remedy for sexual drives which had somehow to be appeased, but that it had a positive, humanizing role. Sexual intercourse was seen not simply as the contact of two bodies, but as a person-to-person act, and so a form of expression, of giving and receiving, a language of love which 'involves the good of the whole person'. All dualism was avoided.

None of this settled the question of birth-control, nor was it meant to. But it laid the foundations for a re-examination of the hitherto accepted doctrine. The constitution *On the Church in the Modern World* conceded that marriage 'is not instituted solely for procreation', that the married have to fulfil their procreative task 'with human and Christian responsibility', and that they are 'co-operators with the love of God the Creator, and . . . so to speak, the interpreters of that love' (50). But the love of God was essentially one of free choice, and 'human and Christian responsibility' suggested that some attention should be paid to overpopulation. Moreover, the text stated clearly that the judgement on the spacing and number of children should 'ultimately' depend on the parents themselves (50). It would prove difficult to wrest back the right to decide once it had been conceded. Even more significant was the Council's refusal to endorse the traditional distinction between the primary (procreation) and the secondary (mutual comfort) ends of marriage. Arriving at the point where it might naturally have made the distinction, the pastoral constitution ostentatiously refuses to make it. True, it regards children as 'the supreme gift of marriage' (50) and the embodiment of the parents' love, but it adds that the 'other purposes of matrimony' are of no less account (*'non posthabitis ceteris matrimonii finibus'*, 50). Though there were balancing passages designed to exclude any judgement based merely on 'sincere intentions or on an evaluation of motives' (51), it was not difficult to derive from these considerations a moral argument which at the very least did not exclude contraception, and might even make it a duty.

But what contributed even more powerfully to the expectations of change was the existence of the Pontifical Commission which had been set up by Pope John in 1962. Membership went from six to eighteen in 1964. Eventually it escalated to reach sixty-four members, some of whom were present not as experts so much as watchdogs of orthodoxy: Cardinals Heenan of Westminster and Doepfner of Munich were vice-presidents. Proceedings were in secret, but inevitably news filtered out. A crucial

turning-point was reached on 23 April 1966 when the four theologians on the Commission who upheld the traditional opinion
admitted that they could not show the intrinsic evil of contraception on the basis of the natural law alone. They were therefore
thrown back on authority as the last line of defence. Dr John
Marshall, an English neurologist who was one of the original six
members of Pope John's Commission, described his reactions to
this damaging admission: 'For me this was certainly the crisis
point in a slow and painful evolution, for if the Church held that
contraception was intrinsically evil because it was contrary to
natural law, it seemed that able and sincere theologians who
earnestly believed in the evil of contraception and had worked hard
at the problem should be able to demonstrate this with some
degree of conviction' (*The Times*, 3 August 1968). Their total
inability to do so was alarming for those who wished to defend the
tradition. Onan was no help either. The attempt to base a scriptural
argument on his case had long since been abandoned, and it was
shown that the unfortunate Onan had been calumniated: his crime
was not any form of *coitus interruptus* but rather a lack of tribal
loyalty in withholding heirs from his dead brother's line (Genesis
38:8–10). But if both scripture and natural law proved to be
fragile and unreliable reeds, the whole case was imperilled.

All the more if a counter-argument could be produced. It was
produced by the fifteen remaining theologian members of the
Commission, and their influence could be seen in the 'majority
report' which was leaked to the press in April 1967 (*National
Catholic Reporter*, 19 April; *The Tablet*, 22 April). It was not in
fact a report of a majority but the report of the Commission itself,
which made it even more significant. In a preliminary section
called 'Pastoral Approaches' it summarized the teaching of Vatican
II to bring out the new emphases developed above. This was
followed by a decisive theological section which argued that the
morality of sexual acts between the married depends on 'the ordering of their actions in a fruitful married life, that is one that is
practised with responsible, generous and prudent parenthood. It
does not depend, then, on the direct fecundity of each and every
sexual act. An egotistical, hedonistic and contraceptive way

followed arbitrarily can never be justified.' The Commission then listed the new factors of which they had taken account, notably 'social changes in matrimony and the family, especially in the role of women; lowering of the infant mortality rate; new bodies of knowledge in biology, psychology, sexuality and demography; a changed estimation of the value and meaning of human sexuality and of conjugal relations; most of all, a better grasp of the duty of man to humanize and to bring to greater perfection for the life of man what is given in nature'.

The Commission's conclusion was that the decision should be left to the individual couple, not as an arbitrary choice but as a conscientious one, made in the light of a complex set of values. These arguments had evidently made an impression on Cardinal Heenan, for in his pastoral letter of Trinity Sunday 1966 he looked forward to the next meeting of the Commission, and hinted unmistakably and in typical staccato style at change: 'Physical science has revealed new facts about nature. Medicine and psychology have made discoveries about human life itself. Although truth remains the same, our knowledge of it is always increasing. Some of our notions of right and wrong have also undergone change.' The pastoral letter made no sense except as a preparation of public opinion for change.

Humanae Vitae cruelly dashed all these expectations. It generated the most passionate and extensive debate that the post-conciliar Church has known: disappointed hopes and off-the-cuff statements were eagerly seized upon by the media. 'Why', asked the editor of *Herder Correspondence*, 'bother with the private theological opinion of the Bishop of Rome?' Dr André Hellegers, an obstetrician who had been a member of the ignored Commission, said: 'I cannot believe that salvation is based on contraception by temperature and damnation is based on rubber.' The riposte was equally vigorous from the other side. Cardinal Pericle Felici, who had been secretary-general of the Council and has since been busy with the revision of the canon law, wrote an article in *Osservatore Romano* which called for obedience to the Pope whether he was right or wrong. 'The possible mistake of the superior', he confidently declared, oblivious of all the harm done in this century by unconditional obedience, 'does not authorize the disobedience of subjects.' Still, this was the first admission in *Osservatore Romano* that there might be some theoretical possibility of a pontifical mistake. For the most part the paper reported only favourable comments on the encyclical, gratefully noted the vast number of letters which had poured in praising the Pope's 'serenity and courage', maintained that only a minority of obstinate and misguided dissidents disagreed, and in its excitement compared the prose of *The Economist* to that of Nazi newspapers like *Angriff* and *Schwarze Korps*. In short, *Osservatore Romano* ran true to form. Cardinal Montini had said in 1961 that it reported not what actually happened, but what it thought ought to have happened.

The questions came crowding in from all sides. The encyclical had not been put forward under the formal label of 'infallible': what kind of assent, then, did it expect and require, and what was to be done about those who disagreed? The proper sphere of the *magisterium* or teaching authority of the Church was the definition of what truly belonged to divine revelation: how far could it go in the interpretation of natural law? What did it mean to speak of 'natural law' when ordinary people, or even theologians using their reasoning powers, could not provide evidence for it? How far was the experience of other Christians, who admitted the possibility of contraception, relevant? Or were they to be dismissed as of no account, despite their having a married clergy which was likely to be better informed on the question? Where were the world's bishops in the shaping and development of the encyclical? Had not the Pope ridden rough-shod over the collegial process? The questions affected the content, the weight, the method, the consequences, and even the meaning of *Humanae Vitae*.

Nor can it be candidly said that any of them have been answered in a satisfactory manner subsequently; they have rather been swept under the carpet. It is a cavalier way to deal with a deep human problem. The American Jesuit moral theologian, Richard A. McCormick, summarized reactions after the encyclical as, in order, 'shock and/or solace, suspension, silence'. Silence prevails, disturbed by the occasional flurry of controversy: the result is that the gap between what is officially declared to be the case and what actually is the case has become embarrassing. In addition to the ordinary difficulties which afflict the honest discussion of sexual matters, the Church has added taboos, restrictions and prohibitions of her own. Insincerity on this question became a way of life.

The bishops were among the most embarrassed. Many of them became spokesmen for a cause in which they did not deeply believe. Hierarchies round the world were ordered by Cardinal Cicognani, Secretary of State at the Vatican, to produce a document in support of the encyclical. Most of them obliged, but introduced various types of 'pastoral approach' which modified the harshness of its impact. The Canadians, for example, stressed the possible conflict of duties between conjugal love, on the one hand, and the care and education of existing children or the health of the mother. Others stressed the rights of conscience, notably the Scandinavian bishops, whose statement cannot have been what Cardinal Cicognani had in mind. 'No one', they wrote, 'is to be regarded as an inferior Catholic on account of his divergent views.' More informal statements went further still. Cardinal Heenan, pressed hard in a television interview with David Frost to say what he would reply to a couple who wished to practise birth-control conscientiously, said without hesitation: 'God bless you. If they're following their conscience, then in the sight of God, which is all that matters – the priest, the bishop, the Pope doesn't matter compared with God – if every person is really dealing with Almighty God' (London Weekend Television, December 1968). The confused syntax could not alter the deep impression made on ordinary people by Cardinal Heenan's 'God bless you'; the falling-off in communion which had been noted in northern parishes was redressed. However, not everyone interpreted 'God bless you' as a legitimation of conscientious dissent: Archbishop Cardinale, at that time apostolic delegate in London, explained to Norman St John Stevas that 'God bless you' really meant 'God help you' (*The Agonizing Choice*, p. 170, n. 2).

It was unwise to cast doubt on the Cardinal's command of the English language. But though the sum-total of guilt feelings may have been diminished by such episcopally provided loopholes, the

graver question was that moral rules or 'norms' had been completely cut adrift from the moral *values* they were designed to
defend. Apologists for the encyclical frequently argued that
contraception was not wrong because it had been condemned, but
had been condemned because it was wrong. But they found the
same difficulty that the theologians of the Pontifical Commission
had encountered when they tried to substantiate this judgement:
so they resorted to attack and denounced what they called 'the
contraceptive mentality'. Thus the Irish bishops in their May
1975 pastoral letter on marriage alleged that 'the contraceptive
mentality is characterized by a lack of generosity of spirit and of
readiness to assume responsibility'. Others were still wilder in their
denunciations of the bogey of 'the contraceptive mentality' and
revealed a celibate's view of sexual pleasure 'for its own sake' as
an abandoned whoopee of mind-blowing selfishness. If Catholic
couples knew from their own experience that although the use of
contraception could be selfish and a matter of preferring the second
car to the third child, it was not always and not necessarily so.
Once the link between the rule ('No contraception') and the value
(an unselfish marriage) had been broken in this way, then the only
remaining grounds for obedience would be authority. But there is
no morality by proxy. Authority cannot substitute itself for the
moral decision. By making exaggerated and unverifiable claims,
authority lost both credit and credibility.

Every parish priest is perfectly well aware of the existence of
the gap between theory and practice. Whatever he may think about
it, he would not dream of denying that it exists. Yet the Vatican
has shown itself to be resolutely determined to pretend that there
is no gap. It is all the invention of 'self-styled liberals'. It is a
feature of strongly ideological modes of thinking that unpleasant
facts can be disposed of by the simple strategy of denial; but in
this instance the Vatican has not been content to wear blinkers – it
has intervened to repress any hint of opposition to its official
teaching. So much energy had gone into preserving the façade of
Catholic unity that some psychoanalytical explanation is called for.
But there can be no doubt about the vigour of the campaign waged
by the Secretariat of State. While most Catholic Christians have

decided that other moral issues such as overpopulation, environmental pollution, drugs, race and poverty are more important, the Vatican remains fixated on contraception.

That was why World Population Year, held in 1974, caused such grave anxiety. An intensive propaganda campaign in favour of birth-control was feared. To counteract this danger, the Secretariat of State produced a long letter, written in French, and sent it secretly to all the world's bishops. Vatican diplomats were invited to submit reports 'on trends of opinion and pressures that might arise', presumably hostile and dangerous trends. Although there was a laudable attempt to widen the debate, to emphasize the need for justice and to show that birth-control could not in itself be the way to solve the world's problem of feeding the hungry, there was also a marked insistence on enforcing the Catholic view, identified *tout court* with *Humanae Vitae*, not only on Catholics but on everyone: 'It is for the Church to guide the whole of mankind – the whole of man and every man – to salvation and to his moral and spiritual elevation' (text in *The Times*, 11 March 1974). This revived a form of Catholic imperialism which had long been supposed dead. The Vatican attached so much importance to the delegation which it sent to the World Population Conference that it screened its potential members with quite unusual thoroughness. Fr Philip Land, SJ, formerly professor at the Gregorian University and a member of the Justice and Peace Commission, was invited to state whether he would uphold *Humanae Vitae* or not. He frankly replied that although he had certain private reservations about the encyclical, he would keep them to himself. This lukewarm assent was not enough for the Secretariat of State and, shortly before the conference was due to start, Fr Land learned that his services would not be required in Bucharest. Cardinal Darmajuwomo of Indonesia, who had been invited privately, was headed off at the last moment on the grounds that his rank would embarrass the official delegation. The appearance of complete unanimity was achieved at this price.

Nor did it enhance the effectiveness of the Holy See's delegation. Their interventions were received with 'hostility, cynicism, boredom and distrust'. When the Vatican spokesmen tried to present their case at a press conference, they 'very rapidly antagonized the audience by their equivocation and evasiveness' ('Bitter Pills in Bucharest', John F. X. Harriott, in *The Month*, November 1974, p. 758). Yet Bishop Sarpong of Ghana gave a moving address on the value of life and the nature of human development which made clear the opportunity that was being missed. He was speaking in his own name. The inflexibility of the Vatican delegation, the fact that it was working to orders, meant that it could make no serious contribution to the debate. After Bucharest the nervousness became positively frenetic as a book commissioned by the Conference of International Catholic Organizations (OIC), due to appear in French, English and Spanish, was ordered to be withdrawn when publication was imminent. When that proved technically impossible, the editors were told to delete all reference to the fact that it originated with OIC. One might think that it must have perpetrated some outrageous crime to deserve such treatment. In fact it had treated the doctrine of *Humanae Vitae* with the greatest respect. It even included Bishop Gagnon's speech delivered at Bucharest as the most recent official statement. Yet the book was alleged to be 'anti-natalist' in tone, to leave the door open for a subjective morality, and to present in one chapter a view of the family 'which does not correspond to what the Holy See demands in such circumstances'. Canon Moerman, editor of the volume and a man of impeccable credentials, was upset. Fr Arthur McCormack, a population expert, was amazed and wrote of the 'clumsy and naïve attempt to suppress a book of this sort and to think that it could be done in secret' (letter to *The Tablet*, 19 March 1975). Like all such interventions, it was counterproductive. But it is another indication of the way literal assent to *Humanae Vitae* was turned into a loyalty test, and superficial conformity secured by repressive means. Only the Vatican shows any enthusiasm for this policy. The thin red line has been drawn, and it will be defended tenaciously. The Vatican officials are like generals who continue to mark the movements of imaginary forces on the map: but nothing happens on the ground.

This obsession with contraception has made it difficult to apply the Council's personalist approach to related questions such as pre-marital intercourse, divorce, homosexuality. 'Catholic sexual morality needs a new start', said Gregory Baum ('Holy Sexuality', in *The Month*, March 1973, p. 108), and he knew that was an understatement. Yet there has been a fresh start among theologians at least, and a serious attempt to overcome the inherited picture of woman as temptress and instigator of evil. Once biological determinism was abandoned, it became impossible to equate sin with the violation of a biological function. Catholic theologians began to discover the ambiguity of sexuality. 'Turning to the insights of depth psychology,' said Baum, 'they became aware that sexuality is not always and not necessarily an expression of love and affection but may also be, and possibly always remains to some extent, an expression of destructive drives such as domination, possessiveness, anger and hostility. The moral quest in man's sexual life, therefore, is to make sexuality as much as possible an instrument of love and affection' (ibid., p. 105). Similar ideas have been developed by Stephan Pfürtner, whose book *Kirche und Sexualität* and public lectures stirred up vigorous controversy among the Swiss. The Swiss bishops were ready for dialogue, but the Congregation for the Doctrine of Faith intervened, judged Pfürtner without a hearing and denied him any possibility of an appeal. In order to continue his work the Danzig-born Professor of Moral Theology in the University of Fribourg left the Dominicans and the university. He did manage to have a final meeting with Cardinal Seper, prefect of the Congregation. He tentatively appealed to the 'rights of man'. Cardinal Seper replied that he did not find this expression in the Gospels.

Pfürtner's starting-point was the wide disparity between the officially received morality of the older generation and the actual morality of young people today, the 'generation without prejudices'. He found that young people, though disconcerting, nevertheless possessed a set of values which are authentic and convincing in their own order. He did not conclude, for example, that pre-marital intercourse should be permitted because it happens; he maintained that the fact that it happens raises a question which cannot be eluded unless there is to be no moral communication whatever between the generations. The questions have to be faced.

Have people been made subordinate to the law? Can intangible and inviolable laws be handed out on every problem of sexual morality as though all the answers were known in advance and possessed an absolute quality? Pfürtner came to believe that 'legalistic moralism' and the repressive 'cult of abnegation' had imposed quite unnecessary guilt complexes on millions of people. The cross was invoked too hastily. 'The cross of Christ', said Pfürtner, 'is altogether too great for us to use it to legitimate precise moral demands or an excessively narrow view of what it means to be human' (*Choisir*, March 1972, p. 7). Pfürtner's 'golden rule' is as follows: 'There is only one inalienable law which ought to prevail always and everywhere: love allied to reason.' As a good Dominican, Pfürtner sought to find confirmation for this principle in St Thomas Aquinas.

But it was not this criterion of morality which aroused alarm so much as his frank recognition of 'happiness' as the goal of sexuality. Pfürtner gave a lecture in Berne in which he developed ten 'theses'. The fourth of them reads: 'Sexuality should be primarily regarded as an opportunity for happiness, and for the fulfilment and liberation of human life. It can be regarded as a source of danger only to the extent that it threatens fulfilment and liberation.' Of course Pfürtner did not imagine sexuality to be no more than the unbridled pursuit of personal satisfaction. On the contrary, the sixth thesis declares that 'gratification at another's expense is immoral', and the seventh that 'sexuality by its very nature has social implications'. He was aware of the dangers of an *égoïsme à deux*. Pfürtner's views were sketchily developed, and took the form of a prologomenon to a future morality which would take seriously the incarnational and personalist principles stated by Vatican II. The Congregation for the Doctrine of Faith, on the other hand, regarded them as a confirmation of the worst forebodings of *Humanae Vitae*. There could be no doubt that the ready availability of contraceptives, by eliminating anxiety about pregnancy, led to greater 'sexual freedom'. But that did not necessarily mean licence or irresponsibility, still less the dire consequences predicted by *Humanae Vitae* for women, reduced to being 'a mere instrument for the satisfaction' of the desires of men (17). Many women claimed the contrary experience. Pfürtner's central question remained unanswered: are we to assume that the young of today, who tomorrow will be middle-aged, have no contribution to make to moral discourse until they have undergone a conversion to *Humanae Vitae*? And how likely is such a conversion?

While theologians were trying not very successfully to understand sexuality positively, canon lawyers were attempting to deal with the sad human consequences of marital breakdown. There was a growing body of opinion among them that the Church's treatment of marriage owed more to law than to theology. Even those canonists who were most opposed to divorce came to accept a widening of the grounds for annulment. They made great use of what is called 'lack of due discretion'. Since this term is not very illuminating for the layman, one needs to have recourse to the definition of a canon lawyer. Mgr W. P. Denning, of the Southwark Diocesan Matrimonial Tribunal, explains: 'It (lack of due discretion) means the inability of one party (or both parties) to establish and sustain a normal marital relationship . . . It is not enough to prove that the couple did not get on together. It has to be proved that from the very beginning there was something in one party which would make it impossible for them to get on together.' One gropes as in a fog to know what that might mean, but we are provided with examples which have succeeded in the courts: 'Homosexuality, serious immaturity, severe psychopathology, inadequate personality, obsessional-compulsive illness, depressive illness with obsessions, as well as the case of the compulsive liar' (*Clergy Bulletin*, January 1973). The scope is wide. But it is far from all-embracing. The victims of many a broken marriage might exhibit none of those symptoms, or they might exhibit them but not be able to prove the point to the satisfaction of the court. Is there any relief for them? Not in public, but canonists talk of a 'solution in the internal forum'. As for those who have civilly divorced and remarried, most of the discussion has centred on the pastoral need to admit such people to the sacraments. There are conditions: provided they show a true Christian spirit in their lives, that their present union is a stable one, and that scandal is avoided, they can be re-admitted to the sacraments. These views were put forward by Fr Bernard Häring in an article in *Concilium* in 1970 and also later by Ladislaus Orsy in *The Jurist*.

Even though canonists continue to reject the old charge that annulment is simply divorce under another name, many have begun to feel that it is not enough to tinker with the existing marriage law, that there is much that is dishonest, underhand or chancy in the present system, that the trying inquisitions of canonists into people's marital intimacies are unworthy or distasteful, and that there is need for a radical rethinking of the Church's teaching on marriage. The Council's stress on marriage as a 'communion of love' and a reflection of the covenant between Christ and his Church provided a clue and a starting-point. To stress covenant rather than contract was to move away from legal categories towards a more existentialist approach. In the contractual legal sense, a marriage might have ceased to exist and become a hollow sham or an agonizing prison, but that was irrelevant since the initial words of commitment had changed the situation 'ontologically', and therefore nothing could be done; but in existential terms the continuation of an intolerable marriage could hardly be considered an enrichment of the individuals or a glowing witness to the values of Christian marriage. Once more there was conflict between a moral (or juridical) principle which had been turned into an absolute, and the requirements of compassion and realism.

Scripture scholars made the first breach and pointed out the difficulty of deriving an absolute teaching from texts which interweave the message of Jesus with the interpretations and adaptations of the early Church. As George McCrae wrote: 'The Church of today must relate, not to an absolute divine law which is in practice inaccessible to our scholarly research, but to the process of identifying what is of Christ and what is Christian and entering into that process of discernment today' ('New Testament Perspectives on Divorce and Remarriage', in *Divorce and Remarriage in the Catholic Church*, edited by Lawrence G. Wrenn). The process of discernment today could also usefully refer to the experience of the first thousand years of the Church's existence, when there was no question of denying the means of grace to those who remarried after divorce; their situation was sometimes tolerated, either tacitly or explicitly. The Oriental Churches have also been less absolute. In his book *Divorce and Remarriage in the Catholic Church* Victor Pospishil argued that the indissolubility of marriage was presented by the New Testament as an *ideal*, and that exceptions might be permitted as 'a concession to human weakness' without undermining the ideal. He drew an analogy with the way widows and widowers were not forbidden to remarry, even though the sacramental nature of marriage implied that it would perdure beyond the grave. Marriage was indeed 'until death', but the death might include the death of the marriage.

The practical implications of these ideas have been developed most outstandingly by Mgr Stephen J. Kelleher especially in *Divorce and Remarriage for Catholics?* Dr Kelleher has worked on marriage tribunals since 1942, and from 1962 to 1968 was presiding judge of the New York tribunal. Experience taught him the inability of the Church to deal with the volume of potential marriage cases, but also that the existing law was the cause of much frustration, misery and injustice. At the insistence of the American bishops he was appointed to the Pontifical Commission for the Revision of the Code of Canon Law, where his views were greeted, according to another member of the same working group, 'with a stunned silence and total incomprehension' (John C. Barry, in *The Clergy Review*, August 1974, p. 508). After doing his five-year stint, Mgr Kelleher was dropped from the Commission without any reasons being given. Perhaps the reason was his insistence on calling a dead marriage a dead marriage. In his book he argues that since marriage is a relationship of love and self-giving, the absence of love and self-giving indicate the death of the marriage; a relationship which has become intolerable for both parties cannot be called a living marriage. According to Mgr Kelleher, the whole cumbersome paraphernalia of tribunal procedure ought to be entirely directed towards answering one question: Is this marriage dead? When it is dead, the fact should be admitted, as the Eastern Churches admit it without denying their belief in the ideal of indissolubility. Kelleher proposes what he calls a 'Welcome Home'

solution: once a marriage was acknowledged to be irrevocably
dead, each party would have a 'clear right to divorce', be able to
marry a second time, and be accepted into the Christian community. He or she would be fully welcomed at the Eucharist and
have his or her second marriage blessed by the Church. This,
concludes Kelleher, 'is the only human and Christian solution for
our time'.

These views have been widely taken up in America. The
National Divorced Catholics Conference assembled over four
hundred people at Boston in October 1974 and passed a resolution
asking the Church to 'change her authoritative teaching concerning
the meaning of Christian marriage so that the rights of Catholics
to divorce and remarry wholesomely and publicly in Christ and in
his Church will be acknowledged when, in fact, their first marriages
are irrevocably broken'. At their 1972 conference, appropriately
on the theme 'Divided We Stand', a liturgy of divorce was
presided over by Fr James Young. Suitable songs were chosen ('All
my trials, Lord, will soon be over' and 'It's too late, baby') and
at the parting of hands the couples were to say, separately, 'I . . .
declare before all present that our marriage has come to an end. I
beg forgiveness for all I have done that has wounded this relationship, and I promise to love you even though we are no longer man
and wife.' This was followed by a blessing that they might 'choose
life and love again' (in *National Catholic Reporter*, 3 November
1972). The divorcés themselves have not been the only ones to
plead their cause. At the eighth National Federation of Priests'
Councils meeting in 1975, Fr Charles Irvin insisted that divorced
and remarried Catholics 'need their daily bread in the Eucharist
just as much as anyone else: the Eucharist is not to be used as
reward or punishment'. However, a substantial minority opposed
this idea and said that any attempt to change the Church's position
would have an adverse effect.

Kelleher's proposals partly reflect the particular American
situation where by 1973 more than 12% of men and 14% of women
had been divorced. In some western states the divorce rate
reached 70% of the marriage rate. Attempts have been made to
draw some consolation from these disturbing facts by explaining

that modern Americans are simply more frank about admitting the failure of their marriage, and that previously unhappily married couples would have struggled along and suffered in silence. Andrew Greeley has tried to find consolation in another way: 'The principal crisis in the American family comes not so much from the fact that the family is going out of fashion as from the fact that Americans have such great expectations for the happiness to be achieved from marriage' (*Divorce and Remarriage in the Catholic Church*, edited by Lawrence G. Wrenn). The role of the Church, in this situation, should be to support whatever is positive and hopeful in marriage, to encourage those trends which realistically make for stability and fidelity. The Council, after all, called marriage the 'school of deeper humanity' (*On the Church in the Modern World*, 52), which suggests that not everything it has to teach can be learned at once. The Christian community plays a vital part in supporting marriage simply by being there. It should also have available counselling services for pre-marriage guidance and to help in crises. But where a marriage has manifestly failed, it is difficult to see how the maintenance of a bond which exists only on paper can be a sign of Christ's union with his Church. Yet it is this, according to St Paul, which constitutes the sacramentality of marriage.

These questions have been raised in America to deal with a situation which exists and which is being faced with some honesty. The same problems can be found in more veiled form elsewhere. But from the reaction of the Italian Church to the referendum on divorce, one can conclude that Rome is most unwilling to open this Pandora's box of problems. Addressing newly-weds after the 59·1% vote in favour of retaining the divorce legislation, Pope Paul said: 'Alas, for us this is a cause of astonishment and grief, since the solidarity of members of the clerical community necessary to sustain the inviolability of marriage was lacking' (*Osservatore Romano*, 16 May 1974). This explanation by clerical disobedience overlooks the changed mentality of the Italian people. It suggests that another distressing gap is opening up between the 'teaching Church' and the Church that is no longer content to be taught. And, as a distraction from the main issue, Italian priests like ex-abbot Franzoni are pursued with disciplinary measures. Similar steps were taken against those who opposed *Humanae Vitae* and Stephan Pfürtner was silenced in a vain attempt to secure uniformity. The more honest have been the more exposed. Those who bide their time survive. Some questions cannot yet be asked. Herbert McCabe quotes the following conversation with a Roman official: 'I told the canonist that all I was asking was whether or not there was injustice in the case. He looked at me with astonishment and said: "You cannot ask that question. What are you trying to do? Destroy the whole system?" ' (*New Blackfriars*, April 1975).

Chapter 15

The Crisis and the Fourth Man

The struggle between the sacred old and the prophetic
new is a central theme of the history of religions

PAUL TILLICH

Systematic Theology, vol. 3, p. 367.

Ten years is not a long time in the history of an institution so
venerable as the Roman Catholic Church, and we are all tempted
arrogantly to overestimate the importance of the recent past. Yet
the last decade of the Church is not just an arbitrary slice of history:
it marks the period in which a prodigious effort was made to
assimilate the achievements of Vatican II. It is this effort, with its
successes, failures, confusions and ambiguities, which has given
the last decade a certain unity. One fairly obvious conclusion has
already emerged from this book: the process of assimilation has
been neither smooth nor harmonious, and gaps have opened up
between the centre and the periphery, doctrine and life, conscience
and authority. There has been intense polarization between
factions.

A decade ago a French writer described the emergence of a
'Third Man' who observed the quarrels between 'progressives'
(First Men) and 'conservatives' (Second Men), and turned away
bored (François Roustang, 'Le Troisième Homme', in *Christus*,
October 1966, pp. 561–7). The 'Third Man' neither hoped for
reform with the progressives nor sought to resist it with the
conservatives; he preferred to cultivate his garden. To say that he
had 'lapsed' would be to put it too melodramatically. It was simply
that he no longer cared about the Church and ceased to identify
with it. Ten years on, the Third Men have not grown fewer, but
the situation has changed again. After a book devoted to a narrative
of what has been happening in the Church, the concluding task is
to interpret its meaning.

Interpretation is not an abstract intellectual exercise nor a luxury for those with time on their hands. It is an urgent practical task. If we do not understand our recent past, we will be unable to foresee the future. Most predictions about the Church's future are little more than hasty extrapolations based on prolonging the apparently successful trends of the present. We cannot predict the future because we are, as it were, in the middle of an unfinished German sentence – and the verb which will give it its final meaning comes only at the end. Some of the most dramatic prophecies prove to be less startling on closer inspection. Thus Malachi Martin begins his book *Three Popes and a Cardinal* with this resounding chord: 'Well before the year 2000, there will no longer be an institution recognizable as the Roman Catholic and Apostolic Church of today' (p. vii). It all depends on what is meant by 'recognizable'. To say that the Church will be different is the most evident of truths, for it is in the nature of all living institutions to adapt in order to survive; and whether the Church will be recognizable or not depends on the selection of features believed to characterize its essential nature. Without presuming to tie down in advance the unpredictable Holy Spirit, some fairly clear picture of the Church of the future is needed, because without it there are no particular reasons for taking decisions now. Every decision is a step towards the future, and too often the Church's leaders have haphazardly resisted change or made only grudging concessions. Hope does not exclude planning.

Planning the future involves understanding the present. One point of general agreement, perhaps the only one, is that a crisis exists, though as we shall see it is capable of many varied interpretations. Few who use this overworked word take the trouble to define it. I shall use it initially in the sense of Henri de Lubac who, following Teilhard de Chardin, defines crisis as 'the disturbance of a state of equilibrium and the search for a new equilibrium' (*L'Eglise dans la Crise Actuelle*, p. 93). It is the feeling of being knocked off balance that produces the sense of crisis. And the simple reason for this feeling is that the Council formulated a new understanding of the Church which affected every aspect of its life. The familiar Counter-Reformation model of the Church as fortress or 'perfect society', complete in itself, able to defy the world and surrounded by formidable enemies was replaced by another model in which Christians mingle freely with the diverse peoples of the world and the Pilgrim Church acts as the sign or sacrament of salvation, though God's grace is not confined to its institutional channels. Many conflicts in the Church arise from a clash of 'models': the disputants are literally talking at cross-purposes, since they appeal to different values and criteria of judgement.

The earlier model was easier to grasp, more immediately consoling and psychologically powerful. Inside the fortress strict discipline was maintained, as befitted the embattled situation. Occasionally a 'convert' was welcomed across the drawbridge, and he was greeted as someone who had 'seen the light'. Identity was never in doubt: it was worn like a badge and could not be forfeited whatever happened ('A bad Catholic remains a Catholic'). Life in the fortress certainly represented one sort of equilibrium, and many remain nostalgic for its apparent peace and tranquillity. To disturb that balance, to break with fortress ways and set off in search of a new balance was a courageous undertaking and bound to be painful. Yet that was what the Pilgrim Church was called to do. It had to begin walking – and walking is a matter of nearly, but never quite, falling over. The balance is momentarily disturbed. There is a feeling of crisis. However, there are various accounts of the crisis, and a critical examination of them will bring us to our conclusion.

A favourite episcopal tactic is to underplay the crisis or even to declare that it does not exist. Since whether a crisis exists or not is partly a matter of definition, this argument can be made to sound plausible. The talk of crisis is said to be the invention of journalists, a disreputable crew, who are only interested in clash, confrontation and conflict and who ignore the solid progress being made in obscurity. This reassuring theory suggests that 'everything will all blow over' or that 'in ten years' time everyone will have forgotten about these controversies'. The crisis is cut down to size by being referred to as 'the so-called crisis' (just as Catholics used to refer to the 'so-called Reformation'), and consolation is drawn from the long perspective of history. This teaches that there has been polarization and trouble after every council. There is even a special Italian word for it, the *dopoconcilio*, but after a while 'things settle down again' and order is restored.

Three comments may be made on the denial theory. First, it does not work. Far from bringing any real consolation to the worried, it plunges them still further into their distress, since they are only too aware of the contrast between the soothing rhetoric and what their experience tells them. Only the truth can console. Denial and deception, even with the best intentions, are counterproductive.

Secondly, although there is something in the idea that clash and confrontation receive more clamorous attention than they did before the Council, this is merely the obverse of a new and desirable openness. In the past every hint and rumour of conflict tended to be suppressed. The front remained solid. The bland led the bland. But what was suppressed did not disappear: it simply went underground and poisoned the Church's life, causing bitterness and frustration. The openness of conflicts in the post-conciliar Church represents a victory for honesty, and it transforms our idea of the Church: no longer a vast monolith marching inexorably forwards and brushing aside the accidents of history, it becomes a people, with all the diversity, turbulence, pressure groups, public opinion and tough argument that characterize a real people.

Thirdly, the notion of the Church 'settling down' at some future date is contrary to its pilgrim calling. There will be no point in the future when everything will fall into place, when all the changes have finally been made and the lost Golden Age restored. The law of the Church's life is what Pastor Roger Schutz, prior of Taizé, calls 'the dynamism of the provisional'. If we take the model of the Pilgrim Church seriously, then we must expect the Church to have hazards and upsets on its journey. We must expect it to be travel-stained, flawed, weary, encumbered with much bric-à-brac and yet trying to travel lightly, for ever picking itself up and starting again. The full reality of the Church has not yet come into existence. It is only the anticipation of the Kingdom, not the Kingdom itself. Perfection, the Golden Age, is a sustaining vision along the way and the gift of God at the end of time, not something that will come about next week or in the next decade or even in the fateful year 2000.

A second interpretation admits the existence of a crisis but attributes it to the work of arrogant and misguided individuals within the Church. If only they could be expelled or curbed, all would be well. This explanation is widespread and profoundly defeatist: an army in retreat always looks around for scapegoats. There were two contradictory versions of this theory: some blamed the 'critics', an ill-defined band of *contestateurs*, while others blamed the mafia of the Roman Curia. The common factor to both versions was that they absolved themselves from responsibility while pinning all the blame on 'the others'.

Hans Urs von Balthasar, otherwise a distinguished theologian, resorted with increasing bitterness to the explanation by villainy. He denounces 'those who have said "no": they burn but they consume themselves. They become cynical and destructive, they smell each other out and hold together. It makes no matter whether they officially leave the Church or remain within it. Anyone who has some facility for distinguishing spirits can recognize them' (*Elucidations*, p. 215). This intemperate, almost incoherent outburst leaves the invisible opponents lost in a fog of unclarity. Using more restrained language, Pope Paul in his Wednesday audiences has rebuked those who 'criticize for the sake of criticizing'. But the notion of someone not actually sick 'criticizing for the sake of criticizing' is as far-fetched as von Balthasar's fantasy of rabid fanatics emerging from the Trojan horse of the Church. To devote oneself exclusively to nit-picking and criticism is both frustrating and futile. And there is an alternative explanation. The critics go to work not to enjoy some perverted satisfaction, but because their hopes are unfulfilled and their love disappointed. If the leaders of the Church could grasp that criticism has a positive role and saw it as an urgent appeal to their pastoral responsibility, then progress could be made. If criticism is dismissed in advance as gratuitous disobedience or mere ranting, then there will be no learning and polarization will grow.

The other version of the explanation by villainy pins the blame

on the Roman Curia. The Curia does indeed bear much of the
responsibility because of the control which it attempts to impose
on the whole Church. Its secrecy, mafia-like tendencies and pre-
conciliar theology have been sufficiently denounced. But we cannot
seriously maintain that if the Curia were miraculously to be
staffed by supermen who happened to be saints, there would be no
crisis. One does not wish to underestimate the power of the
Roman Curia, but it is not solely responsible for the Church's
troubles. Both explanations by villainy must be rejected as the
product of naïve utopianism combined with Manichaeism.

'Liberalism' is sometimes presented as the scapegoat. It is said
to have invaded the Church. Since the Council there has been an
attempt to adapt to the contemporary world with disastrous
results. Cardinal Ruffini, who was Archbishop of Palermo, Sicily,
talked about the Church going down on its knees to worship the
Golden Calf of Modernity. Malcolm Muggeridge in a series of
diverting essays has portrayed the Catholic Church, once the
strongest bastion of world-denying Christendom, as 'succumbing
to the siren voices of material and fleshly well-being wafted across
the Atlantic' ('Backward, Christian Soldiers', in *Tread Softly for
You Tread on My Jokes*, p. 148). Both shared the view that the
success of the Church was built on pessimism rather than the
absurd pretension of improving the world, and that the task of the
Church is to criticize the world, not to ape it. What is at stake here
is the implicit model of the Church. It is possible for the Church
to decline into a sect, and to be content to snatch a few burning
brands from the fire of contemporary life; but if it is to be in
continuity with the great Catholic tradition, it will refuse to be
pushed into the margin of irrelevance, will remain co-extensive
with the whole of human life and take the risk of political commitment. But that supposes a continual conversation with the world.
It cannot be conducted from the battlements of a beleaguered
fortress. If the Church is to teach the world, it must also be ready
to learn from the world.

The grain of truth in the Ruffini-Muggeridge interpretation is
that if the Church and its members were to spend all their time
echoing secular clichés, widely available from other sources, then

we could diagnose a loss of nerve and vitality. But there are situations where the Church alone has the strength to denounce injustice, and the Church does not have to be afraid of ever reinforcing a contemporary trend. The cause of the 'third world' does not become less important because it is fashionable. Christians have been roused from their lethargy and made sensitive to the political and social dimensions of their faith, but that does not mean that the Church has become merely a social-welfare agency or a spiritual Red Cross. The 'politicization' of the Church is a fact. But though politically committed Christians may borrow their categories from elsewhere, their deepest motivation remains Christian.

The search for scapegoats can lead to blaming the crisis on dialogue with other Christians. The Roman Catholic Church has been 'Protestantized'. The Reformation, resisted for so long, has belatedly and bloodlessly triumphed. The Church of Rome has become indistinguishable from Protestantism and is proceeding to repeat its mistakes. It is true that Karl Barth, one of the greatest Protestant theologians of the century, warned the Catholic Church against this danger and notably against the sort of 'biblicism' which ignored history and imagined that one could return to the faith experience of the primitive Church by overleaping the intermediate stages. But this is very much a theologian's observation: most Catholics do not know enough about the first century to make it a norm. The charge of 'Protestantization' is usually based on liturgical change and the remark that 'one can no longer tell the difference'.

It is true that the demand for a vernacular and more accessible form of worship was one of the battle-grounds trampled over at the Reformation, and that Rome has at last conceded the day. It is also true that it has acknowledged that the ministry of the Word is as important as the ministry of the Sacrament, and underplayed specifically 'Catholic' features such as devotion to Our Lady. One can grant the general truth of these assertions, while denying their allegedly ruinous consequences. The polemical situation at the time of the Reformation meant not only that Catholics were unfair to Protestants but that they were unfair also to their own positions.

The Counter-Reformation worked on the principle that if the reformers asserted a doctrine, then Catholics must say the opposite. If they denied the real presence, then it must be honoured in ever more splendid processions. If they rejected auricular confession, then it must be made the centre of the spiritual life. If they dismissed the cult of the saints as idolatrous, then they must celebrate their feasts with even more pomp and construct still more sumptuous reliquaries. But once liberated from the neurotic fear born of the polemical situation, the way was open for emphasizing convergence rather than divergence. This should be a matter for rejoicing rather than lamentation.

Indeed, the question should rather be why there has not been a still greater coming together of Christians. No longer do they grow up in ivory towers, in isolation from each other. They are exposed to the same influences, have the same struggles, and cannot be accused any longer of unfamiliarity with each other's thinking. As Bishop Christopher Butler has said, what keeps them apart are the differences inherited from the past, and he went on to suggest that 'doctrinal agreement will only come about when communion has been established' ('Theology and Life in Community', in *One in Christ*, 1974, no. 3, p. 225). This reverses the usual procedure, which has always assumed that 'communion was the distant goal, possible once doctrinal agreement had been secured'. But Bishop Butler justifies his position (put forward, he hastens to explain, as a question for debate and not a proposal for action) in terms of Bernard Lonergan's distinction between 'faith' and 'beliefs'. Christians already share in *faith*: they differ in the set of propositions in which they have formulated that faith – or rather in which their respective communions have formulated their faith. 'Have we', asks Bishop Butler, 'been too ready to neglect the evidence of shared faith, and to concentrate on the evidence of divisive doctrines?' (ibid., p. 227). That is a *nonne* question, expecting the answer 'Yes'.

There is another type of explanation for the crisis which avoids the temptation of scapegoat-seeking. It sets the crisis in the context of a changing world. What is happening in the Church simply mirrors the crisis of contemporary society which is also off balance, and moreover this is as it should be: the Pilgrim Church would know that it was failing in its mission if it failed to reflect the turmoil and pressures of the age, for then it would be unfaithful to the principle of the Incarnation which implies that it must really live in the *now* of history, and not strive for some trans-temporal escape-route. To take two simple examples. 'Authority' in all its forms is under attack. It is not only bishops but parents, teachers and politicians who have to devise a new style of authority. Paternalism does not work. Values today are communicated horizontally through the peer-group rather than from above. This means, for example, that the priest, if he is to have any effective authority, will have to discover a more involved and fraternal way of exercising it. Likewise, 'institutions' are under attack for their daunting size and impersonality. It would be worrying if the Church came through unscathed, and if Christians did not feel the need to find in the Church a real experience of community.

This is a valuable element in understanding the present situation of the Church. It throws a flood of light on the misunderstandings which have bedevilled the last decade. Different generations operate with different mental maps and judge in the light of different value-systems. The reason why the young apparently 'lose their faith' is not because they are hostile or promiscuous or indifferent: it is simply that they do not find in the Church the values that they cherish. An American sociologist has usefully summed up the features of youth culture: 'Human qualities such as control, planning, waiting, saving and postponing on the one hand, revering, remembering and respecting on the other, are equally de-emphasized. In contrast, activity, adventure, responsiveness, genuineness, spontaneity and sentience are the new experimental values' (Kenneth Keniston, quoted in *School and Christian Values*, edited by Michael Cockett, p. 45). The effects can be seen in the charismatic movement and in the phenomenon of Taizé. It is not a matter of accepting indiscriminately the alternative mental map, which certainly needs supplementing; but the Christian tradition is sufficiently rich and deep to make room for these experimental values. 'The voice of youth', said Pedro Arrupe, General of the Jesuits, 'is the voice of the modern world in the Church.' When that voice is listened to, it makes awkward and stringent demands for 'authenticity'. It insists that orthopraxis is as important as orthodoxy. It is unhappy with any contradiction between theory and practice.

At last, with the youthful demand for authenticity, we begin to come close to the heart of the matter. Throughout this book we have seen so many examples of the gap between rhetoric and reality, between the language of faith and its lived content, between what is officially asserted and what is privately believed, between what authority proposes and what believers accept, between, in short, institution and life. The perennial Christian task is to close those gaps as far as possible: they can never be entirely eliminated, for that would mean that the Christian had arrived at his goal, his pilgrimage over. But that does not mean that he can tolerate their continued existence. It is here that we can speak of a new way of belonging to the Church, characteristic of what may be called, after Roustang, the Fourth Man. For while the Third Man went off to swell the ranks of the post-Christians, the Fourth Men remain within the Church while recognizing that they are in conflict with it on major points. And despite the heavy-handed irony of Hans Urs von Balthasar, they not only remain in the Church out of conviction, they cannot conceive of leaving it, and for a very simple reason: they think of the Church simply as humanity in so far as it has recognized, however falteringly, its vocation in Christ. They can no more leave the Church than they can take leave of humanity. To do so would be a form of spiritual suicide.

Yet the Fourth Man finds himself at odds with the Church. The incurable post-conciliar optimists exhort him to be patient and to bide his time, and remind him of the folly of the cross. The Fourth Man knows about the folly of the cross, but he does not see why it should be compounded by countless other follies which obscure the Christian message and for which no justification can be provided. He learns the truth of Bernanos's maxim: 'It is easy to suffer for the Church – the difficult thing is to suffer at the hands of the Church.' His adhesion to the Church is a form of critical belonging, and he sees criticism not as self-indulgence but as a duty if identification is to be combined with integrity. He forms part of the 'loyal parliamentary opposition' which exercises a watchdog function in the Church. He appreciates the truth of John Stuart Mill's remark: 'My love for an institution is in proportion to my desire to reform it.' And he includes himself in the project of continual reform. But he is keenly sensitive to any attempt to disarm criticism by appealing to faith. This attitude was well expressed by Heinrich Böll, the German Catholic novelist: 'You know that there are two definitions of the Church: on the one hand the institutional Church . . . and on the other the Mystical Body. I refuse to play the game of eternally justifying the first by appealing to the second' (interview in *Commonweal*, 19 May 1974). The strategy to which Böll alludes is very familiar among Roman officials and all who have felt their influence. It consists in switching continually between the severely practical and the loftily spiritual. The critic is discredited and said to be losing his faith or his mind or both. The entire institution, with all its historically conditioned features, is sacralized and treated as though it were wholly of divine origin.

The hypothesis that the Fourth Man has quite simply lost his faith must be taken seriously, for if it were true, he would have nothing to contribute to the Church. Faith can be lost, not in the way one loses a bunch of keys, but in the sense that it ceases to shape a life. But before accusing anyone of losing his faith, we need to define a little more closely the content of faith. The huge theological superstructure erected around faith to elaborate, defend and illustrate it can hide the fact that the content of faith is exceedingly simple. One has Christian faith if one can say that 'Jesus is the Lord' – provided one knows who Jesus is and what 'Lord' means. One has faith if one believes that Jesus died so that we might be reconciled with God and each other, and that he rose from the dead as the pledge of our resurrection. His death and resurrection convince us that hatred does not have the last word, that love is worth-while and hope possible. This is liberating knowledge, bringing freedom from the absurd, from the rat-race, from the bitter taste of ashes which is so much part of the twentieth-century experience. And faith is verified when it casts light on our everyday experience and life acquires a pattern: suffering is no longer mere degradation, fidelity is possible, and death, the last enemy, loses its terror. This is Christian faith. It is not identical with the humanist's faith in man or the Marxist's faith in history.

But what this brief account of faith does not say is how it comes to us. It is not something we invent from scratch, and if we think we do, it is in the manner of an explorer bravely planting a flag on an unknown island only to discover that it is inhabited after all. Faith is mediated through other people. In practice it comes through the Church: but the word 'Church' in itself is an abstraction, and existential faith comes to us through the innumerable believers who, hesitantly and always inadequately, make it come alive for us. Christians mediate faith for each other and the world. They exercise a ministry towards each other and a mission towards the world. The Christian community is a permanent learning community in which all teach and all learn. The mother who teaches her child to pray, the student grappling with the doubt of a friend – they too form part of the *magisterium*. What one asks, then, of an organized Christian body, a Church, is that it should continue to convey the essential Christian message and provide a credible context in which faith is possible. Christianity uses arguments but depends on community. 'We know', says the First Epistle of John, 'that we have passed out of death into life, because we love the brethren' (1 John 3:14). It is unreasonable to ask for perfect faith, hope undimmed, inexhaustible charity in the Church, as Charles Davis does in *A Question of Conscience*. The Church is the flawed embodiment of faith, hope and charity. One cannot ask that it already be at its goal; one can only ask that it should be moving towards it. One can be satisfied if there is enough faith, enough hope and enough charity for it to be a credible sign to the world. The judgement is not made in an instant or a decade. It is the work of a lifetime.

It is at this point that one begins to sense that if the Fourth Man needs the Church, the Church also needs the Fourth Man. His potential role is as the agent or at least the catalyst of change. One of the Church's problems was that the institutionalized use of the image of the Body made for complete immobility: it led to a model of the Church in which unchangeable roles were permanently assigned: hands remained hands and eyes, eyes, forgetting that the hand needs to see, and the eye needs to work. The Pauline use of the image stressed not only the complementary function of the members but also the need for vital, dynamic and life-giving union with Christ, the head. The Council did not make the Body its central and controlling image of the Church. It balanced it with images of growth, and above all with the model of the People of God in history. The People of God is in movement. If it stands still to contemplate its own splendour, it becomes false to its calling; if it absolutizes a moment of its journey, it betrays its origin and its pilgrim destination. The Fourth Men are a part of the Church. Their contribution will eventually be recognized because it will be needed.

There is one simple reason why the Fourth Man can have some confidence in the future: it is that the ancient legal maxim *consuetudo contra legem* operates in the Church – what is actually done overrides the law, and the law eventually catches up. And since at present the Church has no way of enforcing its demands, precedents are being created. The Inquisition happily no longer exists, the kind of theological witch-hunt that first invented and then destroyed Modernism is no longer possible, and even the fact that the Church officially forbids something no longer induces automatic guilt feelings. Most of the bans and prohibitions of the decade have been ineffectual. The official Church may proclaim that intercommunion should cease; but it cannot ensure that it ceases. It may pronounce a ban on birth-control; but it cannot intrude on the privacy of the married. It may revise the code of canon law and present the Church as an authority; but it cannot prevent the experience of the Church from being one of community. It may exhort Christians to shun married priests; but it cannot punish them when they do not. It may hedge theological work around with prohibitions and guidelines; but the work will go on because the questions continue to be asked. It may discourage political priests and committed laymen; but the injustice which prompts them to speak does not go away. The Church is a voluntary association.

To say all this is not to produce a recipe for ecclesiastical anarchy since all the developments mentioned are within the logic of Vatican II. The consequence of saying that the gifts of the Holy Spirit are showered on the whole Christian people will eventually be acknowledged and taken seriously. The Council's statements were clear enough: 'They [the laity] are in their own way made sharers in the priestly, prophetic, and kingly functions of Christ. They carry out their own part in the mission of the whole Christian people with respect to the Church and the world' (*On the Church*, 31). Confidence in the Holy Spirit at work in the whole Church means that ultimately he will bring a greater correspondence between teaching and life, norms and values, institution and existence. Ultimately. But penultimately this cannot be realized in practice without pain, without the prophetically new colliding with the sacred old.

The next twenty-five years will see the emergence of a new principle of relative equilibrium in the Church as the seeds planted by the Council bear fruit. The new model of the Church as a pilgrim and fraternal community serving the world will become dominant. It is not a matter of re-inventing the Church as though it had no history, but of recognizing that the tradition is much wider and richer than we had supposed. The Pilgrim Church has an unfinished quality, it knows that it is still in the making, and that the possibilities are more open-ended than most people thought ten years ago. But if they are to be realized, crippling timidity must be abandoned. As the psychiatrist Dr Jack Dominian has written: 'If I were asked to point to one psychological reason why the hopes of Vatican II are so slow to develop, I would suggest that the retardation occurs at all levels when authority has been challenged legitimately and validly but has not had the psychological resources or insight to cope, and has retreated either in evasion, postponement or repression' ('The Wholeness-Holiness Dimension of the Priesthood', in *The Clergy Review*, March 1975, p. 157). One inevitably thinks, in contrast, of Pope John XXIII, who used to find sleep at night with the thought, 'Relax, Angelo, it's not you who runs the Church, but the Holy Spirit.'

It is fitting to end this book with the memory of Pope John, who launched the Church on the path of the Council without living to see where it might lead. He summoned the Council because he believed that the Church's problems could only be solved with the collaboration of the whole Church, recognizing that 'it takes many to be intelligent'. We have no means of knowing what he would have thought of subsequent developments, except that, having seen the harm done by repression, he would have avoided it. One of his favourite texts was Joseph's disclosure of his identity to his brothers: 'I am your brother, Joseph' (Genesis 45:4). Pope John made this text his own when speaking to socialists, to Jewish leaders, to prisoners in the Ara Coeli prison, and to mankind generally. His listeners were delighted and surprised that a pope should step down, like Joseph, from his throne and overflow his official role. They expected to meet a pontiff and they met a brother.

In Pope John the big abstract words like 'dialogue', 'openness' and 'brotherhood' came alive, and the world hoped again. To speak of the Church is to speak of hope, for the man who does not know hope, does not know God and his promises. Through the present crisis the Church is being tested and purified. Erik Erikson's positive interpretation of crisis applies with precision to the last decade of the Church. 'Crisis', he says, 'is ... not a threat of catastrophe, but a turning point, a crucial period of increased vulnerability and heightened potential' (*Identity: Youth and Crisis*, p. 96). The evidence of the Church's vulnerability should not blind us to its potentiality. And Erikson's definition of crisis can be seen as a secular transposition of the death and resurrection of Christ. In his passion he becomes vulnerable, yet through this experience the power of the resurrection is released upon the world. In this way he becomes 'the first-born among many brethren' (Romans 8 : 29). The Church exists to keep alive that all-encompassing truth.

List of Books Quoted

Abbott, W., and J. Gallagher (eds.), *The Documents of Vatican II* (Geoffrey Chapman, London, and America Press, New York, 1966).

Balthasar, Hans Urs von, *Elucidations* (SPCK, London, 1975).

Berrigan, Daniel, *America Is Hard to Find* (Doubleday, New York, 1972, and SPCK, London, 1973).
   No Bars to Manhood (Doubleday, New York, 1970).

Boros, Ladislaus, *Meeting God in Man* (Burns & Oates, London, and Herder & Herder, New York, 1968).

Bowden, J., and J. Richmond (eds.), *A Reader in Contemporary Theology* (SCM Press, London, 1967).

Brown, Raymond E., *Priest and Bishop: Biblical Reflections* (Paulist Press, Paramus, 1970, and Geoffrey Chapman, London, 1971).

Butler, Bishop B. Christopher, *Searchings* (Geoffrey Chapman, London, 1975).

Chomsky, Noam, *For Reasons of State* (Fontana, London, Pantheon Books, New York, and Vintage Books, New York, 1973).

Cockett, Michael (ed.), *School and Christian Values* (Mayhew-McCrimmon, London, 1972).

Congar, Yves, and M. Peuchmaurd (eds.), *L'Eglise dans le Monde de ce Temps* (Cerf, Paris, 1967).

Cox, Harvey, *The Seduction of the Spirit* (School and Society Books, New York, 1973, and Wildwood House, London, 1974).

Dalrymple, J. (ed.), *Authority in a Changing Church* (Sheed & Ward, London, 1968).

Davis, Charles, *A Question of Conscience* (Hodder & Stoughton, London, 1967).

Desmond, Cosmas, *The Discarded People* (Penguin, Harmondsworth, 1971).

Drucker, Peter, *The Age of Discontinuity* (Heinemann, London, and Harper & Row, New York, 1969).

Edwards, David L., *The British Churches Turn to the Future* (SCM Press, London, 1973).

Erikson, Erik H., *Identity: Youth and Crisis* (Faber & Faber, London, and W. W. Norton, New York, 1968).

List of Books Quoted 243

Fletcher, William C., *Religion and Soviet Foreign Policy, 1945–1970* (Oxford University Press, London, 1973).

Garaudy, Roger, *From Anathema to Dialogue*, ET (Collins, London, 1967, and Vintage Books, New York, 1968).

Gardavský, Vitězslav, *God Is Not Yet Dead*, ET (Penguin, Harmondsworth, 1973).

Gutiérrez, Gustavo, *A Theology of Liberation*, ET (Orbis Books, New York, 1973, and SCM Press, London, 1974).

Haughton, Rosemary, and J. C. Heenan, *Dialogue: The State of the Church Today* (Geoffrey Chapman, London, 1967, and Sheed & Ward, New York, 1968).

Heenan, Cardinal J. C., *Council and Clergy* (Geoffrey Chapman, London, 1966).

A Crown of Thorns (Hodder & Stoughton, London, 1974).

Not the Whole Truth (Hodder & Stoughton, London, 1971).

Jones, David, *Anathemata* (Faber & Faber, London, 1955).

Kelleher, Stephen J., *Divorce and Remarriage for Catholics?* (Doubleday, New York, 1973).

Küng, Hans, *Infallible?*, ET (Collins, London, 1971, and Doubleday, New York, 1972).

Kurtz, Paul, and Albert Dondeyne (eds.), *A Catholic/Humanist Dialogue* (Pemberton, London, and Prometheus Books, Buffalo, 1973).

Lodge, David, *The British Museum Is Falling Down* (MacGibbon & Kee, London, 1965).

Lubac, Henri de, *The Drama of Atheist Humanism*, ET (Sheed & Ward, London, 1949).

L'Eglise dans la Crise Actuelle (Cerf, Paris, 1969).

McDonagh, Enda, *Gift and Call* (Gill, Dublin, and Macmillan, London, 1975).

Invitation and Response (Gill, Dublin, Macmillan, London, and Sheed & Ward, New York, 1972).

Martin, David, *The Religious and the Secular* (Routledge & Kegan Paul, London, and Schocken Books, New York, 1969).

Martin, Malachi, *Three Popes and a Cardinal* (Farrar, Straus & Giroux, New York, 1972, and Hart-Davis, St Albans, 1973).

Moltmann, Jürgen, *Hope and Planning*, ET (SCM Press, London, and Harper & Row, New York, 1971).

Muggeridge, Malcolm, *Tread Softly for You Tread on My Jokes* (Fontana, London, 1968).

Nesti, Arnoldo (ed.), *L'Altra Chiesa in Italia* (Mondadori, Milan, 1970).

O'Neill, David P., *The Priest in Crisis* (Geoffrey Chapman, London, and Pflann Press, Dayton, Ohio, 1968).

Pfürtner, Stephan, *Kirche und Sexualität* (Rowohlt, Hamburg, 1972).

Pospishil, Victor, *Divorce and Remarriage in the Catholic Church* (Herder & Herder, New York, and Burns & Oates, London, 1967).

Ranaghan, Dorothy, *As the Spirit Leads Us* (Paulist Press, Glen Rock, NJ, 1971).

Robinson, Ian, *The Survival of English* (Cambridge University Press, London, 1973).

Robinson, John, *Honest to God* (SCM Press, London, and Westminster Press, Philadelphia, 1963).

Rynne, Xavier, *The Second Session* (Faber & Faber, London, 1964).

Segundo, Juan Luis, *A Theology for Artisans of a New Humanity* (Orbis Books, New York, 1973).

Stevas, Norman St John, *The Agonizing Choice* (Eyre & Spottiswoode, London, and Indiana University Press, Bloomington, 1971).

Stoppard, Tom, *Jumpers* (Faber & Faber, London, 1972).

Suenens, Cardinal L. J., *Coresponsibility in the Church*, ET (Herder & Herder, New York, 1968, and Burns & Oates, London, 1969).

A New Pentecost?, ET (Darton, Longman & Todd, London, and Seabury Press, New York, 1975).

Sweeney, Francis, SJ (ed.), *The Vatican and World Peace* (C. Smythe, Gerrards Cross, 1970).

Swidler, Leonard and Arlene (trans. and eds.), *Bishops and People* (Westminster Press, Philadelphia, 1970).

Tillich, Paul, *Systematic Theology* (Nisbet, Welwyn, 1953–7, and Harper & Row, New York, 1967).

Wills, Garry, *Bare Ruined Choirs* (Doubleday, New York, 1972).

Winter, Michael M., *Mission or Maintenance?* (Darton, Longman & Todd, London, 1973).

Wrenn, Lawrence G. (ed.), *Divorce and Remarriage in the Catholic Church* (Newman Press, New York, 1973).

Zaehner, R. C., *Dialectical Christianity and Christian Materialism* (Oxford University Press, London and New York, 1971).

List of Periodicals Quoted

America, New York
The Catholic Herald, London
Choisir, Geneva
Christianisme Social, Paris
Christus, Paris
Civiltà Cattolica, Rome
Clergy Bulletin, Southwark, London
The Clergy Review, London
Commonweal, New York
Communicationes, Pontifical Commission for the Revision of Canon Law, Rome
Concilium, Search Press, London, and McGraw-Hill, Ontario
The Critic, Chicago
Cross Currents, West Nyack, New York
Dialog, Verlag Herder, Freiburg im Breisgau
Documentation sur l'Europe Centrale, University of Louvain
Evangelische Kommentar, Kreuz-Verlag, Stuttgart
Herder Korrespondenz, Verlag Herder, Freiburg im Breisgau
Informations Catholiques Internationales, Paris
La Libre Belgique, Brussels
Lumière et Vie, Lyons
The Month, London
National Catholic Reporter, Kansas City, Missouri
New Blackfriars, Oxford
Notitiae, Vatican City
The Observer, London
One in Christ, London
Osservatore Romano, Vatican City
La Stampa, Milan
The Tablet, London
The Times, London
Tygodnik Powszechny, Cracow

Index

Adjoubei, Alexis, 164
aggiornamento, 19, 32
Alfrink, Cardinal, 48–50
Almeida, Archbishop, 188
Amsterdam Theological Institute, 68
Anglican Church,
    dialogue with, 127–33
    validity of orders, 132
Anglican/Roman Catholic International Commission (ARCIC), 130
annulment, 221–2
apostolic delegates, 76–7, 78, 80
    see also diplomacy, Vatican
apostolic succession, 106
Apostolicae Curae, 132
Argentina, 65, 159
Arroyo, SJ, Gonzalo, 159
Arrupe, SJ, Pedro, 68, 188, 235
Ascarza, Bishop Santos, 62
Assemblée des Prêtres Solidaires, 65
atheism, 136–7, 151
Athenagoras, Patriarch, 87
Augustine, St, 9, 35, 150
Australia, visit of Pope Paul, 91–2
authority in the Church,
    Vatican approach, 21, 213–14
    bishops lose, 45
    priests lose, 57
    official Church loses, 216, 239
    crisis of, 71, 235, 240
    new ideas on, 42, 49–50
    Anglican approach, 130–1
    see also collegiality; co-responsibility

Bafile, Archbishop Corrado, 77
Baggio, Cardinal, 78
Balthasar, Hans Urs von, 231, 236
'baptism in the Spirit', 206
Barcelona, Archbishop of, 186–7
Barry, John C., 223
Barth, Karl, 233
Baum, OSA, Gregory, 111, 145, 219
Bea, Cardinal Augustin, 81, 119, 124, 127, 129, 135
Beatles, 40
Beaupère, René, 121

Beck, Archbishop, 45, 48
Benediction, 31
Benelli, Mgr Giovanni, 81–5, 95, 125, 183
Berger, Peter, 97
Berlin, Isaiah, 85
Bernanos, Georges, 236
Berrigan, SJ, Daniel, 109, 190–2
Betto, OP, Frei, 183
bidding prayers, 30
birth-control, 210–18
    Paul VI decides alone, 21–2, 51, 93–4
    see also Humanae Vitae
Bisceglia, Don Marco, 201–2
bishops, 71–85
    seen as sacred, 15
    demythologized, 13, 43
    advisory bodies for, 45–6, 49
    diocesan b. in Curia, 80, 93
    see also ministry, episcopal; Synod
        of Bishops
Bishops' Pastoral Office in the Church,
        Decree on the, 73
Bloy, Léon, 182
Böll, Heinrich, 237
Boquen, abbey of, 202
Boros, Ladislaus, 143, 144
Bossuet, J. B., 27
Bourdeaux, Michael, 168
Braun, Dr Cornelius, 78
Brazil, 183–4
British Council of Churches, 122, 129
broadcasting, 141
Brodrick, Robert, 44
Brown, Raymond E., 55, 58
Browne, OP, Cardinal, 31, 74
Bugnini, Fr Annibale, 29, 31
Butler, OSB, Bishop Christopher, 9, 141, 234

Callahan, Dan, 14
Camara Pessoa, Dom Helder, 12, 179
Camus, Albert, 179, 194
Canadian bishops, 22, 52, 56, 77–8, 215
canon law, revision of, 46, 51, 223
Cardinale, Archbishop Inigo, 166, 215

Mary,
diminished emphasis, 233
Paul VI visits Fatima, 90–1
in Communist countries, 175
Mass, *see* liturgy
Mauriac, François, 27
Mawby, Colin, 35
Mazzi, Don Enzo, 199–201
Medellin, bishops' meeting at, 73, 125–6, 157
Mediator Dei, 11
Mendoza y Amor, Benjamin, 92
Methodist/Catholic Joint Commission, *see* Catholic/Methodist Joint Commission
Metz, Johannes Baptist, 105, 108–9, 146, 155
Mexico, 65, 159, 187–8
Mill, John Stuart, 237
Mindszenty, Cardinal, 149
ministry of all Christians, 58, 238, 240
ministry, episcopal, 58, 63, 77–8, 203
ministry, priestly,
m. of the Word, 59–61, 233
m. of the Sacrament, 56, 59–61, 233
function, not state, 16, 62
different roles in different countries, 56
changes in role, 56–7
'president of the assembly', 33
diocesan priests, 59
share in episcopal ministry, 58
ARCIC's report on, 132
International Theological Commission's report on, 105
'71 Synod, 105
validity of Protestant, 121, 122, 132
see also ordination; priests
ministry, sources of, 58–9, 62–3
Missa Luba, 36
Missa Normativa, 31
mixed marriages, *see* marriage
models of the Church, 228–9, 230, 238–9, 240
see also People of God
Modernism, 11, 239
Moerman, Canon, 218
Moltmann, Jürgen, 109, 157
Moore, Sebastian, 104
moral theology,
Council's personalist approach, 210–11, 218–19
norms unrelated to values, 216
existential approach replaces legalism, 222
biological determinism abandoned, 219
influence of psychology, 219

Pfürtner's approach, 219–21
McDonagh's approach, 145–6
see also natural law; rights, human
Mortalium Animos, 117–18
Mounier, Emmanuel, 188
Mozambique, 189
Muggeridge, Malcolm, 232
Murray, SJ, John Courtney, 13, 102
Mystici Corporis, 11

National Conference of Priests of England and Wales, 57
National Council for Pastoral Deliberation (Holland), 49
National Divorced Catholics Conference (USA), 224
National Federation of Priests' Councils (USA), 66–7, 224
National Pastoral Council (Holland), 47–9, 54
National Secular Society (Britain), 138
natural law, 210, 212, 214
New Blackfriars, 13, 19, 182, 203
New Catechism, 12, 95
Newman, John Henry, 29
Norfolk, Duke of, 26
Norris, James, 182
Novak, Michael, 34
nuncio, papal, 76, 80, 84–5
in Bonn, 77
in Chile, 83
see also diplomacy, Vatican

O'Carroll, Fr Joseph, 57
Octogesima Adveniens (Letter to Cardinal Roy), 88, 160–1, 181
O'Neill, David P., 61
Oosterhuis, Huub, 39
ordination,
of married men, 16, 22, 52, 63–4, 67, 92, 93
of women, 16, 51, 63, 64
irreversible, 56, 68
by bishops alone, 58
in context of Mass, 31
Orsy, SJ, Ladislaus, 222
Orthodox Church,
communion with, 121
and intercommunion, 125
problems in Russia, 174, 177
Osservatore Romano, 83, 183, 200, 213–14, 225
Ostpolitik of Vatican, 164–78
Ottaviani, Cardinal, 14
Our Lady, *see* Mary

Pacem in Terris, 150–1
Pangrazio, Archbishop, 105